Triathlon Training

FOR

DUMMIES®

Triathlon Training FOR DUMMIES®

by Deirdre Pitney and
Donna Dourney

WILEY

Wiley Publishing, Inc.

Triathlon Training For Dummies®

Published by
Wiley Publishing, Inc.
111 River St.
Hoboken, NJ 07030-5774
www.wiley.com

WILEY

About the Authors

Deirdre Pitney is a cyclist, a runner, and a writer specializing in fitness and wellness. After completing a 220-mile fundraising bike ride, Deirdre added a third sport, swimming, to her workouts and took on training for her first triathlon.

Donna Dourney is a wellness director, personal trainer, fitness instructor, coach, and accomplished triathlete who has competed for more than 25 years in marathons, duathlons, and triathlons, including a Half-Iron and a full Ironman. She runs a triathlon club for people who want to complete their first triathlons or improve their times and training for their next events. Her experience and knowledge has guided more than 150 nervous beginners from their first training days to the finish line. Donna earned a degree in health and physical education from Seton Hall University. She has held certifications from the American College of Sports Medicine, the Aerobics and Fitness Association of America, and National YMCA Strength and Conditioning.

Dedication

Deirdre Pitney: To Cullen and Margot

Donna Dourney: To my husband, Kenneth York

Authors' Acknowledgments

We would like to thank our agent, Jessica Faust of Bookends, Inc., for her guidance. At Wiley, we'd like to thank Tracey Boggier, acquisitions editor, for her vision and belief in this project. Thank you to our project editor, Elizabeth Kuball, for her much dreaded but greatly appreciated submission schedules and for her professionalism, perspective, and exceptional editing and organizational skills. Thank you also to Graeme Henderson, our technical editor, for his enthusiasm, energy and experience, and to Kathryn Born, our illustrator, for her patience and attention to detail.

Thank you to our models, Sue Diebold, Susan Hoeltve-Ward, Philip Klaas, Daniel Mallery, Linda Oh, and Miguel Rustrian, and to the people at High Gear Cyclery, Trek Bicycle Corporation, Giant Bicycle, and De Soto Triathlon Company, for their support. And a special thank-you to Stacey Smith for her sharing her photographs.

And we'd each like to extend our thanks to each other's family and support networks. Our combined contacts and friendships have made this book possible.

Deirdre Pitney: Thank you to Paul Cullen — his name is now in a book, as he always knew it would be — for telling my favorite cycling story.

An enormous thank-you to the two most fun, insightful, and inspiring people I know — Cullen and Margot. I'd need book after book after book to express all the joy and love you've brought to my life. I am more proud to be your mom than I am of anything else I have ever done or could ever do.

To my friends with whom I've spent many miles on the roads and trails — thank you for always being up for a new challenge and for sharing your passions , knowledge, and experience with me.

Thank you to Kathy Johnson Brown and Ed Pagliarini, wonderful photographers and even better friends.

Thank you to my coauthor, Donna, for bringing to this book and to my life more than she knows and probably would be willing to admit. Her straightforward belief in the people she trains and their ability to reach their goals has guided many beginning athletes, including my daughter, successfully across countless finish lines, whether in 5Ks or triathlons.

Donna Dourney: A heartfelt thank you to the four people who continue to inspire me and bring joy to my life every day, my children, Tommy, Danny, Heather, and Shane. You are the light of my life.

Thanks to my family — my sisters and brothers, who are my best friends and who, even though they sometimes think I'm crazy, always have supported and encouraged me in my endeavors. My dad who has always been there for me and my mom who continues to watch over me.

Thank you to my coauthor, Deirdre Pitney, for giving me this opportunity, for putting my random thoughts in order, for being so wonderful to write with, and for touching my life.

I'd also like to thank Rone Lewis and his staff at High Gear Cyclery (Stirling, New Jersey) for sharing their time and expertise and for the use of his cycle shop. Thanks to my friends and colleagues at the Somerset Hills YMCA for their input and support, as well as the use of the facility for our photo shoots.

Finally, a very special thank-you to my husband, Kenneth York, whose endless love, support, and encouragement have gotten me through many challenges in my life. He believes in me more than I believe in myself and is always there for me at the finish line, regardless of the race.

Publisher's Acknowledgments

We're proud of this book; please send us your comments through our Dummies online registration form located at www.dummies.com/register/.

Some of the people who helped bring this book to market include the following:

Acquisitions, Editorial, and Media Development

Project Editor: Elizabeth Kuball

Acquisitions Editor: Tracy Boggier

Copy Editor: Elizabeth Kuball

Assistant Editor: Erin Calligan Mooney

Technical Editor: Graeme S. Henderson

Senior Editorial Manager: Jennifer Ehrlich

Editorial Supervisor and Reprint Editor: Carmen Krikorian

Editorial Assistants: Joe Niesen, Jennette ElNaggar, David Lutton

Cover Photos: David Madison

Cartoons: Rich Tennant, www.the5thwave.com

Composition Services

Project Coordinator: Katie Key

Layout and Graphics: Melissa K. Jester, Sarah E. Philippart,Christine Williams

Special Art: Kathryn Born

Proofreaders: John Greenough, Penny Stuart

Indexer: Potomac Indexing, LLC

Special Help
Alicia South

Publishing and Editorial for Consumer Dummies

    Diane Graves Steele, Vice President and Publisher, Consumer Dummies

    Joyce Pepple, Acquisitions Director, Consumer Dummies

    Kristin Ferguson-Wagstaffe, Product Development Director, Consumer Dummies

    Ensley Eikenburg, Associate Publisher, Travel

    Kelly Regan, Editorial Director, Travel

Publishing for Technology Dummies

    Andy Cummings, Vice President and Publisher, Dummies Technology/General User

Composition Services

    Gerry Fahey, Vice President of Production Services

    Debbie Stailey, Director of Composition Services

Contents at a Glance

Table of Contents

. . . .

Introduction

. . . .

*T*riathlons are the new black. They're fitness fashion, and they look good on everyone.

Triathlon events are becoming as popular as the weekend 5K road race. But now, instead of closing off a neighborhood loop, race directors are setting up orange cones, yellow tape, barricades, and bike racks throughout cities and entire towns for these multi-sport events that cover anywhere from 8 miles to an awe-inspiring 140 miles.

Still, as much as we're hearing and reading about triathlons and who's training for them, the number of people crossing the finish lines of these events makes anyone who considers participating in the three-sport showdown one of the select few.

Complete a triathlon of any distance, and you qualify as an athlete of exceptional endurance and dedication. If you're considering participating in a triathlon, or you've already started training for one, this book is for you.

About This Book

You can do a triathlon — and *Triathlon Training For Dummies* will add to your confidence and help you improve your performance, comfort, and fun when you do. This book best answers the questions of triathletes who are new to the sport because it was written from that same perspective, focusing on simplifying the complex equipment needs of triathletes and creating training programs you can understand and follow without a calculator, heart monitor, or PhD.

This book is a collaboration of many experienced triathletes who shared their training tips and event expertise. It's the triathlon-training book for *real* people (because not everyone is an Ironman or wants to be), taking you from novice to knowledgeable.

Depending on the length of the triathlon you choose, you'll find that what motivates most triathletes has nothing to do with beating you. What you're more likely to find is team spirit: We're in this together — let's get it done and see how far we can push ourselves.

That's an energy that's infectious. And the discipline, self-confidence, and fitness that come from triathlon training will enhance other areas of your life. So, don't be surprised if you start a mini triathlon trend in your own circle. People will recognize the positive effects that your training has on you. And they'll want some of that for themselves.

Share your gear. Share your knowledge. The book? Sure, you can share that, too — but we're hoping you'll find the information in these pages so helpful to your daily training that you'll tell your friends to buy their own copies.

In this book, we give you answers to the many questions you're thinking right now: What equipment do I need? How do I find time for training? What do I need to know about transitions? Will I make it to the finish? (Trust us, you will.)

Conventions Used in This Book

We've designed this book in a way that makes it easy to read and understand:

- When we refer to distances, we use meters or miles for the swim; meters are abbreviated with a lowercase *m* (so 500m is 500 meters) and the word *mile* is spelled out (as in 1 mile). We use kilometers for the bike and run; kilometers are abbreviated with a capital *K* (so 10K is 10 kilometers).

- Whenever we use a new term, we put it in *italics* and define it shortly thereafter (often in parentheses).

- When we give you a list of steps to follow, we put the action part of the step in bold, so it's easy to find.

- We put all Web addresses and e-mail addresses in `monofont`, so that they stand out from the surrounding text. *Note:* When this book was printed, some Web addresses may have needed to break across two lines of text. If that happened, rest assured that we haven't put in any extra characters (such as hyphens) to indicate the break. So, when using one of these Web addresses, just type in exactly what you see in this book, pretending as though the line break doesn't exist.

One last point: Because we're writing this book as a team, when we want to refer to one of our experiences, we use the person's first name (either Deirdre or Donna), so that you know which of us is behind that anecdote.

What You're Not to Read

You have a lot of training ahead of you. We don't want this book to be an excuse for "not having the time to train." So, we've written it so that you can safely skip some pieces, and still have everything you need to know.

Feel free to pass by anything in a gray box — the text in gray boxes are sidebars. You can always come back to sidebars later, when you've digested everything else in the chapter and want to expand your knowledge, along with your fitness. Same goes for anything marked with a Technical Stuff icon — these are details you won't need to know to participate in your triathlon. Of course, if you're the type who likes to know every last shred of information, have at it — you can impress all your training buddies with your know-how.

Foolish Assumptions

We assume that you know how to swim and you know how to ride a bike — but that's as far as we go. Beyond your basic ability to stay afloat and stay upright, we're prepared for anything.

If you're just getting off the couch, you'll find a training schedule with some tips for you. If you've already tried a triathlon or two and you want to find out how to do them better, faster, or farther, you'll find all you need to do that, too.

How This Book Is Organized

Triathlon Training For Dummies is divided into five parts, each with chapters covering the details of that topic. You can read just one part depending on where you are in your triathlon training or specific chapters within the parts. The organization of this book makes it easy to find what you need. Here's an overview.

Part I: Starting Your Triathlon Training

In this part, you find tools you can use to select the event that's right for you and your schedule. First, we fill you in on the five triathlon distances and how far you'll swim, bike, or run in each one. We offer tips on selecting a triathlon that's right for you. From there, we take a look at the equipment you need to train for, and participate in, a triathlon, and we offer suggestions on picking gear that fits your goals and your budget. We also give you guidelines for evaluating your fitness level and tell you what to expect if you feel you need to get a doctor's approval before beginning your training.

Part II: Taking It One Sport at a Time: Swim, Bike, Run

This part covers the basics of each of the three sports. In your triathlon, you'll start with swimming, then get on your bike, and then head off on foot for your run — we cover the three sports in that same order in this book. From there, we tell you how to put them all together and transition smoothly from one sport to the next. In each chapter, we give you a list of the benefits you'll reap from training in each of the three sports. We provide details on mastering the correct stroke, spin, or form to conserve energy and prevent injury. In this part, we also tell you the benefits of building a support network and training with other triathletes.

Part III: Training for Your Triathlon

In this part, you find out what it takes to live like a triathlete. First, we discuss how what you eat affects how you train. We offer tips on keeping your energy up for training by fueling with the best foods. Here, you also find easy-to-follow training schedules for each event distance, broken out by week, sport, and day. We leave out the jargon and confusing distances and keep it simple, so that you can focus on training and not doing math. After nutrition and training schedules, we present a detailed guide to making your muscles stronger and more flexible to improve your triathlon performance and reduce your chances of being sidelined due to injury. If you do find yourself nursing sore muscles or aching joints, this part is where you can find out what's ailing you, why, and how to make it better.

Part IV: Planning for Race Day

This part is there for you as your event approaches. First, we talk about *tapering* (cutting back on training in the weeks before your event). We tell you why tapering is important and how it can impact your performance. In this part, we also give you a checklist of items to pack for your event and tell you how to catch some shuteye in the nervous nights before your race. This part is where you find details on what to expect when you arrive at your event location and what to do, step by step and minute by minute, as you prepare for your event to start. If you're feeling nervous or doubtful, check this part for tips on staying positive and relaxed. And, after your event, this part is there with tools to help you decide what to do next.

Part V: The Part of Tens

In this part, we give you ten reasons you should do a triathlon — refer to this list anytime you need a little motivation. We also debunk ten common triathlon myths that may be causing you some worry. We give you a great insider's list of ten items that will make you look and feel like an experienced triathlete, even at your first event. And we offer ten Web sites to help you find triathlons based on event distance, time frame, or location.

Icons Used in This Book

We've designed this book so that you can focus your attention on becoming a triathlete, not a research assistant. So, we use icons to identify certain information that you'll find especially useful or important. Here are the icons in this book, along with the kinds of information they signal:

When you see the Tip icon, you'll find information that will save you time or make you a more efficient triathlete.

This book is a reference, which means you don't have to commit it to memory — you won't be quizzed on it. But occasionally, we tell you something that's so important you'll want to remember it. When we do, we use this icon.

People seem to have lots of misconceptions about triathlons. Some of these myths can scare potential triathletes away from the sport; others can just add to their nervousness as they approach the event. The information next to the MythBuster icon sets the record straight.

When we have a story to tell about our own experiences competing in or training for triathlons, we mark it with this icon.

You can get through a triathlon without knowing a lot of technical stuff. We've labeled it with this icon, so you can skip it if you're not itching to know details that won't get you to the finish line faster. Information marked with the Technical Stuff icon offers numbers, formulas, or behind-the-scenes details on gear.

Fortunately, you won't find many Warning icons in this book. When we provide information regarding your safety or health that we don't want you to miss, we identify it with the Warning icon.

Where to Go from Here

You don't have to start with Chapter 1 and read every page of this book in order before you start training. If you've already committed to training and selected an event, turn to Chapter 10 to get a feel for where you are in your training and where you'll need to be — the training schedules in that chapter break down each distance into manageable bits that will get you motivated. As you begin training, be sure to check out Chapter 3 to find out what equipment you need and what you don't. Then be sure to read through the chapters on each sport — Chapter 5 for swimming, Chapter 6 for cycling, and Chapter 7 for running — for an overview of the most efficient form and technique. And don't forget transitions: You have to get from one sport to the next — start practicing now with the tips in Chapter 8. If you're just in the thinking-about-it phase — and, hey, that's where everyone starts! — head to Chapter 16 for the friendly nudge you need to get started.

Wherever you start, with the tools in this book, there's one place you'll finish: arms held high, crossing that finish line, able to officially call yourself a triathlete. We're behind you every step of the way!

Part I
Starting Your Triathlon Training

The 5th Wave   By Rich Tennant

"Why train for a triathlon? I guess after 18 years of raising kids, running a part-time business, and volunteering at the hospital, I wanted to challenge myself."

In this part . . .

We fill you in on the first steps to take now that you've decided to train for a triathlon. In these chapters, you discover how to choose a triathlon event and what to consider if your event is far from home. You're training for three sports — swimming, biking, and running — and you need equipment; Chapter 3 is where you find an overview of everything you need (and don't need) to train for and participate in a triathlon.

In Chapter 4, we give you a list of questions to ask yourself before you start to train. We let you know what to expect at a physical with a doctor and what you could gain from an evaluation with a fitness professional.

You also find out how to enlist the support of family and friends to cheer you on and keep you focused. The triathlon is an athletic event that challenges your personal limits and brings surprising social perks. In this part, you see how training with other triathletes can keep you challenged and motivated.

Chapter 1

Training for a Multi-Sport Event

*W*elcome to the sport of triathlon — a race that combines swimming, cycling, and running in one event. Although the growth of the sport may make it seem as if everyone around you is training for a triathlon, you're actually joining a small minority — a group that the rest of the population might call either remarkably fit and dedicated, or just a little bit nuts. The degree of nuttiness they may attribute to you will be in direct correlation to the distance of your event — the longer the event, the crazier they may think you are.

But while others are scratching their heads, you'll be on your way to complete fitness — improved cardiovascular health and aerobic endurance, as well as powerful, toned muscles. But that's not all. Training for a triathlon is a social event, too — triathlon training clubs are popular with experienced athletes as well as new ones.

So what are you waiting for? This chapter launches you into life as a triathlete.

Defining Your Triathlon

You've decided to do a triathlon. But what exactly does that mean? Going from one sport to the next, and the next again, challenges all your muscle groups — and your mind. The distance of your event will determine just how great this challenge will be. And the goals you set for yourself will determine what you take away from the experience.

A brief history of triathlons

Triathlon is a relatively new sport — the first one took place in San Diego, California, in 1974. Four years later, the first Ironman triathletes crossed the finish line in Hawaii with a time of 11 hours, 46 minutes, and 58 seconds. Since then, triathletes have cut that time to the 1996 record-setting 8 hours, 4 minutes, and 8 seconds.

Triathlon became an Olympic event in 2000, at the standard Olympic race distance of a 1500m swim, 40K bike ride, and 10K run. Once reserved for elite athletes, the growth and popularity of the three-sport event has made it accessible and as easy to find as local road-running races.

Choosing a distance and event

For most first-timers a triathlon is a Sprint-distance event — an 804.7m (0.5-mile) swim, a 19.3K to 25.8K (12- to 16-mile) bike ride, and a 5K (3.1-mile) run. A Super Sprint is slightly shorter than a Sprint, but it's a less common event distance. After you have a triathlon under your belt, you may decide to take on a longer event — such as an Olympic, a Half-Iron, or the extremely challenging Ironman.

Unless you've been drawn to do a triathlon by a specific fundraising race in your area, your first step will be to select an event in a location that's accessible to you and in a time frame that gives you enough time to train. In Chapter 2, we offer tips on how to pick your first race. In Chapter 19, we offer a list of resources for finding local, national, and international races.

Choose a race that's first-timer friendly, close to home, and easy to get to.

Setting your triathlon goal

The reasons for participating in a triathlon are as varied as the athletes you'll see at the starting line — people of all sizes, shapes, and abilities. They're all there to test their endurance and meet their personal fitness or life goals.

Depending on your fitness level, your goal may be to finish your event in a certain time — or simply to finish. And for your first triathlon, that's the best place to start. If you're determined to be a little more specific about how and when, remember these goal-setting tips:

- **Stay positive.** "I will finish" will keep you far more motivated than "I won't finish last." Focus on what you *want* to do — finish happy and strong.

- **Stay personal.** If you want to focus on where you'll place, make this goal about *you*, not the other triathletes. Set your goal about your own personal finish time or how you'll feel when you finish, not about where you'll finish in relation to everyone else. Your triathlon is about *you*.

If you've entered road races, swims, or cycling events in the past, you may be tempted to set a goal time for your event. If you want to set specific time-related goals, set these for your training sessions, not for your first event. So many factors can influence your race time — water currents, wind, course elevations, even the number of other triathletes competing in your event. You don't want to be disappointed that you didn't meet an arbitrary collection of hours, minutes, and seconds for an event you finished successfully in every other way.

Evaluating Your Equipment Needs

You have ambition. You have some degree of fitness. And you have enthusiasm. Still, you may be lacking a few essentials — wheels, clothing, or shoes.

Following is a list of the basic equipment you need to complete a triathlon. Buy them now and start using them in your training. You'll want to use for your event the same clothing and equipment you train in.

- ✔ **Tri suit:** Available in one or two pieces, tri suits fit snugly and feature quick-drying fabrics and padded shorts for the ride — you don't want to have to change any clothing during your event. Tri suits look serious. Even the idea of *wearing* one can be intimidating. You may think that only the experienced or elite triathletes will be in tri suits, but the tri suit is a great choice, especially for beginners, because it simplifies your event and your transitions.

  An optional piece of equipment is a wetsuit. A wetsuit gives you warmth and buoyancy and helps you glide through the water. Water temperature and race rules will dictate whether you can wear a wetsuit.

- ✔ **Goggles:** Goggles protect your eyes from the chlorine or saltwater to help you see where you're going during your swim. Find a pair that fits your face and doesn't leak or fog. Buy a few pairs and pack them in your race bag — you won't want to swim without these.

- ✔ **Bike:** The bike is the most expensive and most complicated piece of equipment you need. If you're in the market for a new bike, visit your local bike shop and share your goals with a salesperson. If you have a bike in your garage or can borrow one from a friend, bring that to a bike shop to have it tuned and to be sure it fits you correctly.

- ✔ **Helmet:** A helmet is an absolute must-have. Don't ride without one — *ever*.

- ✔ **Other bike accessories:** Consider cycling gloves, cycling shoes, clipless pedals, and sunglasses — for comfort and efficiency, and to increase your safety.

✔ **Running shoes:** Just as you have shoes for work and shoes for play, maybe shoes for one outfit and one outfit only, you need shoes just for running. Invest in a good pair of shoes designed just for running, not cross-training or tennis or basketball. You'll appreciate the cushioning on your joints and reduce your risk of injuries.

In Chapter 3, we provide a comprehensive list of all your equipment needs — including what to look for when you're shopping and how much you can expect to spend.

With all the equipment options, it's easy to get overwhelmed and think you need the newest, shiniest, and most aerodynamic equipment you can find and afford. Not so. The most important factor in finding equipment is fit. You can spend a bundle on a high-end triathlon bike, but if it doesn't fit your body, you may as well grab yourself a tricycle.

Taking to Your Sport

Whether you're experienced in one or more of the sports or you're a long-time athlete who's practiced all three of them, putting them *together* requires practice and attention to form.

Finding your form

Even if you already enjoy each of the sports and are comfortable racing or training for a single-sport endurance event, when you train for a triathlon, you'll save energy and improve performance by focusing on the fine points of efficient strokes, spins, and steps:

✔ **Swimming:** There are five basic steps to an efficient and powerful swim stroke: hand entry, catch, pull, push, and recovery. In Chapter 5, we provide details on proper form and body position in the water (complete with illustrations).

✔ **Cycling:** If you remember riding around your neighborhood as a child, you may be surprised to know that there's a *technical* aspect to riding that can make your journey around the block easier and more fun. For more on cycling mechanics and form, turn to Chapter 6.

✔ **Running:** Most first-time triathletes are anxious about at least one of the sports. If swimming isn't your fear, odds are, it's running. For tips on staying on pace with your running, check out Chapter 7.

Making time for transitions

The links between the three sports in a triathlon are called *transitions,* and in a triathlon there are two — one from the swim to the bike (called T1) and another from the ride to the run (called T2). Transitions take place in a designated area where you'll rack your bike and lay out everything you need for your event.

Getting from your swim onto your bike can take anywhere from 5 minutes to 20, depending on how well prepared you are before your event and how much you practice going from one sport to the next.

If you follow the training schedules in Chapter 10, you'll put two sports together before your event, either going from a swim to a bike ride or a ride to a run. You don't have to train in all three sports in one day, but you'll defi-nitely want to get your muscles used to going from one sport to the next in dual-sport workouts.

On your two-sport training days, you can set up a transition area to practice placing your gear and getting it on and off quickly and easily. For transition tips, turn to Chapter 8.

Training on a Schedule

You *can* train for a triathlon and have a life. Training for any distance event is a commitment. We can't promise it won't consume your mind, but we can offer training guidelines so that your time in the water or on the road doesn't chew up every available minute of your day.

In Chapter 10, we offer detailed week-by-week training schedules for each of the event distances. But before you start following the schedules, be sure you can comfortably do the first week's training for each sport. If not, spend some time building your endurance in the sport(s) in which you're weakest.

When you have a solid fitness base, you can train for a Sprint triathlon in as little as four hours a week over a 12-week period. That's doable.

As you increase your event distance, plan to increase the time you spend training — in some cases, double that time. For example, to prepare for an Olympic distance, you'll want to allow for eight hours a week for 20 weeks. A Half-Iron will demand at least ten hours a week for 24 weeks.

An Ironman — well, forget what we said about not consuming your life. You *will* eat, sleep, and breathe triathlon training for the better part of a year, or at least 30 weeks. Everything you do, you'll think first, "How will this affect my training?" But by the time you get to the point where you're ready to compete in an Ironman, you'll be so hooked on triathlons that this will actually sound *good* to you!

Fueling your body and mind

We believe you can fit triathlon training into any lifestyle, but you do need to be prepared for it to take hold in areas you didn't expect. To maintain your energy and your motivation, you'll be making changes to your diet, your sleep habits, and your way of thinking — and if you're following a plan and staying focused, these changes will all be overwhelmingly positive.

After you begin training, you'll find it easy to identify those days when you didn't get enough sleep or eat a nutrition-packed meal. Even what you're *thinking* can affect your workout that day.

As you train, you'll begin to focus on how your body works, not so much on how it looks. Eat a bagel and drink a cup of coffee for breakfast and then try to get through a tough swim or an 80-minute bike ride. You'll notice how it affects your performance — and you'll grab that protein- and carb-rich breakfast and an extra glass of water the next morning. (For specifics on how to fuel your body with good nutrition and hydration, check out Chapter 9.)

Try this exercise some day while you're training: Tell yourself you're tired, you can't do this, you'll never make it to the next telephone pole . . . and you won't. If you focus on bad thoughts, stress, or anger, you'll feel your form fail and your speed slow. Go out and keep your thoughts on your power, your strength, how good it feels to be moving, and you'll keep moving. Yep, your mind is *that* good.

Strengthening and stretching your limits

Training with weights can help you to build stronger muscles, and the power from your pumped muscles can improve your overall triathlon performance and reduce your risk of injury. Don't worry — you don't need to spend hours in a gym. Performing two exercises, twice a week, for each of your major muscle groups — chest, back, biceps, triceps, core, hamstrings, and quadriceps — can yield dividends.

Treat your working muscles right with some gentle stretches, too. Improving your flexibility will ease sore muscles, especially in your neck, back, and shoulders after a long bike ride.

In Chapter 11, we give you a quick and easy strength-training and stretching program to enhance your triathlon training.

Looking Forward to This Race, and the Next One, and the Next One . . .

Thinking about how you'll complete your triathlon right now, as you're reading Chapter 1 of *Triathlon Training For Dummies,* may feel like you're getting ahead of yourself. But visualizing how you'll perform in your event will have two benefits:

✔ It will keep you motivated to get there.

✔ It will help you plan well for your event day.

Beyond sticking to your training schedule and making sure your gear fits and functions properly, preparing for race day by packing well and arriving early can make a big difference in how smoothly your event goes.

Knowing what to expect during your first race

To prepare for your triathlon, be sure to review all the information available on your event's Web site and read Chapter 14 of this book, where you discover what you need to do when you arrive at your event.

Most important of all: Arrive early. Give yourself at least two hours before your event starts to:

✔ Park your car.

✔ Unload your equipment.

✔ Stage your transition area.

✔ Find out how to get to the water and back to the transition area, how to get in and out of the transition area, and in what direction you need to go when you're on your bike and starting your run.

✔ Get your wetsuit on, if you're wearing one.

✔ Stretch and focus.

Thinking about what you'll do next

Yes, we really said it: What's next? If you've accepted the triathlon challenge, be prepared for the possibility that you'll be hooked. And if you are, it's easy to think bigger, better, faster.

Slow down. Remember to give yourself time to enjoy your accomplishment and accurately assess your performance. Chapter 15 is filled with great blah-busters to help you overcome any post-race burnout and helpful tips to get you headed in the right direction for your next event.

Chapter 2

Choosing Your Event

· ·

· ·

*N*ow that you've made the decision to check "Do a triathlon" off your list of goals, you need to get more specific. A triathlon is made up of three sports — swimming, cycling, and running. *That* you know. But how *far* will you swim, bike, and run? And where and when will you do it?

In this chapter, we fill you in on the five race distances so that you can choose the one that's best for you. We also let you know about other logistical considerations that go into picking an event — from course type to location to date.

Going the Distance: Knowing Your Race Options

Your first consideration in selecting an event should be the distance of the race.

When you tell your friends that you're doing a triathlon, you'll probably get a wide-eyed look or two. Most of them will know right away that a triathlon is a three-sport event — they know you'll swim, bike, and run. But their only mental images of triathlons are probably of super-buff athletes dragging themselves across the finish line of an Ironman — a ridiculous distance.

Fortunately for you (and most triathletes), you'll find a calendar full of four other race distances to tackle: Super Sprint, Sprint, Olympic, and Half-Iron.

Triathlon distances are measured in miles, meters, kilometers, or a combination. Although a 20K bike ride may sound like a distance you could never ride, 12.5 miles sounds far more doable — and they're the same thing. When evaluating your race distances, know that 1 kilometer equals approximately 0.62 mile, so a 5K would be 3.1 miles and a 10K would be 6.2 miles. If your mind works in miles and your event is measured in kilometers, simply divide the number of kilometers by 1.61 for the approximate mileage.

For an easy way to convert kilometers to miles or miles to kilometers, go to `www.google.com` and type in the search box *x* **kilometers to miles** or *x* **miles to kilometers** (replacing the *x* with the number you want to convert, of course), and then click Search. (You can do this with meters, feet, or just about any other measurement, too.)

Super Sprint

The common Super Sprint distance is, on average, a 402.3m (0.25-mile) swim, 10K (6.2-mile) bike ride, and 2.4K (1.5-mile) run. If you've already done the slightly longer Sprint triathlon, you'll want to allow at least eight weeks to train for a Super Sprint. If this is your first triathlon, though, allow 12 weeks to train for a Super Sprint.

You won't find as many Super Sprints on triathlon calendars as the other distances, and often the swim leg will take place in a pool instead of open water.

The time to complete this distance ranges from 50 to 90 minutes.

If you're nervous about the open-water swim and just entering a new world of fitness, the Super Sprint may be a good event for you. You also may choose a Super Sprint distance as a "practice" triathlon for training purposes. Super Sprints are also great events for those who don't have four or more hours a week to train.

Sprint

When you search for a triathlon on race-calendar sites, you'll find most of the events will be the popular Sprint distance — an 804.7m (0.5-mile) swim, 19.3K to 25.8K (12- to 16-mile) cycling leg, and 5K (3.1-mile) run. You'll want to give yourself at least 12 weeks to train for a Sprint. And once you're ready to go, this event is so popular, you can probably find one for every weekend of your racing season, depending on how far you can travel — and how intense you are.

Taking a crash course in race culture

Races in each race distance vary in terms of competitiveness, athletes' experience, gender, and organization. All these factors make up a race's culture and can affect how much you enjoy your event. Here are guidelines for determining a race's culture:

✔ **Competitiveness:** Some events have reputations for drawing elite or highly competitive athletes, while others are accessible to beginners. The event's Web site can offer clues as to the type of athlete it attracts. If the site explains each aspect of the event as if it welcomes those who have never done a triathlon before, it's more likely to draw beginners than a site filled with jargon and competitive race times.

✔ **Experience:** Super Sprints and Sprints are the most first-timer friendly events. You

won't find many first-time triathletes at an Ironman.

✔ **Gender:** You can find women-only events, which are especially welcoming to beginners. These races are usually Sprint distances and are first-timer friendly.

✔ **Organization:** Some races are better organized than others, with clearly written guidelines and instructions, well-stocked rest areas and water stops, and plenty of volunteers. Ask other triathletes for their recommendations for well-run races. The race's Web site may also offer clues as to how well organized the event will be. Look for Web sites that are clearly laid out and have straightforward links to course explanations and maps, registration pages, event photos, lodging, and even racer testimonials.

The time to complete this distance ranges from less than one hour for the elite group, to around one and a half to two hours for the majority of the middle-of-the-pack triathletes, to over two hours for beginners who are happy to slowly embrace their time out on the course.

Sprint-distance triathlons are great for every triathlete. They give you the endurance experience without requiring time or training that's not manageable for the average person. You can do a Sprint triathlon and still find the energy to smile as you walk back to your car. Even if you have the fitness required for an Olympic-distance event, it's best to start with a Sprint to learn about transitions, equipment needs, and nutrition and hydration.

Olympic

An Olympic triathlon is the distance sanctioned for the Olympic Games. It's sometimes also referred to as the "standard" distance, although this event is still not as popular as the Sprint. The first Olympic triathlon took place at the 2000 Olympic Games, as a 1500m (0.9-mile) swim, 40K (24.9-mile) bike, and 10K (6.2-mile) run. Plan to give yourself 20 weeks to train for an Olympic-distance event.

The time to complete this distance ranges from 75 to 90 minutes for elite tri-athletes, to between two and three hours for the middle-of-the-pack finishers. Some participants are on the course for four hours.

Pacing is the key to the Olympic triathlon because the distance can be deceiving — it seems only slightly longer than the accessible Sprint distance and acceptably shorter than the more challenging Half-Iron. But this is no Sprint distance. Be cautious about your pace during the swim and bike legs to be sure you have energy for the run. And refuel during the event to keep your energy level high.

If you have experience in endurance training — such as long-distance riding, swimming, or marathon running — you can make an Olympic-distance your first triathlon. But be sure you can comfortably complete the first week of any training plan you intend to follow, such as the one in Chapter 11.

Half-Iron

Calling this race half-anything doesn't do it justice. It's a full challenge, at half the distance of an Ironman. Sign up for one of these, and you'll be swimming 1.9K (1.2 miles), cycling for 90K (55.9 miles), and running for 21K (13 miles). But before you do any of that, you'll be training for at least 24 weeks.

The time to complete this distance is upwards of five hours, with the cutoff time being eight and a half hours. If you haven't reached a certain point in the course by a designated time, the race organizers will most likely pick you up in what's called a *sag wagon* or a *sweep truck.* There's no shame in the sag wagon. Take the ride if you need it — it's for your safety and health.

Don't approach this distance half-heartedly. Plan to devote much of your free time to training.

You'll need to refuel with some combination of gels, energy bars, sports drinks, and food to make it through this race, regardless of your conditioning. Visit the race Web site before your event and research where the fueling sta-tions are positioned on the course and what they'll serve. Train with an eye on these fueling-station distances and options so that you'll be prepared — or plan to bring your own favorite fuel source.

If you're working your way toward an Ironman, you most definitely need to spend some time with the Half-Iron. Still, don't start here. This is *not* a first-triathlon kind of event, regardless of your fitness level and experience.

Ironman

If you got nervous reading about the Half-Iron and thinking about being on the course for eight hours or more, running your body toward empty, or being swept into a truck somewhere just past Mile 63, get your armor on.

The Ironman is the event that causes your friends' jaws to drop when you tell them you're training for a triathlon. The event has earned a reputation so stunning that every triathlete gets to bask in its glory, even if you aren't training for the actual 140-plus-mile event.

Yes, 140-plus miles. It's a number that's hard to wrap your head around. The Ironman is 3.8K (2.4 miles) in the water, 180K (111.9 miles) on a bike, and 42.2K (26.2 miles) running — each event's golden mileage. Swimmers aspire to passing that 2-mile mark, cyclists strive for the century (100 miles), and runners reach for the marathon (26.2 miles). Now, put them all together, and you have the Ironman. The Ironman is the Mount Everest of triathlons, the event just about all serious triathletes aspire to, whether they admit it or not.

You'll need a few Half-Irons under your race belt before you can think of doubling the distance for an Ironman. And you'll need 30 weeks, at least, of training time. You'll also need to register far in advance (possibly a year, depending on your event), and you may need to qualify by offering proof that you've successfully completed other triathlon races.

An Ironman requires your full commitment — mentally, physically, and socially. In fact, the name is all wrong. It should be Ironmen or Ironfamily or Ironfriends. Because everyone you know will need to be along for the miles on this one. You'll need support from your friends, family, coworkers, boss, neighbors, mail carrier. . . . Well, maybe not the mail carrier, but don't rule it out!

An Ironman is not a distance you can conquer without logging the training hours. Even the race itself requires you to commit at least four days to it. You can't just show up that morning as you might for a Sprint distance, complete the race, and go home. You'll need to attend pre-race events and workshops; you'll want to scout the course, swim in the water, and attend all the mandatory safety meetings. And you'll likely have to travel to get to the event — there aren't as many Ironman events as there are Sprints.

An Ironman should not, never, no way be a triathlete's first event.

Checking Your Calendar

After you've selected your distance, you need to make sure you give yourself ample time to train. For example, if you decide on a Sprint event and find a local race that's 6 weeks away, consider how far along you are in your training schedule, because you'll need at least 12 weeks to train adequately for a Sprint triathlon. Start searching race calendars at last three months out from today's date. If today's date finds you comfortably on the couch without a solid fitness base, add another two to three months to that schedule.

Here are some other things to consider when you're checking your calendar:

- ✔ **Weather:** Remember to consider the weather where you live. For example, if it's January and your aim is to get started right away training for a July Sprint, you may need access to a gym, fitness center, or at-home equipment.

- ✔ **Travel:** If it's already July, and you were inspired by a local triathlon in your area and you're eager to get started, consider when you'll be ready for your first event — anywhere from October to December. Depending on where you live, you'll be meeting up with the end of triathlon season, which coincides with warm-weather months, and you may have to travel for your event.

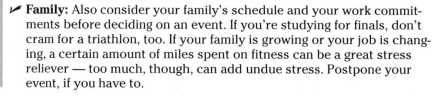

If you find yourself a year away from your event, get started now anyway, building your strength and fitness and perfecting your form. When you're 12 weeks out from event day, you'll be ready to enter your training season strong.

- ✔ **Family:** Also consider your family's schedule and your work commitments before deciding on an event. If you're studying for finals, don't cram for a triathlon, too. If your family is growing or your job is changing, a certain amount of miles spent on fitness can be a great stress reliever — too much, though, can add undue stress. Postpone your event, if you have to.

Getting into many of the most popular events is a little like getting a ticket to the hottest concert of the summer. Okay, so you won't have to sleep out on the sidewalk all night for nosebleed seats, but you will have to act fast or risk being shut out. If the event has an e-mail list, get on it. You'll receive an e-mail when registration opens — be sure to sign up right away.

Considering the Course

After you've picked your distance, it's time to consider the course. No two triathlons are the same — even if they're the same distance. The body of water or the height of the hills can make a huge difference in how you train for and compete in your event. Before you fall in love with a location, think about what kind of course you can handle.

Going with the flow in a lake, ocean, or river

Many people choose a triathlon based on what type of water the swim is in. In an ocean swim, you have to deal with the tide, waves, and saltwater. In a lake, depending on the size, you also may experience large waves and strong currents, both of which add to the difficulty of your swim leg. If you're swimming in a river, you can find yourself swimming against a strong current, which certainly will be more tiring than swimming in a calm pool or placid lake.

If thoughts of the swim cause you anxiety, look for a first race in which the swim is in a pool or in a small body of water, such as a small lake or the bay of an ocean.

If your event choices will have you swimming in an ocean, a vast lake, or anything but a lazy river, don't panic — practice. Work open-water swims into your training schedule. After you're used to breaking through the waves or pushing against a current (or, better yet, letting a current carry you along), you'll feel more confident on race day.

Race organizers will monitor the water conditions. If strong currents or rip tides make swimming difficult or dangerous, they'll postpone or cancel the event.

Striving for peak performance

Knowing the height and frequency of hills on your course is as important as knowing the size of the waves or strength of the current.

Check an event's Web site for course details. Often, you'll find a map of the course showing the elevation or height in feet of each of the climbs.

If you can find only directions along the route or a map of the course itself, use a tool such as www.mapmyride.com to map the course and track the feet you'll climb and over how much mileage.

Some runners or cyclists excel on the long, slow climbs; others are strongest on the steep hills. Know what you're facing and train on hills to mimic what you'll find on your race course. If your event is local or close enough for a day trip, you can do some pre-race reconnaissance and get a feel for the terrain.

If looming peaks scare you, find yourself a pancake-flat course — they're out there.

Planes, Trains, and Automobiles: Traveling to Your Event

You may get lucky enough to roll out of bed and onto your race course —
especially if you're doing a Sprint, Super Sprint, or even an Olympic distance.
It's more likely, though, that you'll have to travel for your event, especially if
it's a Half-Iron or an Ironman. In fact, travel for these distances is often part
of the fun. Would you rather cover 140 miles in your own area, or along the
beach of a tropical island or other exotic locale?

For the longer distances, you may even want to choose an international
event. You can find Ironman races all over the world, including throughout
the United States, Canada, Australia, New Zealand, Malaysia, South Africa,
Brazil, the Canary Islands, and China.

Doing a simple Internet search on your race distance and your locations
of choice will yield hours' worth of leads. Take your time to evaluate the
courses and the cultures of the races. Post to event forums or triathlon discussion boards, or ask friends or fellow triathletes to recommend an event.

For your first event, we recommend you stay as close to home as possible.
Logistically, having nothing to worry about but loading your car will give you
more energy to focus on your triathlon. After you've experienced all there is to
navigate at a triathlon (finding your way around, getting your gear to and from
the transition area, picking up your race packet, convincing a pack of friends
to follow and cheer for you), you can expand your comfort zone — and your
time zone.

If do end up traveling for your event, think ahead and have a contingency plan
for forgotten gear or lost luggage as you would for any travel plans.

Create a spreadsheet detailing all the costs associated with traveling to your
triathlon. You can end up spending as much money as you'd spend on a vacation, which is great — as long as you're exhilarated (as many triathletes are)
by the thought of spending your vacation swimming, biking, and running to
the point of exhaustion.

In the following sections, we offer tips for getting yourself and your gear to
your event, as well as factoring in the costs associated with traveling for a
triathlon.

Getting yourself there

When you're calculating your costs for travel to your destination, be sure to
consider the following, depending on how you plan to get to your event:

- Air or rail fare
- Extra luggage expenses for your equipment
- Car rental
- Gas
- Tolls
- Meals and snacks
- Forgotten incidentals (toothpaste, water bottles, sports drinks, socks, and so on)
- Parking at the airport, train station, or hotel
- Tips
- Internet access (so that you can share your success with your friends and family)
- Local maps, if necessary

Getting your gear there

Your bulkiest piece of equipment is also your most important — your bike. You can ship your bike ahead of time or take it with you on the train or plane:

- **Shipping your bike:** If you ship your bike, you'll be without it for at least a week before and after your event. To ship your bike, visit your local bike store and ask for assistance. Shipping your bike requires that you remove the wheels, pedals, and aero bars (if you're using them), and protect your frame and your fork.

  Find someone experienced in packing bikes instead of trying to do it yourself — especially for your first time; otherwise, you risk damaging your bike. Your event organizer can help you locate a local bike shop in the area where you'll participate in your event. Larger events will even have a system in place to help you get your bike to the event. Check your event's Web site.

  Give yourself enough time to allow for shipping so that you don't have to pay an extra fee to get it there overnight. Also, consider insuring your shipment and make sure you have a way to track your package.

- **Taking it with you:** You have to pay an extra fee to transport your bike on a plane. You also have to plan for how you'll get it to the terminal. A bike shipping box can be bulky and unwieldy, especially if it doesn't have wheels or a handle. You'll need to locate a cart or other means to wheel your bike (without benefit of its own wheels) to the check-in point.

> If you're traveling by train, certain train lines will allow you to wheel your bike (unboxed) right onto a designated area of the train. Check your train line's Web site for requirements, and plan to bring tools and bungee cords in case you need to secure your bike or remove pedals.

Regardless of how you plan to get your bike to your event, unless you're rolling it onto a train with you, you'll need a bike box. These boxes are sized correctly for bicycles and are available in cardboard for around $50 or in plastic for as much as $500.

Trains and airlines sometimes have boxes available for you to use to pack your bike into when you arrive, but we don't recommend this option, because you'll have to worry about bringing tools to disassemble and reassemble your bike and stuff it into a box that may not fit it well.

Be sure to have your bike tuned before shipping. Mark your seat position by putting a piece of tape on the seat post. And be sure to clearly write your name and address on the bike box. Consider also adding a piece of tape with the same information or a phone number on your bike itself.

You may want to consider renting a bike or other equipment for your event if you're traveling. Bike shops offer bike rentals from $50 a day to more than $150 a day. The advantage is that you can get a better bike than you have at home. If this is your first triathlon, though, you'll lose the comfortable fit and feel of the bike you trained on throughout the season.

Eating and sleeping away from home

Depending on where you go and where you're coming from, you can be crossing time zones to get to your triathlon. It's hard enough to sleep the night before your first event as it is. Throw in a transcontinental red-eye flight, and you can find yourself at the race start with less sleep than the time it will take you to complete your event.

Only *you* know how you do with time changes. But add the dehydrating effects of air travel, and you can feel tired before you even begin. If you don't adjust well, don't arrive the day before your event and expect to be rested and ready. Give yourself extra time to adjust to the time change or stay closer to home.

You may also have to battle food differences. Different cuisines can wreak havoc on your digestive system. Try to stick to foods you know.

If you travel far from home, you may be leaving behind your cheering section. Be sure you're up to starting and finishing without them.

Weathering the heat or cold

If you're traveling for your event, the climate and water temperature may be different from what you're used to training in. Check the weather so that you can pack appropriately, adding a wetsuit to your gear bag if the water is colder than you're used to, and tossing in arm warmers or another layer for the bike portion to keep you warm after your swim.

Traveling to a warmer climate can be harder to adjust to than a colder climate. Even with lightweight clothing, you'll need more fluids, and you'll have to avoid going out too hard and risk overheating.

On the other hand, the swim leg that made you anxious during training can be the leg you look forward to most in a warmer climate. And it won't hurt to jump back into the water at the end of your event.

Registering for Your Event

After you know when and where your triathlon will be held, and how long it'll be, you can register for your event. Race registrations cost anywhere from $75 to as much $500 (for an Ironman).

Register as soon as possible after you decide on your event, and consider booking any travel arrangements or hotel accommodations early. Because some races close out within hours after opening for registration, have a second-choice race in mind so that you can avoid being disappointed when you don't get into the race you had your heart set on.

All races max out at a certain number of participants, and that number depends on the race location. Talk to other triathletes to find out which races are more popular to get an idea how early you need to register. Sometimes the less popular races are better for first-timers, because they're less competitive and lower key, and they usually don't have a large number of participants.

To register for an event, you'll need to supply the following:

- ✔ Your name, address, and age on race day
- ✔ Emergency-contact information of someone who will be with you at the event or will be nearby
- ✔ Your USA Triathlon number, if you have one (see the "Becoming a USA Triathlon member" sidebar, for more information)

Becoming a USA Triathlon member

USA Triathlon (USAT) is the sanctioning body for triathlons and *duathlons* (two-sport events). It's a membership-based organization, offering registration discounts to its members for all USAT-sanctioned events. The USAT also ranks members who compete in sanctioned events.

If you hope to become a competitive triathlete, you'll want to join the USAT to take advantage of the ranking program and to save money on your race registrations. You'll also receive a USAT sticker, the organization's quarterly magazine, discounts on triathlon gear, travel incentives, and discounts for events. Basic adult membership

costs $39 per year as of this writing; kids 17 and under can join for just $5 per year.

If you're not concerned about your overall standing among other triathletes, know that events that do *not* have a USAT sanction can be organized just as well as sanctioned events. Don't make your event decision based solely on event sanctioning.

For more information on USAT, go to www.usa-triathlon.org, call 719-955-2807, or e-mail membership@usatriathlon.org.

The registration form may also have an option to check off if you're a first-timer, especially if the event is a Sprint distance. If you enter as a first-timer, for many events, you can't win an award in your age group because you're grouped with all the first-timers. If you're competitive and believe you have a true shot of placing in your age group, register as an age-group participant and not as a first-timer.

Aside from age-group categories, many races have groups for *Clydesdales* (men who weigh more than 200 pounds) and for *Athenas* (women who weigh more than 150 pounds). Within these categories are two age groups — 39 and younger and a masters' division of 40 and older.

When you register online, you'll receive an e-mail confirmation and can go online to check the race Web site to find out how many other participants are registered and how many are in your age group.

Event organizers generally have a no-refund and no-transfer policy. If you can't make the event, you won't get your money back. And you can't give your spot to someone else.

Chapter 3

Gearing Up with the Right Equipment

Triathletes might be eclipsed only by race-car drivers in their desire to compete using the fastest, most aerodynamic, and shiniest gear. Although you'd be hard-pressed to win the Indy 500 in a standard-equipment, off-the-lot hybrid, you can participate respectably in triathlons without burning through the equity in your home.

Still, we *are* talking three sports — so you do need some equipment. In this chapter, we get you geared up for your triathlon — telling you what you need to get started, giving you a list of the basics you need to train and to race, sharing insight into what to borrow and what you shouldn't bother to buy, and telling you where to splurge and where to save — all with an eye on your event goals and your bank account.

The gear doesn't make the athlete — the training makes the athlete. Donna has been living this mantra since arriving in college on a tennis scholarship. In her gym shorts and worn sneakers, she played next to players sporting hundreds of dollars worth of shoes and racquets who couldn't get the ball over the net. Just the same, you can participate in a triathlon in the bathing suit you have, on the bike in your garage, and in your favorite pair of running shoes.

Still worried? Okay, then, we pare down the products to just the essentials, all designed to do two things — get you there and have you convinced you look like you belong.

Saving money on equipment

The good news is triathletes do love gear. And they want the latest and lightest — so finding a gently used bike or other training equipment can be easy to do if you know where to look.

Expensive items such as bikes, cycling equipment, and wetsuits are your best bets for savings. If someone has posted a link to his low-mileage running shoes, garaged in the winter weather, take a pass and go for new.

And if even the thought of wearing someone else's running shoes sends you sprinting, then stop for a second and think about who's been in that wetsuit before you. If wetsuits aren't properly rinsed in clean water after every use, they can take on what is affectionately known as the owner's "funk."

If you're comfortable with a used wetsuit, give it a shot. Or if you have a friend or family member you're really close to — *really* — try out her suit.

This leaves you looking for the most costly equipment — bikes — and it's the place where you can save the most. Spend time trying new bikes at a reputable local bike shop so that you know what type of bike you're most comfortable riding or what size frame fits you best.

When making a purchase, avoid the second-hand sporting-good stores and pawnshops and go right to the source — the athletes. Visit your local cycling store or contact a cycling club or triathlon club and ask around.

Reaching out to friends or family is even better than buying second-hand from a stranger. Chances are, you know someone who has a bike in the garage eager to be taken off the hooks and out for a spin.

Borrowing from friends or family has the added advantage of creating a free trial period. Try out the gear. When you fall in love with the sport (and most likely, you will) and you're ready to commit to a new bike or a wetsuit, you'll know what you like and what you want.

Shopping online for new gear can offer significant savings, too. Still, before you buy online, visit a reputable local shop that specializes in triathlons or in each of the three sports. Fit is important for all your gear, so find out first what fits best. It won't matter how much money you saved on your equipment if you can't use it.

Selecting Comfort First

Every triathlete needs three essential pieces of equipment: a bathing suit, a bike, and running shoes. Beyond that, everything else is about comfort and attempting to improve performance. If your basics aren't comfortable and don't fit correctly, nothing else you add — regardless of high-performance promises — will matter.

So, start with good fit. Only you can decide what feels good. And the best way to determine this is to try on your training clothes and wear them while training.

If your bathing suit doesn't fit, it will rub and chafe, distract you with its falling straps, and create drag, which will slow you down in the water. If your bike doesn't fit, your pedal strokes will be inefficient, you'll waste energy, and you may injure yourself and get off the saddle with aches in your back, knees, or worse. If your running shoes don't fit, you'll be nursing blisters, at a minimum, and possibly dealing with shin splits or knee and back pain. And you won't want to train if you're hurting before you even get started.

Take the time to try on your training clothes and move around in them. Then take them to the water and to the roads.

The day of your event is not the time to try a wetsuit or clipless cycling pedals for the first time. So, if you want a stronger pedal stroke and more efficiency on race day, get a wetsuit or lock into your pedals and start practicing now.

You'll have the best experience on race day if you're not tending to blisters or raw skin. Don't buy new equipment right before your event date. You need time to break it in and get comfortable with it or in it.

Suiting Up: Knowing What Equipment You Need for Swimming

Choosing a swimsuit isn't as simple as throwing on the one you wore on vacation in Florida last year. You need to choose a true racing suit, one that's meant to help you move through the water fast. As important as a good suit are goggles and swim caps. In this section, we fill you in on how to choose a suit (and cover the various types of suits available, including wetsuits), as well as what to look for in goggles and caps.

Hang on to your old swimsuits and even those board shorts. For a challenging workout, put on board shorts or wear two or three slightly worn-out one-piece bathing suits and swim. The loose fit of the shorts or the additional weight of the suits creates drag, making it harder to cut through the water. You'll have to swim harder — like a hill workout for the pool. You can buy drag suits for the same effect.

Think everyone at your triathlon will be sporting a fit physique? Not so. You'll see bodies in every shape and size. In fact, you may be hard-pressed to pick a first-time triathlete out of a lineup of nine couch potatoes and one non-elite participant. In a typical triathlon of 300 participants, you'll find very few elite athletes. So, that leaves the majority of participants feeling just like you. They're all getting into bathing suits of some type. And they're all athletes — including you. So grab your suit, leave your fears on the sand or pool deck, and take the plunge.

Selecting a suit

Triathletes swim in bathing suits designed specifically for the sport, not for lounging or sunbathing. Sport suits are made of snug fitting nylon materials with plenty of Lycra or spandex and generally are treated to resist the harsh chlorine of pools in which you'll most likely train.

Anything that prevents you from cutting through the water smoothly, such as a suit that doesn't fit closely to your body, decreases your *hydrodynamics* (efficiency in the water) and slows you down.

You'll likely wear one kind of suit for training, and another kind of suit for the triathlon itself. In the following sections, we cover both. We also fill you in on wetsuits — when to wear one, when not to wear one, and how to find one that fits.

Training suits

Female triathletes generally choose one-piece sport suits, called *racing suits,* for training. Suits are available with racerback styling or T-backs with thin or thick straps, designed to fit a variety of women's shapes. Try on many suits to find the fit that works best for your body type.

Look for flat seams and locked stitches at the shoulders and around the legs for comfort and to prevent chafing or binding.

When selecting a suit, opt for a snug fit. When the suit gets wet, the fabric stretches slightly. If your suit fits loosely when dry, you can count on uncomfortable sagging during your swim.

Suits for women range in price from $50 to $80 at your local swimming-supply store, but when you know your fit, you can get a good-quality swimsuit for as little as $20 at online sources such as SwimOutlet.com (www.swimoutlet.com).

Most male triathletes prefer jammers, suits that come to the knees. Jammers provide the added benefit of keeping muscles warm for improved performance for your longer swims. You can find Jammers for around $45.

Traditional racing suits, or bikini briefs, are also an option. You'll find briefs in the $25 to $35 price range.

 If you normally take to the surf in your favorite board shorts, test a bathing suit with a slimmer fit for a more efficient swim. Baggy suits slow you down — after a while, swimming laps in board shorts can begin to feel as if you're dragging a piano behind you.

Triathlon suits: Traditional versus multi-sport

After you have your suit for training, it's time to consider what you'll wear at the event. What you wear in the water on event day will be what you'll wear for the entire event (the bike and run, too), so make sure it's comfortable.

You have two main options: traditional sport suits and multi-sport suits (also called tri suits).

Traditional suits

A traditional suit is the same kind of racing suit that we describe in the "Training suits" section earlier. It's a basic racing swimsuit, not specifically geared toward competing in triathlons. You can wear a traditional sport suit during a Super Sprint–, Sprint-, or even an Olympic-distance triathlon.

If you think you may want to compete in a traditional suit, be sure to simulate how the suit will feel when it's wet and you're transitioning from the swim to the bike and run. On one of your training days, immediately after your swim, get on your bike and ride a short distance to see if you'll be comfortable on the bike. Riding without padding in your shorts, especially if your bathing suit seams rub against your body, can be painful.

During your event, you can slip on a pair of bike shorts, but remember, when you're wet, they won't just slide on. And the chamois in the shorts will absorb the water in your bathing suit, leaving you feeling like you're riding and running in a wet diaper.

If you choose to wear a traditional bathing suit and will pull on cycling shorts after the swim, use some Body Glide or other lubricant at the seams to prevent blisters or chafing. Still, pulling cycling shorts over wet skin is difficult and will cost you time in your transitions.

Multi-sport or tri suits

Because of the difficulty of pulling on cycling shorts over a wet suit, many triathletes choose a multi-sport suit, or tri suit. Tri suits (see Figure 3-1), available in one or two pieces, pack all the features of a bathing suit, bike shorts, and running gear into one efficient outfit, eliminating awkward and time-consuming transition changes.

Tri suits wick water from your body and dry quickly, keeping you comfortable. In addition to the efficiency at transitions, tri suits offer a little more coverage and a snug, compression fit with varying leg lengths. And, let's face it, if you're like us and most triathletes, you're not eager to take all your uncovered parts bumping and jiggling along on a bike or run. The flat-stitched seams of a tri suit can also help to prevent chafing. A tri suit with a compression fit can also increase blood flow, bringing more oxygen to your muscles to decrease fatigue

Figure 3-1:
Tri suits are available in one or two pieces and are made with quick-drying, wicking fabric with thin chamois padding in the shorts for comfort on the bike leg of your event.

Courtesy of De Soto Triathlon Company

The shorts on tri suits are longer in the leg than a traditional bathing suit, eliminating the rough elastic seams exactly where you don't need them on the bike. And the shorts have a built-in, lightweight (lighter than traditional bike shorts) chamois, which is padding just where you need it when riding, for added comfort on the bike; the chamois isn't so thick that it will be uncomfortable for the run.

Tri suits are more expensive than traditional racing suits, ranging from $60 to $100 for bottoms and $40 to $80 for tops or $200 for a one-piece suit. Fit is essential — you want a suit that's snug but not tight. Visit a swimming-supply or sports shop that caters to triathletes to try on a suit.

Some women prefer the two-piece tri suits to the one-piece, because they're easier to manage on the last-minute bathroom breaks before the start time. But many women choose one-piece suits which cover their midsections. Women may also want to consider adding the extra support of sports bras under their suits for dual-sport training days and for the event.

A man can choose to wear a tri suit bottom during the swim and add a tri suit top or cycling shirt at the transition to the bike leg, but a one-piece suit (or wearing the top of a two-piece suit during a swim) saves time at the transition to the bike.

When you're shopping for a tri suit, look for the following:

Caring for your suit

Traditional racing suits and tri suits are made of highly technical, manufactured fabrics that require special care to maintain the fabrics' performance. Harsh detergents can damage the fabrics' wicking and quick-dry properties. Here are some tips for caring for your suits to ensure they maintain their fit and function:

✔ Follow any manufacturer's care instructions on your suit.

✔ Rinse your suit in fresh water as soon after a swim as possible.

✔ Use only a small amount of laundry soap free of bleach, fabric softener, and scents, or choose a product specifically made for high-tech fabrics.

✔ Do not twist or wring your suit.

✔ Hang your suit to air dry, and then lay it flat after it's dry.

✔ Smooth, flat seams

✔ A comfortable, non-binding (but supportive), snug fit

✔ Lightweight, easy-to-use zippers for one-piece suits

✔ Lightweight, quick-drying chamois in the shorts

✔ Quick-dry, wicking fabrics with a blend of Lycra and spandex, or a Teflon coating to increase hydrodynamics

✔ Small pockets in which you can place energy foods at the transition to the bike. Choose pockets with zippers. During the swim, close the zippers to prevent the pockets from filling with water.

You'll want to train in your tri suit, but don't wear it for every training session. It's not designed for repeated dunking in a chlorinated pool, and the chamois won't hold up to repeated long-distance rides.

You won't be able to change clothing in transition areas — triathlon organizers don't welcome exhibitionists. (In fact, many event organizers require that men wear shirts on the bike and run legs.) At best, you can remove a wetsuit or add shorts over a bathing suit. In other words, the clothes you'll start in are the clothes you'll finish in, so make sure they're the right ones by training in them a number of times.

Wetsuits

For some beginners and even seasoned swimmers, wetsuits are the security blankets of triathlons. A wetsuit is a one- or two-piece, body-fitting suit made from neoprene rubber. Available with various leg and sleeve lengths, a wetsuit keeps you warm in the water by allowing a little water to enter between your body and the suit, which warms to your body temperature and becomes a layer of insulation.

Wetsuits also bring added benefits:

- ✔ **Buoyancy:** A wetsuit raises you higher in the water and enhances your ability to float.

- ✔ **Efficiency:** The buoyancy of a suit better positions your body, so you swim faster using the same energy or save energy while swimming at your race pace, saving you some steam for your bike and run.

- ✔ **Security:** When you get used to the feel of a wetsuit, it can provide a sense of comfort as you enter the swim leg. So, if an open-water swim scares you — and it does many first-timers — consider wearing a wetsuit.

- ✔ **Glide:** Wetsuits create a smooth and silky form, decreasing drag and increasing speed.

So, if wetsuits keep you warm and help to keep you afloat, why wouldn't you always want to wear one? Well, you have to get it on (no easy feat). You have to keep it on (not always pleasant). Then you have to take it off — quickly. What time you gain in the water, you may lose in your transition times.

Wetsuits can be expensive, too, running anywhere from $200 to $600. Surf wetsuits can be less expensive but are designed for warmth not buoyancy, so what you gain in costs savings you lose in energy savings.

Surf suits are designed to accommodate a paddling motion, not an efficient stroke, and the surf-suit material is tougher to hold up to friction on the board, reducing your smoothness and increasing risk of chafing.

Depending on your event location and the water temperature, event organizers may prohibit wetsuits (to prevent you from getting too warm) or may require wetsuits. Check with the organizer or visit the event's Web site before race day. Generally, if the water temperature is above 78°F (26°C), you won't be eligible to win awards if you're wearing a wetsuit, and if the temperature is above 84° (29°C), the event organizer may prohibit wetsuits.

Shopping for a wetsuit

When you're shopping for a wetsuit, look for the following:

- ✔ **Construction:** Choose a suit designed for swimming, not surfing, scuba diving or water skiing. Look for a wetsuit that features varied thickness around the arms and legs for maximum comfort, flexibility, and range of motion. Suits designed specifically for triathlons will have the thickest neoprene in the legs for maximum buoyancy.

✔ **Fit:** Choose a suit that is snug but does not constrict your movement, especially in your shoulders. A poorly fitting wetsuit can cause your shoulders to tire or your back to ache.

✔ **Smooth seams:** Stitching should be concealed and smooth to prevent chafing.

✔ **Accessibility:** Look for features — such as a smooth, lightweight, easy-to-release zipper — that make your suit easy to get on and off.

There are numerous types of wetsuits available (see Figure 3-2):

✔ **Full:** Features long sleeves and full-length legs in a one-piece suit, designed to keep swimmers warm in waters ranging from 50°F to 66°F (10°C–19°C).

✔ **Sleeveless:** Allows more flexibility in the arms and shoulders than a full suit and is suitable in water temperatures from 66°F to the upper 70s (19°C–26°C).

Figure 3-2: Wetsuits come with sleeves and pants of various lengths for different water temperatures.

Courtesy of De Soto Triathlon Company

✔ **Two-piece:** Provides flexibility in fit with a separate top and pants of various lengths, reducing the possibility of shoulder fatigue that sometimes comes from the limited reach created by a one-piece suit. Two-piece wetsuits also may be easier than full suits to get on and off.

✔ **Spring suit:** Offers buoyancy without too much warmth. Best for temperatures above 76°F (24°C) because a spring suit features short sleeves or no sleeves, and pants to the knee.

Trying on a wetsuit

The first step to consider when trying on a wetsuit for fit is what you'll be wearing under your suit.

During your event, you'll have to peel off your wetsuit and jump on your bike, so many triathletes choose to wear tri suits under their wetsuits. At a minimum, you'll need a bathing suit.

You'll start with your legs when pulling on a one-piece wetsuit, and this will be easiest if you sit down. Be careful where you sit. Sharp objects — or stones and gravel if you're outside at your event — can tear the fabric of your suit. And be careful of long fingernails, which can rip the suit.

Just like pants, you start with the feet first. Keeping your socks on will help you to pull the suit over your feet. Point your toes and slip one foot through one leg and then the other foot through the other leg. When your feet are in, stand up and pull the suit over one calf and then the other calf. Then pull your suit up to one thigh and then up to the thigh on the other leg. Proceed slowly and don't yank your suit from the waist. Continue to pull your suit over your buttocks to your waist.

Next, put on one sleeve at a time. Slide one arm into one sleeve and then the other arm into the other sleeve. Pull the wetsuit up over one shoulder and then the other shoulder, and adjust your suit until the crotch is properly in place.

Ideally, you should be able to zip the wetsuit yourself. Make sure the wetsuit is pulled up and back on your shoulders before trying to zip it. A wetsuit comes with a zip line that you can grab and pull up over your head to pull the zipper to the top. After it's zipped, secure the neck closure (it's usually Velcro) to prevent the zipper from opening.

Expect to spend about ten minutes getting into your suit. (Fortunately, when you put your suit on for the event, you do so before the event starts!) Be sure to head to the restrooms first, and then allow plenty of time to stuff yourself into your suit.

Body Glide or other lubricating product specifically designed for wetsuits can help make the process of getting your wetsuit on and off a little easier. Use a small amount of the product around your neck, wrists, and ankles. Putting socks on your feet as you pull on the pants of your suit can help prevent snags. Take off the socks after you have finished putting on the suit.

Knowing if a wetsuit fits

Wetsuit sizes are determined by height and weight, and a wetsuit should fit you like a second skin — feeling snug but not restricting your movement or feeling so tight around your chest that it compromises your ability to breathe. When you try on a suit, you'll notice it feels hot and uncomfortable out of the water. Don't worry; it's supposed to feel that way. A wetsuit expands slightly when it gets wet, so it'll feel slightly more comfortable in the water.

And don't be surprised if your wetsuit looks even worse on you than it feels. Wetsuits compress your body in all the wrong places, but it's likely that you'll get so attached to yours and all its buoyancy and warmth, you won't care much.

A suit that fits you properly has

- ✔ **No loose spots or gaps.**
- ✔ **A comfortable but not restrictive fit in the crotch.** Move your arms above your head and try your swimming strokes to ensure the suit doesn't pull. If you feel a slight resistance, the wetsuit fits. If you don't notice any resistance, the wetsuit is too big, and too much resistance means the suit is too small.
- ✔ **A zipper that's hard to zip but not impossible to zip by yourself.**

Before your event, wear your suit during a training swim or two. Practice taking it off. Think about what you'll do if you can't get if off quickly enough for that last bathroom break before your wave is called to swim. And know that everyone else is thinking the same thing.

The eyes have it: Finding the best goggles

Sure, you can swim without goggles . . . if you don't mind swimming blind. Goggles are a must-have, both for your swim training and for the event, and the only way to find a pair that works for you is through trial and error. Goggles are one of your cheapest pieces of equipment, but they can be one of the most frustrating to get just right. Why? Because you can't tell if your goggles will leak, fog, or fall off as you dive in until you try them in the water.

Goggles protect your eyes from chlorinated pool waters or the saltwater of an open-water swim, and they allow you to see better in the water. Seeing better isn't a luxury — it's a necessity. If you can't see well during your swim, you won't be able to spot the buoys to stay on course.

Goggles are made of lightweight plastic. Each eyepiece on a pair of goggles features a foam, rubber, or gel cushion to create a watertight seal between the goggle and your *ocular bone* (the bone around your eye) to prevent leaking. Still, even with the seal, goggles can leak, fog, or just fall off.

You'll find many sizes and styles of goggles, but they all fall into one of two main categories:

- **Traditional goggles or race goggles** (shown in Figure 3-3) cover each of your eye sockets individually and sit close to your eye. Race goggles come in a variety of styles, but they're all small, light, and low in profile to reduce drag. Lens sizes vary, with some offering better visibility than others. The amount of gel or rubber around the lens varies as well; less rubber means less drag but also less comfort. Race goggles are inexpensive, starting at only $6.

- **Triathlon masks** (shown in Figure 3-3) cover your entire eye area, including the bridge of your nose. Triathlon swim masks are larger than goggles but not as big as a scuba mask. The size makes them more comfortable to wear and offers better peripheral vision, allowing you to easily see other swimmers and buoys, and some triathletes find they leak and fog less than traditional goggles. Masks cost around $12 to $35.

Treating your wetsuit right

- Use only lubricating products designed for wetsuits. Do not use petroleum jelly, cooking spray, or other oils on your wetsuit — they can cause the neoprene to break down and crack.

- After each use, rinse your wetsuit with cool and soft water, being sure to get any sand or salty water from the teeth of the zipper. Do not put your wetsuit in a washing machine.

- Use a wetsuit-specific cleanser, if necessary, and rinse off your wetsuit as soon as possible after your swim. Leaving your wetsuit in a crumpled ball will cause mold to develop, ruining your suit.

- Hang your wetsuit on a thick plastic hanger to air-dry. Never put your wetsuit in the dryer.

- Take your wetsuit off the hanger when it's dry to prevent it from stretching at the shoulders.

- Store your wetsuit, lying flat and inside-out, in a cool, dry location.

Figure 3-3:
Traditional
goggles
or race
goggles,
center, are
available in
a variety of
sizes and
cover each
of your eye
sockets
individually.
Swimmasks,
right and
left, are
larger than
goggles and
cover the
entire eye
area and the
bridge of the
nose.

Photo by Ed Pagliarini

Regardless of the type of goggles you choose, look for:

✔ **Easily adjustable head straps:** Goggles head straps adjust at the temple to give you a snug fit. Goggles in the $25 to $30 price range feature an easily adjustable buckle system with one strap. Goggles with double straps have an S-bracket type of adjustment. To adjust the strap for the best fit, you need to pull the straps to lengthen or shorten them.

✔ **Tinted lenses or the option to change out lenses depending on weather conditions:** Not sure which tint is best? Here's a quick guide to selecting tinted lenses:

• Clear: Good for indoor pool use or on overcast days.

• Yellow, amber, or red: Improves visibility on overcast days.

• Blue: Best for early mornings or evenings.

• Gray: Best for sunny days.

• Mirrored: Reduces glare on bright-light days.

✔ **UV protection:** Choose goggles with UVA and UVB protection to shield your eyes from the sun's rays during open-water swims. UV rays can cause eye injuries, including cataracts, pterygium, macular degeneration, and sunburn to skin around the eyes.

✔ **Anti-fog lenses:** Manufacturers apply coatings to the lenses of goggles to help prevent mist from covering the insides of the lenses and blocking vision. *Remember:* Even with anti-fog coatings, you may find your lenses will still fog on occasion.

You can find anti-fog solutions to apply to your goggles if they didn't come with an anti-fog coating. The solution can prevent your goggles lenses from getting cloudy, but they don't work any better than a little spit. Take off your goggles and dip them in the water. Add some saliva to your finger or spit on the lenses and rub it in. Use this trick every time you get in the water.

✔ **Scratch-resistant lenses:** Even tiny scratches to your lenses can affect visibility. Look for goggles that feature a coating to prevent scratches.

✔ **Different or adjustable nose bridges:** If you have a broad nose bridge, you'll want to use goggles with a wide setting between the lenses. Look for traditional goggles that come with adjustable or different widths of nose bridges. You can install them by using the supplied Allen wrench to loosen the tiny screws in the rubber around the lenses, removing the existing bridge, inserting the new bridge, and retightening the screws. Swim goggles made of silicone rubber stretch slightly for comfort around the bridge of your nose.

✔ **Prescription lenses (if you need them):** Some goggles can be fitted with lenses to match your prescription for improved visibility. Some brands allow press-on prescription lenses to adhere to the goggles lenses.

✔ **Gel or padding where the goggles frame your eye sockets:** Gel or padding helps to seal out water and offers additional comfort — without the harsh, but temporary lines, that traditional goggles leave on a swimmer's face.

Clean your goggles with water or, if they're very dirty, use a small amount of baby shampoo. Do not use abrasive cleansers on your goggles — they can damage the anti-fog coating and reduce visibility.

Ask friends for their recommendations for the best leak-free brands of goggles — but don't just take their word for it. What works for your friend's face may not work for your face. Start with a recommendation; then see if you can borrow a pair of your friend's favorite goggles (or even a pair that a friend might not like but that he still has lurking in his swim bag), and go for a swim. You might find the perfect pair for you.

Goggles have to fit correctly or they can end up causing you frustration, headaches, and time. The way goggles fit your face is the most important factor to consider in making your selection. When you're searching for the pair of goggles that fits you best, head to a local swim shop where you can try them on. Then follow these steps:

1. **Pick a pair of goggles — any pair — and start there.**

   Don't be afraid to try kids' goggles if you have a small face.

2. **Press the goggles over your eyes, positioning them over the bridge of your nose, without putting on the head strap.**

   Do they stay in place for at least a few seconds? If so, move to the next step. If not, pick up another pair of goggles and start over.

3. **Adjust the head strap so that it's tight but comfortable.**

4. **Notice how the goggles feel.**

   Goggles should not create pressure on your sinuses, which can reduce your ability to breathe. Pay attention to areas where the goggles pinch or press uncomfortably across your temples, on your forehead, or against your eyes. If you notice any pressure or pain, start over with another pair.

5. **When you find a pair that fits comfortably, buy one pair and head to the water to try them out.**

   If the goggles leak or fog up excessively or fall off when you dive into the water — yep, you guessed it — head back to the store and start over with another pair.

   Don't just throw out the pair of goggles that didn't work for you. Donate them to your pool, give them to a friend, or hang onto them until someone asks *you* which goggles you recommend. You can tell him about your favorite pair of goggles and also let him try the pair that didn't work for you — maybe they'll work for *him*.

6. **When you find a pair that fits comfortably *and* performs well in the water, head back to the store and buy at least a few more pairs.**

   Keep the spare pairs handy in case you lose your first pair. (Every swimming pool has a box of lost goggles — proof of how often swimmers seem to misplace theirs.)

A no-hair day: Selecting a swim cap

Swim caps cover your head, hair, and ears, providing warmth, keeping the hair out of your eyes, and improving hydrodynamics. Hair slows you down; caps provide a smooth glide. Swim caps also provide some protection against the harsh chlorine of the pools or from the sun, both of which can damage your hair.

Although some pools require swim caps for swimmers with longer hair, not everyone trains with a swim cap. Caps are required by many triathlon organizers, however. So if you don't train with a cap, be sure to give one a try before your event, just to get a feel for it. And if you train with a cap, don't fall in love with it — event organizers who require caps most likely will supply them on race day.

If you're training in open waters, wear a brightly colored swim cap to make you more visible to lifeguards.

Event organizers who require and supply swim caps don't really care about protecting your hair or improving your time. Their main concern is knowing where you are, so they'll provide a cap color-coded to your age group and your *wave* (your grouping for the swim).

The caps supplied at triathlons typically have the event name on them, so triathletes save the caps as souvenirs. Long after your event, your swim cap tells others that you're a triathlete, and it often becomes a conversation piece.

Swim caps are made from latex, silicone, or neoprene, and each material has its benefits and best uses:

- ✔ **Latex:** Latex is the cheapest option for a swim cap — latex caps cost $3 to $5 apiece. And latex caps stay put on your head. On the downside, latex caps can be uncomfortable, and they tend to tear and wear out easily.

- ✔ **Silicone:** Most triathletes who wear caps like the thicker material of silicone. Silicone caps provide insulation, and their softness makes them stretchy and adjustable for comfort. They don't pull your hair as much as latex does, and they last longer. But a silicone cap can move around on your head, creating a distraction. Silicone caps cost from $8 to $20.

  Choose a silicone cap for your longer open-water training swims to help you stay warm.

- ✔ **Neoprene:** Sometimes called "hot heads," neoprene caps keep you warm in cold, open waters. The thicker fabric raises your core body temperature by as much as 5°F (3°C). A neoprene cap isn't the best choice for pool training, but for a cold, open-water swim, it may be a necessity. Neoprene caps come with chin straps to keep them in place. Costs start at $20.

You'll also find caps available in nylon or Lycra, the same material as your swimsuit fabric. Although these caps are the most comfortable, they allow water into your hair, which means they create drag and are not as hydrodynamic as the other materials. Nylon and Lycra are best if you're looking just to keep the hair out of your face and eyes and not planning to swim many laps. We don't recommend them for training.

Latex and neoprene swim caps can be tough to get on, especially if you have longer hair. Dip your cap into the water and fill it, and then dump out the water. If you have long hair, secure it in a ponytail or scoop it up and twist it; stuff the twist under your cap after you put it on.

Ride On: Choosing a Bike and Bike Gear

During your triathlon, you'll spend the most amount of time — as much as half of your total race time — on your bike. This is the only leg of the race for which you'll need a machine, with gears and wheels and tools for maintenance. And this makes the bike and bike accessories the most expensive and technical purchases you'll make to prepare for your triathlon.

Bikes come in as many shapes and sizes as triathletes do. And in bike purchases, the adage "You get what you pay for" holds true. As you select features that contribute to aerodynamics, smooth gearing, and light weight, you'll find that the price of the bike increases.

But nowhere else in your event will the equipment you choose have such an impact on your overall performance. A well-equipped, well-maintained bike with correct tire pressure and fit can shave minutes from your bike-leg times.

Still, a high-performance and high-priced bike is no substitute for training. So, select the bike that works best for your lifestyle and your triathlon goals; then ride, ride, ride.

There are three steps to deciding on a bike:

1. **If you don't already have a bike you'll use for your triathlon, decide how much you're willing to spend.**

   You can spend as little as a few hundred dollars for a bike that's decent enough to get you there or more than $10,000 to get you there fast (providing you've trained well).

   You don't need to go out and spend thousands of dollars on a high-performance bike for a triathlon. Most triathletes, especially first-timers, participate on bikes that cost an average of $500. You may even be able to ride the bike you have sitting in your garage, providing you get a tune-up and adjustments for fit.

2. **Choose the type of bike that will work best for you and your riding style and needs.**

   Bikes that are acceptable for riding in triathlons come in five major categories (see the "Looking at your bike options" section for more). Within each category, features and components you add will affect the price.

3. **Do your homework.**

Visit your local bike shop and try many models and styles to see what feels best for you. Bike shops will allow you to ride the bike outside. Take for a good spin any bike you're considering buying — change gears, climb and descend a hill, test the cornering (turning). Then hop on another bike and try that one, too.

In the following sections, we go into more detail on the five major categories of bikes. We also let you know how you can tell if a bike fits you. And we cover your clothing and accessories options, including pedals and shoes.

Looking at your bike options

When it comes to competing in a triathlon, there are five major categories of bikes:

- Tri bikes
- Road bikes
- Touring bikes
- Mountain bikes
- Hybrid bikes

In the following sections, we fill you in.

Tri bikes

If you plan to train and ride your bike only in triathlons, then you might find that a triathlon-specific bike (or tri bike) is a good choice for you. A tri bikes is designed to put you in a better aerodynamic position than a traditional road or mountain bike. Better aerodynamics and lightweight materials mean faster performance.

And the tri bike's angles and frame geometry (the way the bike is made) allow you to pedal in a position that makes it easier for your legs to transition from the bike to the run. Tri-specific bikes also feature *aerobars,* specific handlebars on which you rest your forearms. The thinking behind aerobars is to make your body compact and tight, or low and small. On a tri bike with aerobars, your arms and elbows are pulled in close to your body, reducing the amount of surface area that needs to cut through the wind (see Figure 3-4).

Here are the features you'll find in a tri bike:

- **A short top tube to permit the rider to comfortably lean forward onto the aerobars.**

✔ **Lightweight frames made of aluminum, aluminum plus carbon fiber in the seat stays, or all carbon fiber:** The advantage of carbon fiber is that it absorbs road vibration, which reduces rider fatigue, and is lightweight. Less weight means less effort required to power the bike, which translates into speed.

✔ **A narrow and hard saddle with a long nose, positioned higher than the handlebars.**

Figure 3-4:
A rider on a tri-specific bike is more aerodynamic than riders on other types of bikes, such as road or mountain bikes.

Courtesy of Trek Bicycle Corporation

✔ **A seat angle of 76 degrees to 78 degrees to engage the large muscles of the leg.**

✔ **Two chain rings in front and nine or ten in the rear for maximum speed.**

✔ **Wheels with as few as 24 spokes to reduce wind drag, or a solid-disc rear wheel:** Disc wheels eliminate wind drag that can slow you down on the bike (that is, as long as the wind is either in your face or at your back or there is no wind at all). In a crosswind, disc wheels make it difficult to keep the bike straight, which can make you tired fast and increase your risk of falling. Spoked wheels, while less aerodynamic, offer improved efficiency over disc wheels in crosswinds. The fewer spokes on a wheel, the less wind drag they create.

✔ **Narrow tires pumped to high pressure, such as a 700C by 20mm tire.** (For more on tires and how they're measured, check out the nearby sidebar, "Tire me out: How tires are measured.")

If you decide to continue training for triathlons after your first, and you plan to participate in six or more races a year, you'll want to consider two bikes: a tri bike for racing and a road bike on which you'll log most of your training miles and participate in group rides. Tri bikes are good for events, but uncomfortable to use for daily training or for long rides.

Tri bike prices begin at $1,800 for an entry-level bike. Expect to spend about $3,000 for a tri bike with a lightweight and strong carbon-fiber frame. When you add high-performance components (better quality gearing systems and brakes) and disc wheels, you can invest $8,000 or more.

Tri-specific bikes facilitate faster triathlons, especially for beginning triathletes who benefit most from the aerodynamics and decreased muscle fatigue when they transition from the bike to the run. What you gain in speed, though, you lose in control and comfort. Tri bikes are single-purpose machines, and their purpose is to go fast. Don't get a tri bike if:

- ✔ You're a beginning rider and you plan to participate in group training rides.
- ✔ You'd like to use your bike for activities other than training for and participating in triathlons.
- ✔ You're a first-timer and you aren't yet sure if you'll want to pursue triathlons.
- ✔ You often ride hills with many turns and curves.

Don't expect to see all the athletes, even those who look like elite triathletes, riding tri bikes. You don't need a tri bike to participate in a triathlon, and you'll see more road bikes at a first-timer friendly triathlon than you will tri bikes.

Road bikes

Road bikes are for use on paved road surfaces. A road bike positions you comfortably for everyday training or for extended distances (see Figure 3-5). Brake levers and shifts for gears are within easy reach on a road bike's drop handlebars, giving you maximum efficiency and safety, especially important when training on public roads with traffic.

Road bikes offer versatility and are able to handle hills and longer rides more comfortably than tri bikes.

If you haven't ridden a road bike in while, you may find it a little awkward and find yourself holding tight to the handlebars. Your road bike will respond to your body movements, so at first, the bike can feel twitchy. With time and practice, you'll feel more connected to your bike and think nothing of reaching down for your water bottle or wiping sweat from your face.

Look for these features in a good-quality road bike:

- ✔ **A longer top tube and compact wheelbase for control and comfort.**

- ✔ **Two or sometimes three chain rings in front:** The third smaller chain ring makes hill ascents easier.

- ✔ **Gear shift levers and brake levers within easy reach on a drop handlebar.**

- ✔ **Nine to ten gears in the back for efficiency and speed.**

- ✔ **Wheels with 32 to 36 spokes and thin, high-pressure tires, generally 700C by 23mm, 25mm, or 28mm.** (For more on tires and how they're measured, check out the sidebar, "Tire me out: How tires are measured," in this chapter.)

You'll find road bikes in a variety of price ranges — from $500 for an entry-level aluminum-frame bike to $3,500 and up for a full carbon-frame bike. As with tri bikes, as you select high-performance wheels and components, you can expect to pay more for your bike.

An entry-level bike will cost around $900 and up. A midrange bike, around $1,750, offers a combination of aluminum and carbon fiber in the frame, providing the weight-saving benefits of carbon with the cost-saving benefits of aluminum.

Figure 3-5:
The short wheelbase of a road bike makes it responsive to turns, and its frame geometry allows you to feel more comfortable on extended rides.

Courtesy of Trek Bicycle Corporation

Tire me out: How tires are measured

Tires you will want to use for training or participating in a triathlon are measured in diameter and width. A 700C tire is used on tri, road, touring, and hybrid bikes. 650C tires are best for mountain bikes.

The width of the tire and the air pressure determine how much rolling resistance your tire will have on the surface on which you're riding. The higher the pressure and narrower the tire, the faster you'll ride with less effort. The most common tire width for comfortable road riding is 25 to 28mm.

You can reduce rolling resistance to increase speed by using a narrow tire, such as a 20 or 23mm-wide tire pumped to its maximum pressure, but you'll sacrifice comfort — narrow, high-pressure tires do not absorb vibration or bumps well, and they increase your potential for flats.

Some triathletes add aerobars to their road bikes to put them in a better aerodynamic position. But you may not find aerobars comfortable, and they aren't safe on a road bike. A road bike has a longer wheelbase than a tri bike, so you have to stretch farther to rest your arms on the aerobars, compromising comfort and leg power. Clip-on aerobars also don't generally come equipped with brakes, so when you're in the compact, race position, you don't have access to your brakes without lifting yourself off the aerobars and moving your hands. Sometimes, that takes more time than you have to avoid an accident. Bottom line: Because of the safety issues involved, we don't recommend using aerobars on road bikes.

Touring bikes

The features of a touring bike are similar to those found in road bikes, but touring bikes are meant to be used to carry loads on long trips. Touring bikes feature sturdy and strong frames and wheels with more spokes than a road bike. All this adds weight (about 8 to 10 pounds), and more weight means you have to work harder.

Invest in a touring bike if you think you'll ride for long distances for extended bike trips. You can always change out the tires for narrower and higher-pressure tires and remove racks meant for carrying packs to reduce the weight.

Here are the additional features of a touring bike:

- ✔ **700C tires that are slightly wider than tires on a road bike (from 28mm to 33mm) with as many as 36 spokes on the wheel for comfort when riding long distances and for strength when you encounter pot holes or rough roads.** (For more on tires and how they're measured, check out the sidebar, "Tire me out: How tires are measured," in this chapter.)

- ✔ **Additional space between frame wheels to allow for attachment of fenders and packs.**
- ✔ **A wheelbase that's slightly longer than a road bike and a design that allows a more upright sitting position.**
- ✔ **Fenders and racks for carrying packs.**
- ✔ **Additional water bottle mounts for extra hydration on long journeys.**

You can pay as little as $1,200 for a touring bike. Or you can spend more than $3,000 for a solid, good-shifting machine that can take you the distance.

Mountain bikes and hybrids

If your triathlon is a first-timer-friendly event, you'll see many participants on hybrid bikes or even mountain bikes. Hybrids combine comfort with the efficiency of a road bike. Mountain bikes add features, such as suspension and wider, heavily lugged tires, for tackling rugged, off-road terrain (see Figure 3-6).

Everything about hybrid and mountain bikes is heavier than road bikes, and the wheelbase is longer, so a mountain bike or hybrid is less responsive than a road bike. These bikes are not designed to go fast and straight — they're all about overcoming obstacles. But some riders prefer the less twitchy, more secure feeling of a hybrid or mountain bike.

Figure 3-6:
A mountain bike or hybrid offers a more relaxed frame geometry, which means you'll sit in an upright comfortable position.

Courtesy of Giant Bicycle, Inc./Giant for Women

Here are the features common to mountain and hybrid bikes:

- **650C wheels with fat (up to 38mm), low-pressure, lugged tires.** (For more on tires and how they're measured, check out the sidebar, "Tire me out: How tires are measured," in this chapter.)

- **T-bar handlebar for upright riding.**

- **Smaller chain rings in front and bigger cassette gears in the rear — ideal for handling rough terrain, loose gravel, mud, and steep hills.**

- **Disc brakes to ensure stopping when brakes and tires are wet and muddy.**

Mountain bikes fall into two basic types:

- **Hard tail,** which has only front suspension (the rear stays firm)

- **Full suspension,** in which both front and rear wheels are fit with shocks

Although you'll do just fine on a hybrid or hard-tail mountain bike, we don't recommend full-suspension mountain bikes for triathlons. As you pedal downward, your pedal force is absorbed by the suspension and not directed to moving you forward quickly. The suspension also adds to the weight of your bike.

A mountain bike can be a good choice if, after your event, most of your riding will be tours around your neighborhood rather than tours of triathlons across the country. And if you ride more often on packed gravel or bumpy trails than you do on roads, a mountain bike may be a good choice for you.

By design, though, mountain bikes move slowly. You'll find that the low tire pressure on the smaller 650C wheels and the single hand position creates fatigue on rides longer than 10 miles. Wind resistance adds to that fatigue, as you'll be in a full upright position on your mountain bike.

You can find a good-quality hybrid bike for as little as $500, while solid cross-country racing mountain bikes can cost $1,400 and up.

If you decide to use a hybrid or mountain bike for your triathlon, consider changing the tires. The feature that makes mountain bikes efficient and comfortable off-road makes them inefficient and lumbering on paved surfaces. The big lugs on mountain-bike tires require more energy on the road. Consider a narrower, smoother tire and one you can pump to a pressure higher than 70 to 80 pounds per square inch (psi), the standard for mountain-bike tires. Treadless tires, called "slicks," cost around $30 but can be as much as $100 per tire.

Getting fit first: Why the proper bike fit is important

After choosing the bike that meets your goals and your lifestyle, the way that bike fits you is the most important aspect of a comfortable, enjoyable, and efficient cycling experience. A bike that fits you properly helps you to deliver power to the pedals, moving the bike forward as efficiently as possible.

A reputable bike shop will measure your *inseam* (leg length) and even your torso and arm length to guide you in selecting a bike. Manufacturers offer sizes based on centimeters, but like clothing sizes, they vary from one company to the next. Your best bet is to get on the bike and ride it.

A proper fit is based on the biomechanics and the size of your body, and a certified bike-fitter is best qualified to make adjustments to your bike to maximize comfort and efficiency and to reduce fatigue, soreness, and chance of injury.

Expect to put your bike on a stationary wind trainer in the store, where you'll ride it while the fit expert evaluates and compensates for saddle height, handlebar height, pedal position, and saddle angle. This type of basic bike fitting takes about 20 minutes. If you haven't purchased your bike at the store, you can expect to pay around $30 for a basic fit, plus any parts you need. If you've purchased your bike at the shop, they should be sure you are comfortable on it before you leave the store.

A comprehensive "professional" fit can take about two hours and allows you to alter your bike to account for your muscle flexibility and the way you pedal. A professional bike fit can cost from $100 to $200, in addition to any parts you might need, such as a new saddle or handlebar stem. In addition to measuring basic fit, a professional fit will take into account:

- **Crank length:** A measurement based on the length of the pedal cranks as it relates to the diameter of the circle created by your pedaling motion and the angle of your knee as it completes the rotation.

- **Handlebar size and position:** The angle and height of your handlebars and their width can affect your comfort. Adjustments can also be made to bring the bars closer or move them farther away from your saddle. Some adjustments can be made with positioning, while others will require new handlebars or a new handlebar stem.

- **Saddle tilt:** The angle of your saddle can affect your comfort. A saddle that's tilted too far forward puts pressure on your arms as they hold you up on the handlebars.

> ✔ **Saddle position:** Adjusting the saddle position is a compromise between comfort and power. The fore-aft (forward-backward) position of the saddle in relation to the crank allows you to maximize your muscle power.

Whether you're buying a new bike, borrowing a bike, or breaking your bike out of the garage, bring it to your local bike shop and ask the people there to make any necessary adjustments for proper fit.

Picking pedals and shoes

Pedals come in three styles:

> ✔ Flat pedals that you use with sneakers or running shoes
>
> ✔ Toe clips into which you slide your feet while wearing sneakers or running shoes
>
> ✔ Clipless pedals into which you lock a cycling-specific shoe with an adjustable cleat

Few things about cycling are as frightening to first-timers as locking into clipless pedals, but clipless pedals offer an increase in pedaling efficiency because you can spin rather than pump. And through the spinning motion, you'll be pulling up one pedal as you push down on the other.

We recommend clipless pedals for the increase in power and speed they provide. In addition, cycling shoes fit for a clipless pedal system provide extra stability for your feet, keeping them flat through the pedaling motion and correctly positioned on the pedals, further contributing to efficiency.

If you're nervous about being locked in, visit a cycling store that has stationary wind trainers set up. Put on your cycling shoes and clip into the pedals and practice clipping and unclipping. Then take your bike out onto a flat lawn to try them out while you're moving. Before you head out onto the roads, take some practice rides in a parking lot.

What to wear: Clothing and accessories

It's possible to jump on your bike in running clothes or other casual wear and head off, but what you wear can greatly affect your comfort, your efficiency, and your safety. In this section, you'll find out what to wear — from head to toe — and why.

Staying safe with a helmet

The first and most important article to put on your body before you set off on a bike ride is your helmet. Never ride without a helmet. Event organizers will require one for the bike leg. Expect to pay $50 to $70 for a good-quality helmet made from sturdy foam molded into a hard, thin, plastic outer layer.

Here are the features to look for in a helmet:

- ✓ **American National Standards Institute (ANSI), Snell, or Consumer Product Safety Commission (CPSC) certification.**

- ✓ **Bright colors for better visibility on the road:** A helmet is a safety statement, not a fashion statement, but selecting a bright color can help make you more visible to drivers on public roads.

- ✓ **Openings for ventilation to allow air flow, keeping your head cool and improving aerodynamics:** Expect to pay more for helmets with wide-open vents because they'll be constructed with reinforcements, much like rebar, built into the foam to maintain strength while allowing for maximum airflow.

- ✓ **Easily adjustable chin and ear straps using a flip-lock system and a dial-adjustment for head straps inside the helmet:** The ability to adjust your helmet while it's on your head, instead of having to take it off and fumble with straps, can help you create a secure fit.

If you fall and your helmet makes contact with the ground, replace it immediately. Helmets are not designed to withstand multiple impacts. Even a minor blow can compromise the integrity of the helmet. For this reason, do not buy or use an old helmet, because you can't be certain of its crash history.

When you're shopping for helmets, follow these steps:

1. **Place the helmet on your head and evaluate its initial fit.**

   Is it way too big or too tight? If so, you'll notice that right away. Small adjustments can be made with the head, chin, and ear straps, but if the helmet doesn't fit onto your head or flops around, try another style or size.

   The front rim of the helmet should go across your forehead just above your eyebrows.

2. **Adjust the straps inside the helmet so that it fits securely around your head.**

3. **Adjust the lengths of the chin straps to ensure that they fit tightly under your chin and that you can move comfortably.**

4. **Adjust the strap around each ear to create a triangle that outlines your ear.**

   The ear strap adjustments should sit slightly below your ear lobes.

5. **Place your hands on the helmet and try to move it back to front or side to side.**

   If you can move your helmet, it's not the right fit. Adjust the straps again for a secure fit or try another helmet.

Dressing for comfort and visibility

There's a reason cyclists sport bright colors and bold graphics: They want to be noticed. When you're shopping for cycling clothing, look for colors that will be easily visible to drivers.

Clothing choices are more about function than fashion. Choose cycling jerseys, shells, or jackets that fit closely to your body. Clothing that billows away from the body creates drag and slows you down (not to mention irritates you with its flapping). When you try on a cycling top, lean forward and stretch your arms out in front of you to ensure nothing binds or restricts your movement.

Cycling clothes are designed to fit closely to your body so that the technical fabric can wick away moisture from your skin. This helps to keep you cool in the summer and keeps you from getting clammy in the cold weather.

Jerseys can cost from $24 to $100, while shells and wind- or rain-resistant outerwear can start at $50 and cost up to $200 or more.

A cycling top and jersey has the following features:

✔ **A zipper that ranges from a quarter of the length of the shirt to the full front of the shirt** to allow you to pull it open as you heat up on a sprint or uphill and quickly zip it back up when the wind picks up on your descent.

✔ **Pockets in the back of the jersey or at the sides in which you can store essential items,** including nutritional bars and snacks, or a cellphone for emergencies. Pockets with elastic at the tops are easy to access while riding, but they may not be secure enough for storing ID or money. We've ridden along many times only to have a nutritional bar bounce from a pocket onto the road.

✔ **Mesh fabric for breathability or a combination of wicking and mesh fabrics.**

✔ **Longer length in the back and elastic waistband** to keep the shirt in place and covering your back as you bend forward to reach the handlebars.

Cycling shorts are essential for any training rides more than 10 miles long. They're made of wicking Lycra and spandex fabrics to fit your body closely, reducing drag and minimizing the risk that loose pants or shorts will get caught in your gears or get bunched up and cause chafing.

Cycling shorts come with built-in padding, called *chamois,* in the crotch area of the shorts to provide comfort and minimize possible chafing. Choose the thickness of padding that's most comfortable for you. If you head out for a ride, and you're experiencing soreness, consider investing in a pair of shorts with a thicker chamois.

Cycling shorts can range in price from $30 to $100. Invest in the best pair of shorts you can afford.

Wash your shorts immediately after wearing them and allow them to air-dry inside out.

Socks, gloves, and sunglasses

Most lightweight socks that are made of a blend of fabrics designed to wick away moisture will work for cycling. Expect to pay $10 for a pair of cycling socks.

Fingerless gloves (or full-fingered gloves in colder weather) help keep you comfortable during long rides. Gloves often have gel padding in the pressure points. After miles of road vibration, your hands can get tired and ache if you're not wearing gloves. Gloves cost from $20 to $60. Expect to replace them at least once every season.

Any sport sunglasses will do to wear on the bike to protect your eyes from road debris and wind. Glasses specifically designed for cyclists, though, often come with interchangeable lenses to provide maximum visibility in different lighting conditions. Cycling sunglasses cost from $40 to $200.

Pounding the Pavement: Getting What You Need for the Run

When you're ready to hit the road, nothing is more important than your running shoes, so in this section we start from the bottom and work our way up.

Choosing a good running shoe

There are two basic types of running shoes:

- ✔ **Shoes designed for motion control and stability:** You'll need a stability or motion-control running shoe if you *overpronate*. Overpronating occurs when your foot rolls significantly inward as you move from your heel to your toes.

- ✔ **Shoes designed for cushioning:** Cushioning, or neutral, running shoes are best for runners who supinate, or underpronate. Runners supinate if they roll very little from the outside of their feet to the inside as they move from their heels to their toes, creating a more rigid step. There are three levels of cushioning — minimum, normal, and maximum — and the amount of cushioning you need can depend on many factors, including your body size, the distance you're running, the existence of current foot problems, and what surface you're running on.

So how do you determine which of the 300 pairs of sneakers that are out there is right for you? For your first pair of running shoes, start by visiting a reputable running store, as opposed to a sporting goods store or an online retailer. Employees at running stores are runners — that's why they're there. They're knowledgeable about the different types of shoes and will talk to you and ask you questions to determine which shoes are best for you.

Expect to pay as much as $80 or more for your running shoes.

Then follow these five guidelines to select shoes that fit:

- ✓ **Take the shoes you use now for walking or running to your local running store.** A knowledgeable sales person will be able to look at how your shoes are worn to determine if you are in the correct type or if you might need shoes that offer more motion control or cushioning.

- ✓ **Shop for running shoes late in the day, when your feet are at their largest, espccially after an evening run.**

- ✓ **If you wear *orthotics* (inserts in your shoes to alleviate a foot problem), be sure to bring them with you.**

- ✓ **Wear the socks you plan to use when you run.**

- ✓ **Run in the store with them to see how they feel or outside on the side-walk to ensure that they feel comfortable.** Don't worry; in running shoe stores, everyone does it — in fact, it's expected.

Dressing for the occasion: Clothing and accessories

Running socks generally are made of *CoolMax* (fabric designed to pull mois-ture and offer breathability) or other fabrics to keep your feet cool and dry. These fabrics not only add to your comfort but also help alleviate blister-causing friction. In the interest of saving money, drawer space, and time in transitions, you can wear the same socks for cycling as you do for running. Socks come in various heights, thicknesses, and degrees of cushioning. Determine which type is right for you and buy many pairs.

When selecting clothing to wear for training or for your event, you'll find that clothes designed specifically for athletes work better than your old cotton T-shirts. Here are six features to look for when selecting clothing for training:

- ✔ **Wicking fabrics:** *Wicking* is the process of pulling wetness away from the body, keeping you dryer. Wet cotton feels heavy and sticks to your skin. Wicking fabrics keep your skin dry, and the fabrics themselves dry faster, helping to keep your body temperature stable in extreme heat or cold.

- ✔ **Form fitting:** There's a reason triathletes wear clothing that fits tightly, and it's not to show off their fit physiques (of course, that doesn't hurt!). Loose-fitting sleeves can bunch up while you move your arms, creating chafing. You want clothes that are form fitting, not baggy.

- ✔ **Smooth seams:** Rough seams and tags can irritate skin after miles of a repetitive motion.

- ✔ **Hi-tech fabrics:** Materials such as Gortex make it possible to train in extremes of heat or cold without adding bulk. They also trap air (and keep it warm) or breathe (and keep you cool).

- ✔ **Layers:** As you warm up, run, and then cool down, you'll find that you start cold and warm up, then get a chill again as you slow down toward the end of your training. Dressing in layers gives you the flexibility to remove an article of clothing when you're hot or put back on when you're chilled.

- ✔ **Pockets:** Look for concealed pockets, particularly ones that have zipper closures, to keep items such as house keys safe. You may even find pockets where you can stash your iPod or MP3 player, as well as extra nutrition on the go.

Chapter 4

Getting Ready: Body and Mind

. . . .

In This Chapter

▶ Deciding if you need a physical

▶ Determining how fit you are

▶ Building your support team

. . . .

If you have your gear and you've decided on your event, you're probably eager to get started with your training program. But before you get going, you'll want to make an honest assessment of your fitness level — for your safety and to help you gauge how far you've come by event day.

In this chapter, we give you questions to ask yourself to determine whether you should visit a doctor before you start training. We also provide a summary of what to expect at your physical and at a professional fitness evaluation with a trainer at your gym. If you don't have a gym membership, you still can assess your cardiovascular fitness, strength, and flexibility yourself with the simple do-at-home tests in this chapter.

We also fill you in on the importance of generating a support network and training with other triathletes so that you're ready mentally as well as physically.

Let's Get Physical: Checking In with Your Doctor before You Begin

If your decision to train for a triathlon coincided with your decision to exercise after being a couch potato for many long years, then you need to begin your training with a visit to your doctor. On the other hand, if you've been exercising regularly three to four times a week for months or, better yet, years, you likely have a good impression of your overall health. Unless you're experiencing pain, dizziness, or unusual symptoms, you may not feel a visit to your doctor, aside from your regular physical, is necessary. In this section, we help you make that decision.

Knowing whether you need a physical

For most people, starting a fitness program should not pose any risk. But just *assuming* you're one of those people is not a risk you want to take.

If the first step in your training program was to join a fitness center, take advantage of the complimentary fitness evaluations most centers offer to their new members. If you're already a member, approach the staff and tell them you're planning to train for a triathlon. They should take the time to help you evaluate your fitness level to get you on the right path.

Most fitness centers or personal trainers will use the standard Physical Activity Readiness Questionnaire (PAR-Q) to evaluate your need to see a physician before starting an exercise program. The PAR-Q is based on the following seven questions. Think carefully about each question and answer honestly, yes or no.

- Has a doctor ever said you have heart trouble?
- Do you frequently have pains in your heart and chest?
- Do you often feel faint or have spells of severe dizziness?
- Has a doctor ever said your blood pressure is too high?
- Has your doctor ever told you that you have a bone or joint problem such as arthritis that has been aggravated by exercise or that may be made worse with exercise?
- Is there a good physical reason not mentioned here why you should not follow an activity program even if you want to?
- Are you older than age 65 and not accustomed to vigorous exercise?

If you answered "yes" to any of these questions, visit your physician for a physical. Be sure to tell your doctor of your intent to train for not one, but *three* sports.

If you don't have any "yes" answers and you answered each question honestly, you can be reasonably assured of your ability to begin training. Still, it's always a good idea to visit your doctor regularly and share your plans to train for a triathlon.

Believe it or not, some people lie on these forms, sometimes merely because they don't want to take the time out of training to visit their doctors, or because they may have skewed perceptions of their fitness levels. Be honest. And if you have any doubt or just want reassurance, visit your doctor. On your harder training days, you may find yourself climbing a hill on a hot, sunny day fairly sure that your heart is going to pump right out of your chest. Give yourself the added confidence of knowing it's just doing its job.

Knowing what to expect if you get a physical

Depending on your age and fitness level, when you visit your doctor and tell her that you're planning to train for a triathlon, she may order additional tests to best assess your health. Use the results of your visit as solid knowledge of where you're starting and a great baseline against which to judge how far you'll have come after you complete your triathlon.

Be sure to explain exactly what you intend to do — the types and intensity of exercise, how often you plan to exercise, and the complete distance and time frame of your event.

Your doctor will ask you about your family history and evaluate your primary risk factors for heart disease, including your diet, whether you smoke, your stress and activity levels, and your weight, age, and gender.

From there, you'll undergo a standard physical, during which your doctor will take your blood pressure and resting heart rate (remember this number — you'll be excited to see the drop after you train for your event). After evaluating your basic vital signs, your doctor will decide whether you need any further testing to determine your heart health, such as an electrocardiogram (EKG).

An EKG, also referred to as a stress test or treadmill test, monitors the changes in your heart as you exercise. During the test, you'll walk on a treadmill while connected to a machine that tracks your heart rate. The test takes place in three stages of three minutes each, gradually increasing in speed and incline. You'll walk until you reach your maximum heart rate or until you can't continue; you'll also be stopped if the monitor indicates an abnormality, such as a decrease in blood flow to your heart. After the test, you'll lie down for five to ten minutes, so that the medical staff can continue to monitor your heart rate and blood pressure. Your doctor will discuss the test with you afterwards, but a complete report usually takes two to three days to be available.

After you've received physician's clearance to begin or resume your training program, your next step is a complete and honest evaluation of your fitness (see the next section).

Evaluating Your Fitness

A fitness assessment will help you set realistic goals, as well as offer a starting point for charting your progress. Assessments are best performed by certified fitness professionals, such as the staff at your gym or a personal trainer. In your assessment, you'll get information about your cardiovascular fitness, including your resting heart rate and blood pressure; body-fat composition; muscular strength and endurance; and flexibility.

Cardiovascular

Your cardiovascular fitness is based on two measures: heart rate and blood pressure.

Resting heart rate

Your resting heart rate, or pulse, is the number of times your heart beats per minute while you're sitting and relaxed. The better conditioned you are, the lower this number will be. The average heart rate for men is 70 beats per minute (bpm). For women, the average is slightly higher: 75 bpm. Well-conditioned athletes often record resting heart rates as low as 40 bpm.

If your resting heart rate is as high as 100 bpm, visit your physician before you begin your exercise program.

Many factors can affect your heart rate — stress, anxiety, certain medications, or even a few cups of coffee before your assessment.

For your true resting heart rate, measure your beats per minute when you wake up in the morning and before you get out of bed. If a fitness professional will be taking your measurement during the day as part of your overall fitness evaluation, sit down quietly for 15 minutes beforehand.

To take your own resting heart rate, you'll want to measure your beats per minute for three days in a row and take the average number from these three measurements. Follow these steps to take your heart rate:

1. **Place the tips of your first three fingers of your right hand on the pulse point under your left wrist or take your first two fingers of your left hand and place them on your carotid artery (the area on your neck just below your jawbone on the left side of your windpipe).**

2. **Press slightly until you feel your pulse.**

3. **Using a watch or clock with a second hand, count the beats for one minute.**

If you have a heart rate monitor, which you'll need for training, you can also put it on when you go to bed at night and check your heart rate when you wake up in the morning.

Your number probably will fall somewhere between 60 bpm and 90 bpm. As you become more physically fit, and your heart becomes stronger and more efficient, your resting heart rate will decrease.

Blood pressure

Your blood pressure measures the force with which your blood presses against the walls of your arteries — essentially how hard your heart has to work to pump blood through the blood vessels. The lower the number, the easier it is on your heart. Higher numbers indicate the heart is working hard.

Blood pressure is a combination of two numbers:

- ✔ The systolic number measures the pressure when the heart beats while pumping blood.
- ✔ The diastolic number measures the pressure when the heart rests between beats.

Blood pressure readings list the systolic number over the diastolic number, such as 120/80 (which is read, "120 over 80"), the ideal number.

As you age, your blood pressure naturally increases. Stress, obesity, smoking, and other lifestyle factors can contribute to high blood pressure. Living with high blood pressure for a long period of time can lead to health problems, such as heart disease or heart failure, stroke, and kidney failure. Exercise can keep your blood pressure in check.

The most accurate means to determine your blood pressure is by visiting a medical professional who will use a blood-pressure cuff. As with heart rate, what you did just before you had your blood pressure checked can contribute to a high reading. If you continue to get high readings, talk to your physician.

Body composition

Body composition is the percentage of your body weight that's comprised of fat — and this is a number few of us want to know! But it's a more accurate measurement of your overall health than weight itself.

Throw out your scale. Instead, judge the changes in your body by how you feel in your clothes and how toned and fit you look.

The weight charts that so many people still refer to can be misleading. Take a 250-pound bodybuilder, for example. Regardless of height, this person would be considered overweight using traditional weight charts. But a bodybuilder has a high percentage of muscle mass (and muscle weighs more than fat) and only 8 percent body fat. Women typically have body-fat percentages of 22 percent to 25 percent. The average adult male has a body-fat percentage of 15 percent to 18 percent, although athletes — male and female — generally are at the lower end of this range.

You can find many scales and handheld gadgets to help you measure body fat, but use these with caution — they have a large margin of error. In fact, no body-fat tests can be completely accurate, but they can give you a starting point from which to chart your progress.

Hydrostatic weighing (which involves weighing a person under water) is the most accurate and scientific way to measure body-fat percentage — and it's the most expensive. You won't find hydrostatic weighing machines at your neighborhood gym.

Instead, fitness centers use skin-fold measurements — your trainer will place a measuring device, called *calipers,* at various points on your body — usually the parts you'd least like to have pinched, such as the abdomen, backs of the arms, backs of shoulders, and upper thighs. The calipers pull the skin away from the muscles and bones. The measurements are used as variables in a formula that determines overall body-fat percentage.

Testing your limits: A submaximal evaluation test

A submaximal test (or submax for short) measures your overall cardiovascular fitness in relation to how well your heart recovers from exercise. This test is performed to evaluate how efficiently your heart works when you exercise at less than your hardest, or maximal, effort. Having a submax test will offer a benchmark for your fitness level.

Submaximal tests take you to just below your absolute hardest exertion point. Because the test takes you so close to the point of exhaustion, these tests require supervision for your safety.

A submax test may be done on a treadmill, a stationary bike, or a 12-inch step bench. For example, during a three-minute step-bench test, your trainer sets a metronome to a count of 96 bpm. You step up and down on the bench, alternating right and left feet and keeping in time with the metronome. You keep stepping for the full three minutes — or until you just can't take another step at that cadence. At this point, you have your heart rate taken for one minute. The result of this one-minute heart rate is your score, which can be compared to averages for men and women in various age categories.

In general, your maximum heart rate is 220 bpm minus your age. Your heart rate on the submax test, whether it's higher or lower than the average for a person your age, will give you an idea of your overall fitness level.

Where you store the fat on your body can be an indication of your risk for health problems, regardless of whether you're considered obese. For example, carrying excess weight around your waist — even if you're not obese — puts you at greater risk for heart disease and cancer then extra weight around your hips.

To determine the ratio of fat around your waist to the amount around your hips, you need to calculate your hip-to-waist ratio. This number will help you more accurately assess whether you need to lose body fat than the number on your scale. Here's how to get your hip-to-waist ratio:

1. **Using a tape measure, measure your hip circumference at its widest part.**

2. **Measure your waist circumference at the belly button or just above it.**

3. **Divide the waist measurement by the hip measurement.**

Table 4-1 fills you in on the level of risk associated with your waist-to-hip ratio.

Table 4-1	What Your Waist-to-Hip Ratio Means	
Risk	*Male*	*Female*
Low	0.95 or lower	0.80 or lower
Moderate	0.96 to 1.0	0.81 to 0.85
High	1.1 or higher	0.86 or higher

Muscular strength and endurance

Your fitness professional may choose a variety of tests to determine your muscular strength and endurance. Two simple tests you can perform yourself without equipment are the push-up test and the sit-up test.

Push-up test

The push-up test measures upper-body strength. To perform this test, men should do traditional military-style push-ups; women should do modified push-ups, in which the knees are bent and positioned on the floor with feet raised and crossed at the ankles.

For accuracy, you have to perform "real" push-ups, not the fake ones you see in the gym all the time in which people bend their elbows and drop their heads to make it look like they're actually lowering themselves to the floor. Refer to Chapter 11 for a description of the correct form.

Count the number of push-ups you can complete in one minute and compare that to the average for your gender and age group, shown in Table 4-2.

Table 4-2	Push-Up Averages (Per Minute)				
Gender	Ages 18 to 29	Ages 30 to 39	Ages 40 to 49	Ages 50 to 59	Ages 60 and Older
Male	19 to 29	13 to 24	11 to 20	9 to 17	6 to 16
Female	11 to 22	10 to 21	8 to 17	7 to 14	5 to 12

Sit-up test

A one-minute timed sit-up test measures your core strength, important for all three sports in a triathlon. To perform a sit-up, lie flat on the floor with your knees bent, your feet flat on the floor, and your hands crossed over your chest, with your elbows up. Curl up until your elbows reach your knees. Return to the starting position and repeat as many times as you can in one minute.

Your core strength can be determined by charting the number of sit-ups you complete against the average for your age group, shown in Table 4-3.

Table 4-3	Sit-Up Averages (Per Minute)				
Gender	Ages 18 to 25	Ages 26 to 35	Ages 36 to 45	Ages 46 to 55	Ages 56 to 65	Ages 66 and Older
Male	35 to 38	31 to 34	27 to 29	22 to 24	17 to 20	15 to 18
Female	29 to 32	25 to 28	19 to 22	14 to 17	10 to 12	11 to 13

Flexibility

The ease with which your muscles stretch to allow you to move in certain positions is your *flexibility*. You may find it easy to bend at the waist and to touch your toes or even to place the palms of your hands on the floor. Or you may struggle even to touch your knees.

People vary in their flexibility and, as they age, their muscles loose elasticity. But gentle stretching and exercise can help you to maintain your flexibility. Fortunately, being inflexible does not harbor the same health risks as high blood pressure or poor cardiovascular fitness. But it can make you more susceptible to injuries and influence your comfort performing certain exercises, such as riding your bike with your hands on the drops of your handlebars.

As part of your overall fitness evaluation, your trainer will ask you to perform various flexibility tests. We've included two common tests — the sit-and-reach test and the shoulder-flexibility test.

Sit-and-reach test

The sit-and-reach test is a common measure of flexibility, especially for cyclists, because it measures flexibility in your lower back and your *hamstrings* (the muscles in the backs of your legs).

To perform the sit-and-reach test with your trainer, follow these steps:

1. **Sit on the floor with your legs straight out in front of you, your knees flat against the floor, and your feet (without shoes) flat against a *sit-and-reach box* (a box constructed to allow you to place your feet flat against one side — the top of the box is marked with measurements).**

2. **Position one hand on top of the next and intertwine your fingers.**

3. **Lean forward to stretch as far as you can reach, keeping your knees flat, and repeat this motion three times to practice.**

4. **Inhale deeply. As you exhale, reach forward as far as you can along the top of the box and hold this position for 2 seconds.**

Your trainer will record your score based on the number on top of the box and measure it against the norm for men and women.

If you don't have access to a sit-and-reach box or you want to do this at home, simply sit on the floor with your legs straight out in front of you. Lean forward from the waist reaching your hands toward your knees, your calves, or your toes. Make a note of where you can reach. In a few months, test yourself again. Or you can have a friend hold a ruler straight in front of you at your feet. Your feet are point zero. If you can't reach your feet, your measurement will be a negative number. If you can reach your toes, you have average flexibility.

Shoulder-flexibility test

The shoulder-flexibility test measures the elasticity of your shoulder joint, particularly important in swimming. It's a test you can do easily at home:

1. **Stand with your feet shoulder-distance apart.**

2. **Raise your right arm straight up above your head, with the *bicep* (the top of your arm) near your ear.**

3. **Bend your elbow and drop your hand behind your head and toward your back, between your shoulder blades, with your palm facing your back.**

4. **Keeping your upper arm still, reach your left hand hard around behind your back with the palm facing outward, reaching up until you can touch the fingers of both hands together.**

5. **Reverse hands and repeat.**

If you can touch your fingers, your shoulder flexibility is good. If you can clasp your hands, even better! If your fingers are 2 inches or more apart, add stretches to your routine to improve the flexibility in your upper back, shoulders, and upper arms (see Chapter 11).

Building Your Support Network

If you've read this chapter from the beginning, you have a better understanding of your body. Now it's time to think about your mind. If you're thinking you'll only need your legs and arms to swim, bike, and run, you're missing one critical component — a positive state of mind.

What you do with your body starts first with what you're *thinking* your body can do.

No matter how positive you are, you'll hit days when you'll awake to pouring rain, and you'd much rather roll over in bed than head out for a long run or ride. This is when you need the support of friends and family — in other words, someone to roll you *out* of bed.

Share your goals with people you know. You may motivate others to join you, and you'll build a wide network of people who will encourage you. Your spouse, partner, children, siblings, parents, aunts, uncles, friends, and neighbors can be a tremendous source of support. If you have children, share your goals with them and let them know how they can help you achieve those goals. The more people you get excited about your event, the easier it'll be to stay motivated!

Developing your own cheering section

If your family and friends are willing to be by your side on this triathlon-training journey, you'll also want them there when you get to your destination — the race.

It's easy to head out on the morning of your event, thinking that this is a personal challenge and not wanting any of your loved ones to feel obligated to stand around for a few hours simply to clap for a few minutes as you cross the finish line. Wipe this thought out of your mind.

There are two reasons to encourage friends and family to join you on event day:

- ✔ **To spread the energy:** Many people get caught up in the positive experience of the triathlon. Let them see what it's all about. Others get a great sense of fulfillment by volunteering and can help out at the event.

- ✔ **To support you:** The more people you have scattered throughout the course to cheer you on as you pass, the easier it is to smile as you forge ahead. You'll be so proud of yourself, and words to express your joy will be hard to find. Have someone there to share it with you.

If you're traveling far, or commitments keep friends or family from joining you, it's great to have a support team with you at the race or someone's arms to run into as you cross the finish line, even if it's the friend you started the race with or the friend you made along the way. Triathletes are an encouraging and supportive group — you'll easily find someone to give you a kind word on the course and tell you you're doing a great job.

Training with other triathletes

One the best pieces of training advice we can offer is to join a triathlon club. You're less likely to decide not to go for a training swim, ride, or run when you know that people are waiting for you — and if you bail, they'll be sure to give you a hard time the next time they see you. Or they may be too busy raving about the fun training session they had or how beautiful the weather was. Either way, you'll be sorry you missed out.

Don't be afraid to join a triathlon club or look for group rides or runs through cycling or running clubs. You may be thinking that everyone in a club will be much faster than you and will have been training and racing for years. Not true. There are just as many, if not more, athletes new to triathlon training as there are veterans.

Triathlon clubs are made up of experienced veterans and beginners, and you'll learn from both. All new triathletes feel just the way you do — sharing your fears can help you feel more confident. And the veterans can help you with tips and training advice; most are more than happy to go out on a ride or run with you.

If you prefer to train alone, you can do that, too. We often train that way. Maybe you're home all day with your kids or you work a job where you talk to people all day. Training can be the only time you have to be alone. Take advantage of that quiet time and focus on you. You can use the triathlon club or online forums to talk with other triathletes about your training or to relieve any feelings of doubt, taking advantage of the networking but still having your focused time to train.

Part II
Taking It One Sport at a Time: Swim, Bike, Run

The 5th Wave   By Rich Tennant

"Listen, thanks. I'll return them as soon as I get the wheels fixed."

In this part . . .

This part covers all the basics of the three sports. Here you find out what you need to know if you're new to swimming, cycling, or running. We cover each sport in its own chapter, with information on mastering technique and form. We also fill you in on the physical benefits that each sport brings to your overall fitness. This part is where you find training tips and drills to get you started and get you performing at your peak, as well as tips for staying safe while training in open water or on the open road.

Triathlons are about putting the three sports together. In Chapter 8, you find out how to add dual workouts to your training and how to practice transitioning from one sport to the next.

Chapter 5

Swim: Taking the Plunge

In this chapter, we give you everything you need to prepare for the swim leg of a triathlon, including the secret to enjoying your swim training and how to get the most out of it in the shortest amount of time.

If you aren't already comfortable in the water, we help you do that. From there, we show you the basic elements of an efficient swim stroke and offer tips for working on *bilateral breathing* (breathing to your right and to your left).

Speed is the least-important concern for the swim leg of your first triathlon. Instead, you want to focus on making it through the swim while conserving as much energy and muscle power as possible to help you through the cycling and running legs. To help you swim with efficiency, we give you a dozen drills you can use to break up your lap training and help you to focus on overall body balance, which is everything that encompasses swimming: stroke, kick, breathing, pulling, and body rotation.

Looking At the Benefits of Swim Training

Of the three sports in triathlon training, swimming creates the most anxiety for many first-timers. Most people learned to swim as children because of swimming's biggest benefit — it's just plain fun. But, for most people, swimming endless training laps and entering the ocean in a pack of hundreds of flailing arms and kicking legs doesn't hold the same appeal as a game of Marco Polo. But if you learn to relax and perfect an efficient stroke technique, you can learn to love swimming, if you don't already.

If you're new to swimming

The idea of running toward a body of dark water amid a herd of rubber-suited triathletes may sound anything but relaxing and rejuvenating. If you're a beginning swimmer, take your time — but don't put it off. Unfortunately, your running or cycling conditioning will not translate well in the water. So, get in the water and make yourself comfortable there. Here, more than in either of the other two sports, we encourage you to seek the assistance of a trainer to help you one-on-one or in a small group until you feel comfortable and confident in the water and in your technique.

Swimming is a total-body exercise, pulling every part of you into the action, including your mind. You can emerge from a great training swim feeling refreshed and focused — an immediate benefit. Meanwhile, you'll be gaining all kinds of benefits:

- ✔ **Your muscles will be toned.** Swimmers are known for their long, lean, and well-toned bodies. Your muscles will benefit in the same way.

- ✔ **You'll improve your cardiovascular fitness.** Swimming improves your aerobic conditioning and endurance, bettering your body's use of oxygen and increasing lung function. All this makes you a stronger cyclist and runner as well.

- ✔ **You'll be more flexible.** While you're building core strength, the movement of a technically correct swim stroke also improves your range of motion.

- ✔ **You'll run a low risk of injury.** As you swim, you're virtually weightless, supported by the water, so you don't experience the impact and jarring on your bones and joints that you do with other sports. In fact, swimming is the ideal sport for healing from injuries endured from pounding the pavement during running or other high-impact sports.

- ✔ **You'll participate in a sport you can enjoy for life.** Because swimming is gentle on your joints, you'll see swimmers of all ages in the pool, and quite possibly they'll be lapping you into their 70s and 80s.

- ✔ **You'll be relaxed and rejuvenated.** When you submerge yourself into a pool at the end of a long or stressful day, the world drifts away. You can't hear anyone under water, so your time in the water is time all to yourself. If you focus your mind on what your body is doing, you'll emerge from the pool with a sense of calm.

Mastering the Strokes

You'll spend less time training for the swim leg than you'll spend training for the cycling or running legs of your event. Swim training is not about time spent in the water; it's more about technique.

If you're a land athlete who trains thinking mostly about power, speed, and distance, you may find yourself dumbfounded when you take your fitness to the water. You can't power through water for long if you're not using the correct form. Becoming an efficient swimmer requires a commitment to practicing and perfecting your stroke.

Even if your event will take place in open water, don't rush right out to the ocean just yet. Mastering your strokes in a pool where you can focus on form is more important. After you have the strokes down, you can add some open-water training to build your confidence there.

In the following sections, we explain how good body position and an understanding of how to use your arms as levers will propel you forward better than the splashing and kicking many beginning swimmers resort to.

First things first: Relaxing in the water

The first step to swimming effectively is relaxation. You need to get comfortable in the water. Breathe. Feel how your body moves. Tension in your body will prevent you from floating and propelling forward properly. In order to swim well, and conserve energy while doing it, you must first at least feel safe in the water, if not completely relish it.

If you're new to swimming, before you even *begin* to work on form or to swim laps, spend a few 20-minute sessions in the water to build your confidence level. If you're afraid of the water, try this exercise until you feel more comfortable:

1. **Hold a foam swimming noodle in front of you or at your waist for buoyancy.**

2. **Gradually release control of the noodle, allowing it to support your weight in the water.**

   As an alternative, you can ask a friend to hold your hands while you float, supported by the noodle under your arms or at your waist, with your legs extended behind you. Your friend should continue holding your hands until he feels you relax.

3. **Slowly work up to floating, independent of help.**

   Ideally, before you begin your swim training, you should be comfortable enough to float on your stomach with your face in the water for a count of ten.

If you're still anxious about floating in the water, try floating in the fetal position. Take a breath, lower your face into the water, and pull your knees up toward your chest. Your back will rise to the surface. Hold this position for a count of ten and release.

Chalking it up to chin position

How you hold your face in the water determines how well you'll float.

As a child, you may have been taught to float and glide face down, with the water level at your hairline just above your forehead and your eyes looking forward just under the surface of the water. Although this was a great way to prevent you from bashing into the wall as you swam, what you didn't notice — and wouldn't have cared much about then — was that keeping your head up lowers your hips in the water, which means slicing through the water is more difficult.

Instead, tuck your chin slightly toward your chest, focusing your eyes on the bottom of the pool, bringing the water line to the center of the top of your head (see Figure 5-1). Your back and hips will rise to the surface, making you more buoyant.

Figure 5-1: Lowering your head into the water raises your hips, making your body more buoyant.

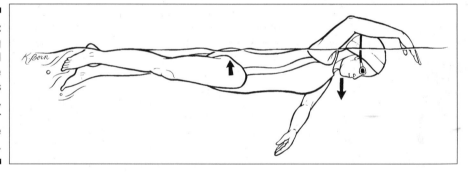

When floating on your back, the same principle applies: Position your head back so that your chin is pointing up. You should be looking up at the ceiling or the sky, not at your feet.

Stroke . . . stroke . . . stroke: Getting down the fundamentals

You'll swim your triathlon using a freestyle stroke (sometimes referred to as the crawl). In order to swim an efficient freestyle, you need to visualize yourself swimming on your *side* rather than flat. In a side position, your body is streamlined and hydrodynamic. As you rotate from side to side during the *stroke cycle* — which is one right arm pull and one left arm pull — you'll increase the distance per stroke, allowing your body to relax and take fewer strokes per lap, which uses less energy in the process.

Here are the steps to an efficient and powerful swim stroke:

1. **Reach with your arm, elbow bent, and slice your hand into the water 6 to 12 inches past your head (see Figure 5-2).**

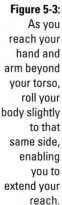

Figure 5-2:
Slice your hand into the water 6 to 12 inches past your head.

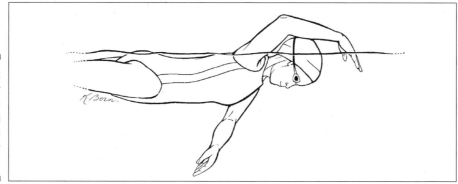

2. **When your hand is in the water, roll your body to the same side, as you extend your arm and reach your hand forward as far as you can (see Figure 5-3).**

Figure 5-3:
As you reach your hand and arm beyond your torso, roll your body slightly to that same side, enabling you to extend your reach.

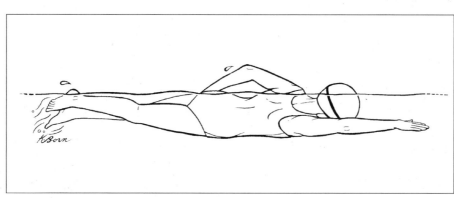

3. **Catch the water with your hand.**

   The catch is the first action of the pull, the downward motion of the hand. Imagine that, as you reach for the water in front of you, you're using it as leverage to *pull* yourself forward (see Figure 5-4).

Figure 5-4:
Reach for
the water
in front of
you, imagin-
ing that the
water itself
is giving you
leverage.

4. **Pull back with your hand flat and your elbow bent at 90 degrees as it reaches under your body (see Figure 5-5); rotate and roll your hips back toward the center as you do so.**

   This is the part of the stroke that moves you forward.

   As you begin pulling back with one hand, you'll start Step 1 with your other hand.

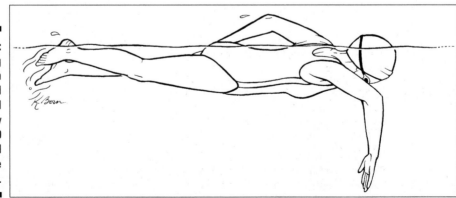

Figure 5-5:
Pulling
back with
your hand
flat and
your elbow
bent at 90
degrees will
help move
you forward.

5. **As your hand reaches your stomach, press your hand and forearm to give you a push forward, straightening your arm toward your thigh as you do (see Figure 5-6).**

   At this point, you'll start to turn your head to take a breath, if you need one (see the next step).

Figure 5-6: As your hand reaches your stomach, press your fingers and forearm to push the water back and propel your body forward.

6. **When you finish Step 5, relax your hand and arm.**

   Your thumb should brush past your thigh. Now lift your arm, elbow first, from the water, taking a breath if you need one (see Figure 5-7).

In order to accomplish an efficient stroke, you need to roll your body to the side and glide at each stroke. Imagine you have a skewer through your body from your head to your ankles. When you swim, that skewer should move straight through the water in the direction you're going, while your body, guided by your shoulders and hips, rotates around the skewer without interrupting the straight, forward motion.

Each time your hand enters the water, count that as one stroke. Over the course of a 25-yard pool, an efficient swimmer will do no more than 14 to 16 strokes; beginners average 18 or more. Gauge your progress not by the speed of your laps but by counting your strokes per length to see how the number drops as you train.

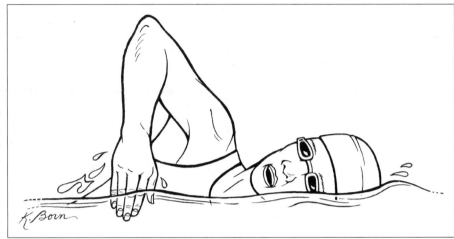

Figure 5-7:
Recover
your arm
from the
water with
your elbow
high.

Kicking it up a notch: The flutter kick

Your goal should be to develop an efficient straight-leg flutter kick. Your kick is not what powers your movement — instead, think of your feet as the rudders that will help lift and balance your body in the water. In order to do this, though, you need to establish a kick that's powered by the hips and not by bent knees.

When you're swimming a freestyle stroke, only your heels should break the surface while you're kicking. Keep your legs relaxed and straight out behind you and point your toes. A powerful flutter kick is a shallow and fast-paced kick, as well as a relaxed and fluid movement.

A good way to test what kind of kick you have is to kick while swimming on your back. Glance down as you kick to see if your knees are coming out of the water as if you were riding a bike. A correct flutter kick on your back should not expose your knees. Instead, you should only see a small amount of white water being kicked up by your toes.

(Not) waiting to exhale: Breathing

As you swim the freestyle stroke, your face will be submerged in the water. You'll need to turn your head with your shoulders on occasion to take a breath. We recommend learning to breathe to your right *and* your left as you swim; this is called *bilateral breathing,* and its advantage over breathing to one side only is that, when you swim in open water, you'll be better able to look up to either side to position yourself on the course.

An efficient breathing cycle is one in which you're either breathing in or blowing out. Don't make a habit of holding your breath in the water — this will deprive your muscles of much-needed oxygen and drain you of energy. Ideally, you want to take a breath every third or fourth stroke.

As you enter Step 5 of your stroke (see "Stroke . . . stroke . . . stroke: Getting down the fundamentals," earlier in this chapter), turn your head enough to allow yourself to take a deep breath through your mouth. Return your face to the water and release your breath through your nose, keeping your mouth closed until you're ready to take your next breath. On your third or fourth stroke, when your opposite arm is in Step 5, pulling back, turn your head to that side and take a breath.

I spy: Sighting your way in the water

Sighting is what helps you know where you're going in the water. To see where you're going, you need to be able to fix on an object. In the pool, you'll use the black lines down the center of each lane to make sure you stay straight. In open water, though, you won't find a black line on the ocean floor.

Buoys will mark the course in open water. As you take a breath, before you put your face back in the water, look up and forward slightly for the next marker.

Some swimmers like to incorporate one breaststroke into their freestyle strokes every five to seven strokes to look for course markings. If this style works best for you, feel free to do this and give yourself a small break from the harder freestyle stroke.

Most of your training will be in pools, but you can still use this technique in the pool to help you practice sighting as you would in open water. Choose a day when you're alone in your lane and close your eyes as you swim. Every four to eight strokes, open your eyes and look up at a fixed object (such as a chair at the side of the pool or a clock or object on the wall) to keep yourself on track or to get back into position.

Finding Water to Train In

With running or cycling, you can train right outside your front door — or, if you have the right equipment, you can even train right in your own house. But unless you have a lap pool in your backyard (which is longer than the average backyard pool), finding water in which to train can be a bigger challenge than finding the time to train.

If you live in a warm climate, your possibilities may be endless — indoor pools, outdoor pools, or open water. In milder climates, though, you'll be limited to indoor pools. For most people, the idea of swimming back and forth in a straight line has about the same appeal as spinning on a trainer or running on a treadmill, but pool training has distinct advantages.

Perfecting your swim skills is easier to do in a lap pool — which doesn't have currents and waves. If you have a local swim club or YMCA in your area, check out its lap-swim schedule or masters'-class schedule. (Don't be fooled by the name — a masters' class is simply for people older than 19. Masters' classes are offered in a variety of skill levels.)

Never swim alone without a lifeguard on duty.

If all your swim training is done in a lap pool, be sure to find an open body of water — a lake, a river, or an ocean — to swim in before the triathlon. If you can, train at least once in the same body of water you'll swim for your event.

Pass the kickboard, please: Pool etiquette

No splashing. Yes, that rule still applies. And here are some others that will you help you find — and keep — your place in the pool:

✔ **Do not dive in.** Enter at the steps or by sliding your body into the water from the side.

✔ **Pick the appropriate lane for your pace.** If you're not sure of your pace, choose the slow lane or an empty and unmarked lane.

✔ **If you'd like to swim in a lane already occupied by a swimmer, ask first before you enter.**

✔ **Split or circle when sharing a lane.** If you're sharing a lane with another person, either you can each stay to your own side (to the right or left of the center line for every lap) or you can swim in a circle, going down the right side and returning on the left. Circle swimming is best if you're sharing a lane with more than one person.

✔ **If you need to rest for a moment, swim to the wall and then move far to the side.** If you need an extended break and are sharing a lane, pull yourself out of the water until you're ready to swim again.

✔ **If a swimmer in your lane taps your foot, that means she'd like to pass.** Continue swimming to the wall, then move to the right as far as possible and stop to allow the other swimmer to turn and begin swimming ahead of you.

✔ **If you'd like to pass a swimmer, tap his foot to let him know — but only tap once.** If the swimmer doesn't move to the right at the wall, it's possible he's not aware of the etiquette and thinks you're merely being annoying. If you have an opportunity, let him know of your intention verbally — just say, "I need to pass you, please."

✔ **Ask the lifeguards for permission before you use kickboards or flippers.** If equipment is positioned at the end of a lane, a swimmer probably left it there to use for a drill after finishing some laps. Don't take it.

You'll find open-water swimming distinctly different — and more challenging — than swimming in a pool. You won't find that black line on the bottom of the lake or ocean, and you won't have *lane lines* (ropes of buoys that divide a pool into lanes) to keep you going straight. In the open water, sometimes you can't see your own hand in front of your face. Add currents and waves to these challenges and you have the recipe for panic (or at least some anxiety).

For open-water swimming, remember these tips to help keep you safe:

- ✔ **Schedule your training time when a lifeguard is on duty.** Currents, *rip tides* (fast-moving forces of water that move quickly from the shoreline), and other hazards can overwhelm even the strongest swimmer.

- ✔ **Swim parallel to the shoreline, just far enough out that you're not hitting the bottom with your hands.** This way, if you do get tired or experience a cramp, you can get to land quickly or enable someone on the shore to get to you quickly.

- ✔ **Swim with other people.** The more people you have to train with you, the safer you'll each be as individuals. If you don't have a friend to swim with, be sure to bring a friend to wait and watch carefully at the shore with a means to support you in the water if you need assistance.

- ✔ **Check the weather.** Pay attention to weather reports and to lifeguard warnings. Even the most serene lake can create unmanageable swells in a sudden storm.

- ✔ **If the warning flags are up at the beach, schedule your swim for another day.** Rip tides and strong currents can be dangerous. If these conditions are present on race day, your race will be cancelled for racer safety, so don't feel as though you have to train for rough conditions.

If you do get caught in a rip tide, don't panic. Swim along it, parallel to the shore, until you can get past it and in to the beach. If you're feeling nervous or tired, signal to the lifeguards for assistance. Don't swim against the strong current, because you'll exhaust yourself before you reach the shore.

Don't make the race your first open-water swim experience. With just a few open-water training sessions, you'll learn to sight to stay on track and to swim with currents and waves.

Training for the Swim

Don't expect to jump in the water, swim the laps you'll need for your race distance, and be done. You need to master your form so that efficient strokes come naturally to you during your event and you don't find yourself panicked and heading back to shore.

Swimming lap after lap without paying attention to technique won't do much to improve your overall triathlon performance. Your goal is to expend the least amount of energy possible, in order to reserve your strength and endurance for the bike and the run.

Work on your technique before worrying about your speed; power will come as your efficiency increases.

Before you run from the pool in fear of lap after endless lap, remember that swim training is less about how far you go than it is about how you get there. During your swim training, you'll break your laps into *sets,* designated distances followed by rest periods. You'll also add sets of *drills* (exercises that help you build strength or endurance or practice your form) followed by rest periods. In fact, many swim coaches tell their athletes that if they're short on time during their swim workouts, they should focus on drills as opposed to swimming "junk" miles just to get the distance in.

A sample training session using drills and sets might look like this:

> **Warm-up:** Swim four lengths.
>
> **Drills:** Swim eight lengths of four drills for two lengths each. Choose drills from the following sections that will work the techniques you're struggling with the most. Do these at a moderate pace.
>
> **Main set:** Swim two sets of eight lengths each, with a 20-second rest in between, then another eight lengths followed by 20 seconds of rest.
>
> **Cool-down:** Swim four lengths.

At the end of this workout, you'll have covered about a half-mile. But you'll benefit much more from this half-mile than the one in which you dive in and trudge through 36 lengths, half the time losing count, and most of your technique, by the halfway point.

When we refer to a *length,* we mean one full length of the pool. Standard pools are either 25 yards or 25 meters. A *lap* is two lengths — down and back.

In the following sections, you'll find a variety of drills — from the very basic front-float check to tips on improving your stroke mechanics. Start with the more basic drills and work your way toward the ones you find more difficult.

You can use swim fins to help you maintain the proper technique until you become more proficient at the drills.

Drill 1: Front float

In this drill, you practice floating on your stomach. You're more buoyant in this position than you are with your hips lower. This drill helps you prepare to be in the right position for swimming. Here's how to do it:

1. **Float face down.**

2. **Tuck your chin so that your eyes are focused on the bottom of the pool.**

3. **Press your chest down toward the bottom of the pool.**

4. **Feel your hips lift toward the surface.**

Drill 2: Streamlined front glide

This drill helps you feel the benefits of elongating your body. When you make your body as narrow as possible, you slice through the water more easily. Here's what to do:

1. **Push off from the side of the pool.**

2. **Place your face down and into the water and your arms overhead behind your ears, with your elbows straight.**

   Your hands should be flat, with your finger pointed, and one hand should be on top of the other.

3. **Keep your feet together, check your chin position (see "Drill 1: Front float"), and press your chest down to lift the hips.**

Drill 3: Streamlined front glide and kick

Practice this drill to experience how your body glides through the water when you're in a hydrodynamic position. Follow these steps:

1. **Follow the instructions for Drill 2 (see the preceding section).**

2. **As your momentum gives way and you slow down, flutter-kick your legs from your hips.**

   Focus on keeping your body long and using a shallow, steady kick. Breathe when necessary.

Drill 4: Body position

This drill helps you return your head to the correct position after breathing. It also helps you perfect your kicking motion. Here's how to do it:

1. **Position your body face down in the water with your arms at your sides and your chin pointing toward the bottom of the pool.**

   Position your head so that the water breaks at the top of your head, not on your forehead.

2. **Press your chest toward the bottom of the pool and feel your hips rise to the surface.**

3. **Flutter-kick forward in this position until you need to breathe.**

4. **Lift your head forward out of the water to take a breath.**

   Your hips will drop as you lift your head.

5. **Return your head to the starting position and complete the drill.**

   Do this drill with or without fins.

Drill 5: Body balance

This drill will help you maintain your forward momentum and keep your balance. Here's how to do it:

1. **Position yourself in the pool, face down, eyes focused on the bottom of the pool.**

2. **Flutter-kick forward in this position and begin your stroke as you rotate your head to the side.**

3. **Allow your shoulders and hips to follow as you turn your head.**

4. **Continue to rotate until you're on your back.**

   Keep kicking as you rotate, especially when you're on your side. Keep half of your head in the water throughout the rotation.

5. **When you're on your back, rotate back in the same direction until your face is in the water.**

6. **Repeat the drill, rotating to the opposite side.**

Drill 6: Statue of Liberty

This drill will help you perfect your balance in the water. Here are the steps:

1. **Begin to swim and then roll to your side.**

2. **Kick as you swim on your side, with the arm closest to the bottom of the pool extended in front of you, with your ear resting on your shoulder.**

   Position the palm of your hand facing the bottom of the pool. Your arm should be just under the surface of the water.

3. **Keep your top arm stationary on your top hip.**

   Pull your top shoulder slightly back to find the position in which you can balance.

4. **Flutter-kick to the side with a straight, steady beat.**

   Keep your head positioned so that your eyes are focused up and back, with your chin pointing toward your top shoulder. Don't look forward — this will cause your hips to sink.

Drill 7: Ten snap ten

This drill helps you focus on your balance, as well as on each of the individual elements of your stroke and on making your stroke strength even on the right and left sides. Here's how to do it:

1. **Perform the Statue of Liberty drill (see the preceding section) for ten kicks on your right side, and then roll your face into the water and begin your recovery stroke with your left arm.**

2. **Begin the pull portion of your stroke, in which you bend your elbow and pull yourself forward, increasing the speed of your hand movement as you move toward the left hip.**

3. **As your hand reaches your hip and you push the water back, rotate your left hip so that you're on your right side.**

4. **Repeat the Statue of Liberty drill on this side.**

Drill 8: Ten-three-ten

This drill will help you to improve your balance and bilateral breathing. Here are the steps:

1. **Perform ten kicks on your side in the Statue of Liberty position (see "Drill 6: Statue of Liberty," earlier).**

2. **Take a deep breath as you tuck your chin and look toward the bottom of the pool.**

3. **Release your breath and start pulling your hand out of the water with your elbow high, taking three strokes in the forward position.**

4. **Rotate your hips to the other side, as in Drill 7 (see the preceding section), and perform ten more kicks in the Statue of Liberty position.**

   Be sure to kick steadily on your side and as you roll from one side to the other. When swimming the three strokes between breaths, keep your head still and your eyes focused on the bottom of the pool.

Drill 9: Front kicking with a board on an interval

This drill will help you to improve your balance and bilateral breathing. Here's how to do it:

1. **Using a kickboard, position your hands at the curved edge at the top of the board.**

2. **Rest your elbows on the board.**

   Your shoulders should be at water level.

3. **Kick, with your heels barely breaking the water surface, fast enough to agitate the water.**

   Your kick should be shallow and have a fast enough cadence to create propulsion.

4. **Try to do as many as ten lengths kicking in this way.**

   If you get tired, you can use fins for the last laps. Challenge yourself to do more laps without fins as you train.

Drill 10: Proper push-off

This drill will help you to feel the momentum you gain in a streamlined position. Here are the steps:

1. **Start on your side with one hand holding the wall and the other straight out in front, pointing toward the opposite end of the pool.**

   Your shoulders should be at water level.

2. **Place your feet against the wall, with your toes pointing toward the side wall and both knees bent slightly.**

3. **Drop under the water, releasing your hand from the wall and extending to reach the other hand.**

4. **In the same movement, as the hands touch, push against the wall with your feet, propelling your body forward.**

   You should be about 18 inches under the water.

5. **Hold a tight streamlined position as you kick and roll to your stomach.**

6. **When you reach the surface in this streamlined position, begin your first stroke and continue to the next wall.**

Drill 11: Fingertip drag

This drill helps you focus on a high elbow recovery. Practice a high elbow recovery, relaxed and controlled, for a clean slice through the water. This drill also helps you to focus on a full-body rotation at the end of each stroke. Here's how to do it:

1. **Swim freestyle, but instead of lifting your hands completely out of the water during your stroke, drag your fingertips across the top of the water, never losing contact with the water, as you bring your arm from your hip back to the catch position.**

   Keep your hand and arm relaxed during the recovery portion of the stroke.

2. **As your hand passes your head, continue to reach forward until your shoulder and body rotate to the side. Continue your stroke.**

Chapter 6

Bike: Cycling Strong

· ·

In This Chapter

▶ Adding up the many benefits of cycling

▶ Spinning for power and efficiency

▶ Maintaining your bike for best performance

▶ Staying safe on the roads

▶ Adding drills for speed

· ·

*Y*ou don't need to be reminded about how much fun you had riding a bike as a child. It's *still* that fun. In this chapter, we review the many benefits of cycling that are sure to put a smile on your face. You find out how riding as an adult for a triathlon takes the joy of riding as a child and adds the technique and form that will see you comfortably through many miles, with energy leftover for the run. You find out how your body position can make hill ascents and descents easier and safer, and discover just what to do with all those gears.

You don't need to be a bike mechanic to make some minor adjustments and repairs that will keep you riding smoothly, and here you find out which ones you can do yourself and when to take your bike to your local bike shop.

Perhaps most important, you find out how to stay safe when riding on the roads — and where and how to ride when you can't get outside.

Identifying the Benefits of Cycling

When you ride your bike to a destination that's 50 miles away, you feel as if the world is within your reach. And when you ride that far, you see roads and scenery that you would have missed in a car, exposing you to a broader view of the world around you.

If you're new to cycling

We'll spare you the cliché about bike riding, but know that if you're just getting back on a bike after many years or you're ready to take your leisurely rides around the block to a new level, you'll have little trouble mastering the mechanics and techniques you need to complete a triathlon. And, as with many sports, technique can make up for what biology lacks. Although some bodies with obviously strong legs, seem custom made for bike riding, good bike fit and proper riding position can take you from a neighborhood rider to a competitor.

It's a safe bet that the last time someone instructed you on cycling is when your parents took the training wheels off your bike. Before you begin your cycling training, we recommend you visit a certified fitter at your local bike shop to help put you in the correct biomechanical position on your bike, as well as instruct you in proper riding technique. This can cost anywhere from $25 to $150, but it's money well-spent as it can make a huge difference in your pedaling efficiency and your comfort on the bike. When you're fit, head out onto quiet roads or an empty parking lot to practice shifting gears and cornering (turning). You'll want to ride straight and confidently before you venture onto well-traveled roads. And if you need support, experienced cyclists usually are more than willing to show off — er, show *you* — their skills.

As you explore the countryside, you experience your surroundings in a way that driving a car doesn't allow. And while you're enjoying yourself, your body gets stronger — your heart pumps more efficiently, your lung capacity increases, and your leg muscles grow stronger and more toned. All the while, you're burning calories and losing excess body fat.

You can ride your bike for life. As a low-impact sport, riding a bike is gentle on your joints. Don't be surprised to see cyclists in their 60s and 70s out for a Saturday-morning century — and passing you on the hills.

Mastering the Spin

You are the engine of your bicycle. You pedal to power the movement in your wheels. Just as we talk about an automobile's efficiency in terms of gas mileage (how far you can travel on a single gallon of gas), you need to maximize the efficiency of your pedal stroke (how far you can travel on your leg strength and endurance). Refueling your body's engine isn't as easy as refueling your car's engine.

Spinning is to cycling what cruise control is to driving. The rate at which you *spin,* or rotate your pedals, determines how much fuel you burn. Ideally, you'll spin your pedals between 80 to 100 revolutions per minute (rpm), with a preferred cadence of 90 rpm. A revolution is one complete circle, and the number of revolutions per minute is called your *cadence.*

In the 80- to 100-rpm range, your body works at the most aerobically efficient rate and can continue for extended periods of time without burning quickly through all its fuel.

 Many beginning cyclists believe they go faster if they "mash" on their pedals in a high gear and a low rpm, meaning their legs push hard on the pedals and move more slowly around than 80 to 100 rpm. Sure, you'll go fast, but not for long. Constantly pedaling in a high gear puts strain on your knees and requires more of an up-and-down piston-like motion than a smooth circle. All this will cause you to wear out quickly. Professional bike racers in the Tour de France operate within a 90- to 100-rpm cadence range for 23 days every July. If it works for them, it'll work for you, too.

Finding your cadence

You can prove the effectiveness of an ideal cadence to yourself by first practicing pedaling at 90 rpm on a flat road until your legs are accustomed to the feel of this spin rate (see the "Measuring your cadence" sidebar). Then pedal up a hill, shifting the bike to successively lower (easier and smaller) gears in order to maintain that 90 rpm. Success! You're at the top.

Next time, pedal up that same hill, but don't shift to lower gears. Your cadence will drop to 70 and 60 rpm and then 50 (even lower if it's a steep hill), and your leg muscles will develop a burning sensation, signaling the buildup of lactic acid. If you keep pedaling at this rate on a long hill, your legs will tire, and you might even need to stop.

If your revolutions per minute reach beyond 100, you're riding in a gear that's too low (and it's likely you're bouncing slightly in your seat, too).

Adjust your gears (after all, you have as many as 30 of them) until you find the combination that allows you to spin comfortably at least at 80 rpm. You'll most likely not be able to maintain 80 rpm when climbing a hill in the same gear you used to approach the hill. And it's easy to spin well over 100 rpm on a downhill. That's why you have so many gears on your bike. An experienced cyclist changes gears often. Not only is it acceptable to shift and reshift as you ride a road with rolling hills, it's expected. Your goal is to use your gears to maintain the same cadence, regardless of terrain.

Measuring your cadence

If you're riding the ten-speed bike you pulled from your garage and you're not ready to commit to a new bike or a multitude of accessories, simply count your revolutions to measure your cadence. Using a timer or the second hand on your watch, count each time your right knee comes up on the pedal, aiming for a count of 22 to 23. Count for 15 seconds, and then multiply that number by four. This is your cadence.

A bike computer with a cadence counter is the best way to determine your cadence; it constantly reads your revolutions per minute as you're pedaling. A basic bike computer, which measures average speed, maximum speed, distance, and time, starts at around $30. As you add features, such as the cadence counter and average overall speed for your ride, the price

can reach $100 or more. The computer's screen attaches to your handlebars or stem, where you can easily see it. Some computers have a wire from the screen to sensors on your front fork and your front tire, and on your pedal's crank if you have a computer with a cadence counter. Or you can purchase a wireless version that sends messages to your computer from the sensor on the fork or the crank.

To use your computer to measure cadence, find the cadence screen and begin riding. Adjust your gears until you find the gear that will let you spin your pedals comfortably in the 80- to 100-rpm range. As a beginner, you'll find yourself closer to 80 than 100, and that's fine. After this rate feels easy to attain, gradually increase your spinning rate during flats on your ride.

Circling the issues

When you rode a bike as a child, you hopped on your bike and pedaled, engaging mostly your quadriceps as you pushed on alternating pedals. You can ride your triathlon in this way, but you'll sap your legs of energy for the run and sacrifice power and speed.

For the most efficient spin, you want to engage all your leg muscles when you train for a triathlon. To do so, practice spinning in full circular movements, rather than in an up-and-down motion.

The best way to take advantage of all the muscles in your legs is to use pedals onto which your feet are attached so that you can pull up on the pedals as well as push down. Regular platform pedals only allow for a pushing motion.

Toe clips allow you to insert your running shoes into cage-like fittings on the pedals — but clips have their drawbacks. When you're rushed in an intersection — or a triathlon — it's easy to misjudge the location of your toe clips, or the pedal itself might have turned upside down, making it hard to secure your foot in the clip. Toe clips don't provide the same efficiency on the upstroke, and they don't keep your foot stable for maximum leg power.

Experienced cyclists prefer clipless pedals. These oddly named pedals actually do clip your pedal onto a steel cleat that's fit onto the bottom of a firm-soled cycling shoe. The name *clipless* refers to the lack of the toe clips, the types of pedals that were created before the higher-tech clipless pedals.

If you're nervous about wearing clipless pedals and being "locked in," practice clipping in and out with your bike position on a wind trainer. If you don't have a wind trainer, visit your local cycling shop and ask someone there if you can spin for a short time to practice clipping in and out of your shoes. Practice allows you to get the feel for how much pressure you need to secure your foot into your pedal and to release it.

You also can practice clipping in and out on grass, which will keep you moving slowly and provide a soft place to land should you fall. Once you are comfortable on the grass, move to a parking lot and practice some more before heading out on the streets.

Someone in your cycling shop can also help you adjust the tension on the pedals, making it easier to release your feet until you get more comfortable with the motion.

To clip in, you simply position the ball of your foot on the pedal and press down until you hear a click. You should be able to pull straight up on the pedal without disengaging. If your foot comes loose, adjust the tension to tighten the pedal slightly.

Practice removing one foot at a time and make the foot you're most comfortable removing be the one you use most often to position on the ground when you come to a stop. To release your shoe from the pedal, twist your heel outward while pulling your foot up and back.

When you're on the road, during the first few rides, it's easy to forget that you're clipped in as you come to a stop and are thinking about shifting, braking, and traffic. Try unclipping long before you get to your stop. And practice unclipping from the same pedal each time. If you've unclipped but feel yourself falling to the opposite side where your foot is clipped in, turn your handlebars slightly so that your wheel moves toward the side you've unclipped. That should help you shift your weight, giving you time to put your foot down.

Cyclists will not laugh at you if you fall because you forgot to unclip from your pedals. Well, actually, yes they might — but only your friends and only because they know the feeling. They've been there, too, and will be there again. Expect to fall at least once when you're learning to ride with clipless pedals. Even the most experienced cyclists get caught off-guard every so often and forget to unclip before they come to a complete stop. Generally, these falls are not serious, because you typically aren't moving forward. You'll be surprised at how slowly you fall, too, which will make you wonder why you didn't have enough time to get your foot out in the first place. With practice, unclipping will become second nature, and you'll manage even if you wait until the last minute. When you get used to riding with clipless pedals, you'll wonder how you ever rode without them.

Whether you're using toe clips or clipless pedals, concentrate on spinning your feet in complete circles, applying equal pressure through the entire circle, or one revolution of the pedal. The down stroke is easy; it's how you start and how you've been pedaling since you were a child. Focus also on the upstroke, or the continuation of the full circle.

As you push down on your right foot and reach the bottom of your pedal stroke, imagine pulling your heel out of your shoe, or scraping something off the bottom of your shoe, as you pull around and back up to the top of the pedal stroke in one continuous motion.

Technique and form

Maintaining proper form keeps your cycling efficient, enabling you to ride longer distances than you ever thought yourself capable of riding. And proper form and a high cadence will make your transition to the run easier on your leg muscles.

In triathlon training, the more efficient you are on the bike, the easier the run will be.

In this section, we give you guidelines for proper cycling technique, including how to get started, cornering, braking, and shifting gears.

Starting smoothly

Here's how to get started:

1. **Stand over your bicycle with both feet flat on the ground.**

2. **Shift all your weight to your left foot.**

3. ***If you're wearing cycling shoes with clipless pedals,* snap your right shoe into the pedal, and raise your foot to the two o'clock position.**

4. ***If you're wearing running shoes,* use the toe of your right shoe to position the pedal at two o'clock. Place your right foot on the platform pedal or into the toe clips.**

5. **Push off with your left foot and step down forcefully onto your right foot, driving the pedal straight down and standing on it.**

6. **Slide onto the saddle and keep pedaling.**

Cornering

When approaching a turn, most beginning cyclists slow down, and then steer with the handlebars through the turn and speed up again. This technique can be dangerous, especially when riding with a group or in a race where people are cycling behind you. Instead, you want to focus more on adjusting your weight than turning your handlebars. You can complete the turn safely while continuing to maintain your speed by braking softly as you approach the turn.

Here are five steps to proper cornering:

1. **As you approach a curve or a turn, decrease your speed slightly before you enter the turn.**

2. **Approach the turn wide, and shift your weight slightly into the turn.**

3. **As you enter the turn, lift your inside pedal up to the 12 o'clock position and press down on the outside pedal at the 6 o'clock position.**

   Point your inside knee slightly toward center of the turn. Keep your weight on the back of your saddle and on your outside foot.

   When you're taking a corner, be sure the pedal on the inside of your bike, toward the turn, is at 12 o'clock. If you take a corner at a steep angle on your bike and your inside foot is at 6 o'clock, your foot can make contact with the ground — and then so can you.

4. **Cut in toward the apex of the turn and then complete the turn wide again, accelerating out of the turn.**

   Keep your eyes on where you want the bike to go, not on your front tire. Your bike will go in the direction you're looking, so "steer" your eyes in the direction you want to turn, rather than looking at your front wheel.

   When you're avoiding a hazard in the road, also look to where you want to go, not at the hazard. If you look where you want the bike to go, your body will take over, and your hips will subconsciously press in the proper direction.

5. **Resume pedaling when you're exiting the turn, with your bike in the upright position.**

Practice cornering in a quiet parking lot to get the feel for how your bike adjusts to your weight shifts. Also, practice cornering at slower speeds and away from traffic areas until you're comfortable with the technique.

Shifting gears

If you're using an older bike, you may be shifting using cumbersome levers on your handlebars or down tube that you need to pull forward or move back to change gears, which then usually adjust with a clank.

If you've purchased a newer model bike, you'll find shifting to be an easy task — new bikes do the work for you. Small levers near your brake levers and the brake levers themselves act as shifters. They need just a slight hand motion inward to engage them and move the chain from one ring to the next.

Your bicycle will feature between 14 and 30 gear choices, depending upon the configuration. The purpose of all those gears is to help you ride efficiently and allow you to maintain your ideal cadence regardless of the terrain.

Don't worry about what "number" gear you're in. Find the gear that allows you to maintain that steady, 80- to 100-rpm cadence.

Road bikes have two or three chain rings in the front and seven to ten cogs or gears on the rear wheel in a *cog set*. A front derailleur helps to guide the chain from ring to ring in the front. A rear derailleur helps to guide the chain from cog to cog or gear to gear in the back.

The smallest of the three chain rings makes it easier when climbing, which minimizes leg fatigue on long hilly rides. Or you can take advantage of the extra power of the large chain ring when you're riding on rolling or flat roads.

The smaller back-wheel cogs are for bigger gears (bigger resistance) and used for downhills; the bigger cogs are for smaller gears, or when you're cycling uphill.

Familiarize yourself with the gear shifters and how they operate. The right-hand lever operates the rear cogs; the left operates the front chain rings.

Practice moving the gear levers into the various positions to become familiar with which way they move and the spot that they engage the gears. If the lever is not in the proper position, you're between gears; you'll hear a clicking noise and will need to *feather* (gently adjust) the lever until the chain engages correctly with the ring.

Avoid crossing your chain from your smallest ring in the back to your largest in the front or your smallest in the front to your largest in the back. Crossing gears creates tension on your chain. Your chain can drop or pop off the rings. If you find yourself in this position, adjust your rear gears before you attempt to shift rings in the front. If you're crossing your chain, you'll usually hear a slight "clicking" noise in the gears. Once you shift, the noise will go away.

Gear shifting should be done with very little pressure on the pedals and at a high cadence. Practice shifting in a parking lot or on quiet roads. Be comfortable with your shifting before riding in high-traffic areas. With enough practice, gear shifting will become instinctive. You'll know the gears by the way they feel.

The larger the ring you use, the more power you have. But the larger the ring, the more power you need to apply. Big rings, then, are great for sprints (when you need a short burst of speed) or for downhills when you want to take advantage of gravity for speed. You'll use a ring somewhere in the middle for flat riding and your smallest gears for going up hills.

Proper shifting is more about when to shift than how. *Upshift,* or move to a gear that requires more power output and increases your speed, when going down hill or on a flat road. *Downshifting,* moving to lower gears to make your hill climb easier, requires good timing. Your goal is not to lose momentum, so begin shifting to a lower gear as soon as you begin to go uphill. Shift successively lower to maintain your optimal rpm or a resistance at which you can continue to pedal yourself up the hill.

Form

The power in your cycling comes from your lower body. Your upper body should be relaxed with very little movement. If your upper body is not relaxed, you'll feel pain in your shoulders, neck, and wrists.

To prevent this, bend your elbows and keep your shoulders down and relaxed. Maintain a neutral or flat spine, and avoid hunching over. As you lean slightly forward, you should be carrying most of your upper-body weight with your lower back, not resting it all on your arms. If you are locking your elbows as you ride, this is an indication that you may be relying on your hands and arms to take your weight. Consider having your seat adjusted for a more comfortable riding position.

Lean forward from the hips and keep your shoulders square. This helps to relieve tension in your neck and shoulders and also opens up your lungs and sends more oxygen to working muscles.

Position your hands on the hoods of your handlebars, where you can reach your gear levers and your brakes (as shown in Figure 6-1). Maintain a light grip with two fingers on your brakes at all times. Change positions often, especially during long rides (resting your hands on the tops of your handlebars to give your upper body a rest and to relieve the pressure on your hands) or on your drops when you descend a hill or are looking for an aerodynamic advantage.

If you find that your hips are rocking from side to side when you pedal, you may need to adjust your seat height, or you may just be pedaling in a gear that's too low to maintain the proper pedal strokes.

As you reach the bottom of your pedal stroke, your knee should be slightly bent, just shy of straight. If your knee is bent, your seat is too low. Raise your seat to give you full extension on the down stroke of your pedaling for maximum power.

Figure 6-1:
You'll ride most often with your hands on the hoods of your handlebars.

Photo by Ed Pagliarini

Braking

Proper braking is essential to riding efficiently and safely. The brake levers on the right side of your handlebars control the brakes on the back wheel of your bike; the left side controls the front brakes. When braking, apply the brakes gently, and then increase pressure gradually as needed, being careful not to apply all the pressure to just one brake.

If you brake hard with only your back brake, you may find yourself in a skid. If you apply all the pressure to the front brake, you'll send all the weight of your bike onto the front tire and perform an "endo," a great trick if you're intending to lift your rear wheel off the ground — but not so great if you're going "end over end" (or somersaulting over the front wheel).

If you're descending a hill and you aren't comfortable with your speed, *feather* your brakes (press them lightly and then release them and repeat) to slightly reduce your speed.

If you need to brake strongly, use mostly your back brake and lighter pressure on the front brake, while you shift your body weight toward the back of your saddle.

Beware of wet pavement, especially painted white lines on wet pavement, sand, or gravel when you are braking. Hitting any of these on the road while you are braking can cause you to skid.

Stopping

To stop your bike and dismount like a pro, begin braking early to avoid skidding. Slow down gradually, placing your right pedal at the six o'clock position, or the bottom of your pedal stroke. If you're using clipless pedals, disengage your left foot by turning your heel out as you pull up. As you bring your bike to a stop, put all your weight on your right foot and stand up off the saddle. Step forward with your left foot and place it on the ground, leaving your right foot on the right pedal.

If you prefer, you can disengage your right foot, put all your weight on your left foot, and step forward with your right foot, leaving your left foot on the left pedal. But decide which way you want to do it, and stick with it so that stopping becomes second nature to you.

Hills

After you're comfortable with shifting gears, you can tackle your first hill. You'll need an understanding of gearing to get comfortably up a hill and safely back down.

Getting up any hill

Climbing hills is as much about confidence as it is about strength. And so cyclists develop their own ways to "talk" themselves up hills. Some don't look at what's ahead. Others keep an eye on the peak, never losing sight of their goal.

To prove that hills are a mental as well as a physical challenge, talk to cyclists about their hill strategies. You'll hear as much talk about how they refer to hills as you hear about correct form and gearing. You'll hear seriously steep uphills described as *reverse downhills*. You'll be told to focus on getting just to the next driveway or the next telephone pole. You'll be advised to not make eye contact with a hill. You'll get stories of songs to the top or counting to distract you. We both count while we climb. Deirdre works on a four count, while Donna prefers ten. Either way, the effect keeps us from focusing on the hill and instead on the power in our legs.

A positive mindset, good form, proper gearing, and plenty of practice can help you tackle any hill. Don't avoid hills. When you get stronger, believe it or not, you'll start to look *forward* to the hills for the challenge and the reward at the other side.

Standing on the uphills

Standing on hills, or "getting out of the saddle," will help propel you forward over a difficult part of the hill by moving more of your body weight over your legs, allowing you to apply more power downward. Standing moves you forward, but it takes a great deal of energy. You'll know at what point you need to stand — your cadence in the seated position will become too slow to maintain the climb.

If your hill is a half-mile or more, you can alternate between sitting and standing, doing each for approximately one minute. For shorter climbs, you may not need to stand at all. Your legs will tell you when they need to stand up. And as you get stronger, you'll find that you can stay seated longer during a climb before you need to stand, if you need to stand at all.

To stand, move your hands from the top of your handlebars to your hoods and keep a light grip. Lift your weight from the saddle, leaning forward slightly. As you push down on your right pedal, rock your body and your bike slightly to the left. As you push down on the left, rock gently to the right. Find a rhythm that's comfortable and take the hill.

Using proper climbing technique enables you to climb more efficiently, expend less energy, and save your legs for the rest of your ride. Try these steps for climbing:

1. **As you approach the hill, shift into a lower gear (the larger cog in the rear). If the hill is steep or long, shift onto a smaller chain ring in the front to allow minor adjustments in the rear that make your ascent easiest.**

2. **As you begin your ascent, continue to downshift to find a gear that allows you to maintain your cadence, or stay as close to it as possible.**

   It's better to be in a gear that's too low and ascend the hill with some energy left over than to burn yourself out halfway up the hill.

3. **Start the climb in the seated position — shift your weight (and slide your butt) to the back of your saddle.**

   This position engages more of your larger and more powerful upper leg and gluteus muscles.

   Don't hunch over the handlebars or lean forward as you ascend a hill. Sit up straight to open your lungs and permit easier breathing.

4. **Keep a light grip on the top of your handlebars, and pull up with your legs in addition to pushing down. Try not to swing back and forth. Keep your upper body "quiet," concentrating the movement in your legs.**

5. At the peak of your hill, keep pedaling over the hill until you resume your spin at a high cadence, and then begin to shift up to smaller rings (higher gears) in the rear. If you've dropped into a small chain ring in the front, remember to move back up to a larger ring before you descend.

Descending hills safely

Every hill has its reward — as long as you know how to get down it safely. Depending on the size of the hill and your body weight, you can easily find yourself bombing down a hill at 35 to 40 mph, making it important to maintain control.

You can put yourself into the proper position for descending hills to help yourself maintain control of your bike:

1. **Position your weight at the back of your saddle, to put your weight on the rear wheel.**

2. **Move your hands to your drops, and position your fingers ready on the brake levers.**

3. **Position your right foot at three o'clock and your left foot at nine o'clock and press your knees tightly against each side of your top tube to help you stabilize your bike.**

4. **Continue to look down the hill, scanning for any potential hazards.**

   If you're descending a winding hill and can't see far enough ahead of you, maintain a slower speed by feathering your brakes as you descend.

Performing Basic Repairs and Maintenance

You can save yourself time and money if you learn to perform maintenance and basic bike repairs yourself. If this isn't something you have any desire to do, don't feel bad — many people arrive at the bike shop with a flat tire to be changed.

Even if you stay on top of basic maintenance, you'll feel more confident, secure, and comfortable on your bike if you bring it to your bike shop at the beginning of the season for a tune-up.

Still, there are simple things you can do to keep your bike functioning properly:

✔ **Clean and lube the chain.** Use the following steps to clean and lubricate your chain, minimizing wear on the gears and promoting smooth shifting:

1. Wet an old towel with an environmentally friendly citrus-based degreaser diluted with equal parts of water and clean your chain after every three or four training rides.

2. Lean your bike against a stable surface, and with your bike's chain in the middle gear on the rear cogs, use one hand to spin a pedal in reverse, while the other hand holds the degreaser-soaked towel around the chain as it moves backwards. Continue for two minutes or so.

3. Spin the chain through a dry towel and let the bike sit for 10 minutes to allow any remaining degreaser and water to evaporate.

4. Apply one drop of a light, evaporative bicycle lubricant (do not use household oils or lubricants) to the center of each link connection.

5. Spin the chain backward for 10 to 15 strokes, and then wipe again with a dry, clean towel to absorb excess on the outside so that it doesn't attract dirt as you ride.

✔ **Replace worn brake pads.** Check your brake pads frequently. If you notice squeaking, rubbing, or excess black dust on your legs or your bike, or if the pads show obvious signs of wear, purchase new pads and follow the directions that come with the replacement pads. Be sure that the pads are aligned with the rim and aren't touching the tire.

✔ **Clean the rear cogs.** Remove the rear wheel as you would when changing a flat tire. Using a rag, clean the grease buildup from each ring and between each ring. Replace the rear wheel, remembering to secure your quick release and lower the lever for the brake pads. If you regularly clean and lubricate your chain, you shouldn't need to clean the rear cogs often.

✔ **Replace worn tires.** When you notice cuts, or your tire looks squared off when you examine the tread, it's time for a new tire. Remove the old tire completely from the rim. Mount one side of the new tire first on the rim, and then install the tube and complete the job as you would when fixing a flat.

✔ **Check bolts for tightness.** Using the appropriate size Allen wrench, check the rear derailleur cable bolt, the front derailleur bolt, and the brake pad bolts to ensure they're tight.

✔ **Run through the gears.** Make sure all your gears are working properly. Ask a friend to lift the back wheel of your bike and crank the pedals to spin the wheel as you use the levers to shift from gear to gear. Check that the chain shifts smoothly from gear to gear without slipping or skipping a ring. If your gears or chain need to be adjusted, bring your bike to your local bike shop.

If you're not mechanically inclined, take your bike into the shop where you purchased it for a yearly "tune-up." Many shops offer free tune-ups for the life of your bike.

If you like the idea of saving money and taking control of your own bike repairs, check out *Bike Repair & Maintenance For Dummies,* by Dennis Bailey and Keith Gates (Wiley).

Checking your bike before you ride

To have a safe enjoyable ride, check the components on your bike before you ride.

Wheels and tires

Inflate your tires before every ride. Your tires lose air pressure when you ride and even when they sit waiting for their next ride. Tires pumped to the correct pressure will help to make your ride more comfortable and easier.

It's best to purchase a floor pump to have on hand. You can buy a pump with a pressure gauge for $20 to $30 at your local bike shop. Pump your front and back tires to the pressure designated on the side of the tire.

Also check the tires for areas that are worn or for road debris that can puncture your tubes. Lift your bike slightly to lift the front tire off the ground. Spin the tire and, as it goes around, watch to see that it spins steadily and doesn't wobble. Then, with your riding glove on (to protect you from sharp objects or glass), place your hand lightly on top of the tire as it spins to remove anything attached to your tire. Repeat with the back tire.

If you have a computer on your bike, with a sensor on the spoke, spin your tire to make sure that the computer can read the sensor and also that the sensor hasn't slipped and is, therefore, clicking against another part of the tire or your bike.

Brakes

Check to be sure you've engaged the lever to position the brakes close to the tire. If you had to remove your tire to transport your bike or for maintenance, you had to lift this lever to release the brakes to allow the tire to come off.

Standing next to your bike with your hands on the handlebars within reach of the brake levers, move your bike forward and squeeze the brake levers to be sure they engage the tires and stop the bike. You also can check just the front and just the back brakes in this same manner. Move the bike forward and squeeze the lever on the right handlebar to check the back brake and the left lever to check the front brake. If you hear rubbing or squeaking, check the brake pads or adjust the braking component to center it on the tire.

Fixing flats on the fly

Flats happen. Sometimes you'll ride a whole season without a flat. Other times, you'll find yourself fixing a flat every time you head out for a ride. Expect them and be prepared to change them, and they're nothing to worry about. If you're not prepared, you can find yourself sitting roadside or with a very long walk ahead.

Keeping your tires properly inflated will help to prevent flats. If flats are becoming the norm, bring your bike into your local bike shop to have someone look at your tires and your wheels.

Fixing a flat on the road is easy when you have a couple of tools and a spare tube. You'll need a set of tire levers and either a small pump or a CO_2 cartridge and inflator, all available from your local bike shop.

To change a flat tire, follow these steps:

1. **Bring your bike to a safe place off the road to change the flat.**

2. **Open the brakes so that you easily can remove the wheel.**

   To open side-pull brakes, fully rotate the lever on the brake upward.

   To open linear-pulls (also known as V-brakes), lift the end of the noodle (the solid, right angle tube) out of its holder.

   To open cantilever brakes (these feature a cable that runs over the top of the tire), lift the cable end on one side out of its holder.

3. **Remove the wheel with the flat.**

   Lay your bike down with the gears facing up. If your rear wheel went flat, shift gears to the smallest cog in the rear so that you can remove and replace the wheel. Open the quick release on the wheel with the flat, lift the bike, and pull down on the wheel to remove it. To extract rear wheels, it helps to pull the derailleur back slightly to clear the axle parts as the wheel passes through.

   For the front wheel, you'll need to hold one side of the quick release and turn the other counterclockwise to create clearance to get past the wheel-retention tabs on the fork.

4. **Remove the tube.**

   Tubes come with two different valve types: Presta and Schrader (see Figure 6-2). Most new bikes use tubes with Presta valves. Remove the valve cap and nut (sometimes found on Presta valves). For a Presta valve, unscrew the tip and press down to let all the air out. For a Schrader valve, use the end of your tire lever to release all the air.

Figure 6-2:
Tubes feature one of two types of valves: a Presta valve (left) or a Schrader valve (right).

Photo by Ed Pagliarini

5. **Lift the tire from the rim.**

   Holding your wheel and using your body or the ground for stability, position your hands directly opposite the valve. Take a tire lever and near a wheel spoke, slip the lever under the bead (the hard lip of the tire that keeps it secure against the rim) and pry it down to lift the tire. Hook the lever onto a spoke. Place another lever about 2 inches away from the first and pry again, lifting the tire away from the wheel (see Figure 6-3). Use that lever to slide around the wheel, pulling the tire up and out of the rim. Remove only one side of the tire, leaving the other side on the rim. When you have removed the tire from the rim, you'll be able to reach in and pull out the tube.

6. **Remove the tube.**

   Slide the tube out from under the tire, without removing the tire entirely from the wheel.

Figure 6-3:
Use tire levers to lift the tire from the rim so that you can pull the tube out from under the tire.

Photo by Ed Pagliarini

7. **Inspect the tire.**

   It's important to look for whatever caused the flat. If you don't, a sharp item may still be in the tire where it will just puncture your new tube. To find it, remove your glove and use it to run around inside the tire. If something sharp is still stuck in your tire, it'll snag the glove. Remove whatever is poking through your tire. Then examine your tire for cuts.

   Any rip in the tire longer than about ab inch will need to be reinforced so that the new tube will not slip through it and pop when it's inflated. Use folded paper money, the Mylar wrapper from an energy bar, or even a small piece of an old tire that you keep in your saddle bag as a temporary patch.

8. **Install the tire and tube.**

   First, put a small amount of air in the tube to give it some shape. You can do this by opening the valve and blowing into it (or use a hand pump), and then closing the valve. Insert the valve into the valve hole inside the tire and then tuck the tube into the tire, working your way around the rim. Beginning at the valve, press the tire's bead (the edge) under the rim, working a few inches to the right of the valve and then a few inches to the left of the valve. Continue alternately working a few inches to the left side and then a few inches to the right side until you've completely worked the tire bead under the rim, finishing on the opposite side to the valve.

As you tuck the tube into the tire, be sure the tube is not getting caught between the tire and the rim. If it does, you can end up with another flat, as the tube may puncture when you inflate it.

9. **Inflate the tire.**

   Place your pump on the valve, bracing it by wrapping a finger behind a spoke so that you're pushing against your hand, not the valve. Inflate the tire until it's just firm (not fully inflated). At this point, inspect the tire to make sure it's *seated* (sitting correctly on the rim). Check that the bead line on the side of the tire is equidistant from the rim all the way around on both sides of the tire. If it's not, or if you see a section of tube peeking out from under the rim, let the air out, work the tube back into place, partially reinflate it, and check the tire again. When the tire is correctly seated, fully inflate it.

   When you're on the road using a hand pump or a CO_2 cartridge, you'll have to estimate the air pressure in your tire by feel. One full CO_2 12g cartridge should inflate your road-bike tire adequately to get you through the remainder of your ride. You'll need a 20g cartridge for hybrid or mountain-bike tires. You'll notice that your tire is low on air the next day, because CO_2 escapes quickly from the tube. Before you ride again, be sure to fill your tire with air from your floor pump.

10. **Reinstall the tire.**

    Place the tire back on the frame. Make sure you've secured the quick release and re-engaged the brake by closing the brake quick release or reattaching the noodle or cable.

11. **Pick up after yourself.**

    Look around your work area and gather up your tire levers, punctured tube, and spare tube's packaging. Put everything you can in your saddlebag or in the pockets of your riding jersey. If you can't fit the scrunched-up tube, drape it over your shoulder and across your chest and back as you would a messenger bag.

You can get more than one flat on a ride. Be prepared by bringing more than one tube and CO_2 cartridge on long rides. If you're riding in a group, another cyclist will most likely have a spare if you don't. If you're alone and other cyclists pass you, they'll usually ask if you have everything you need. Do the same in return.

Handling repairs on the road

If you're inspecting your bicycle before each ride and staying on top of its normal maintenance schedule, the likelihood of a breakdown on your ride is small. However, traveling with a multipiece tool kit is important, in case you do encounter a problem when you're on the road. Bike shops sell this kit, which is small enough to fit in a jersey pocket or in your saddle bag, for around $20. The tools are all secured together, much like a pocket knife, and feature Allen wrenches in a variety of sizes. Some kits include tools to fix broken chains, as well.

The most important "tool" you can bring on your training rides is your cell phone. If you need assistance or cannot repair your bike, it's best to call someone for a ride home.

Riding with a broken spoke

A broken spoke will cause your wheel to wobble because the tension is no longer the same on both sides of the wheel. Spokes usually break on the rear wheel and can cause the wheel to rub against the brake. If the wheel wobbles severely, making it difficult to ride, you need to *true* the wheel, which means adjusting the spokes to correct the wheel.

To true a wheel, you need a spoke wrench to loosen and tighten the spokes in the area of the broken spoke to equalize tension on both sides of the wheel. This is best done by a bike mechanic. If a spoke breaks during a ride, pull off the road and call a friend or family member to pick you up.

Poor rear shifting or chain skipping

You may notice problems with shifting if you've accidentally dropped your bike or fallen. If the *rear derailleur* (the component that guides the chain as it moves from one cog to the next) gets jarred or out of alignment, your chain can skip gears or change gears poorly.

Don't try to fix this problem yourself — you can damage your gears, chain, derailleur, or the spokes on your wheel. Minimize shifting and end your ride as soon as you can. Then take your bike to your local shop for repairs.

Loose bolts or slipping components

Occasionally, check your brake cables and seat posts to be sure they're secure. Use your multitool to tighten any loose fittings.

A dropped chain is an easy fix and can be performed without any tools. Use a rag or tissue (a leaf will do) to protect your hands from grease and guide the chain around the middle chain ring on the front of your bike and the middle cog in the rear. To give the chain some slack and help you position it on the cogs, move the rear derailleur forward. Lift the back of your bike with one hand and spin the pedals with your other hand to make sure the chain is in place (see figure 6-4). Lift the back of your bike with one hand and spin the pedals with your other hand to make sure the chain is in place.

Figure 6-4:
To fix a dropped chain, reposition the chain onto the middle ring in the front of your bike and the middle cog in the rear. To give the chain some slack, move the rear derailleur forward.

Photo by Ed Pagliarini

Staying Safe

When you're riding, you're sharing the road with cars — many of which are being driven by distracted drivers. Never assume that a driver sees you or will give you the right of way. Most drivers will go out of their way to give you room on the road, but don't be surprised if you encounter the occasional hostile driver who believes bikes have no place on the road. Be as courteous as you would expect any driver to be.

There are two critical things to remember when riding your bicycle:

- ✔ You are a vehicle, governed by the vehicular operating laws of your state — a human-powered vehicle, but a vehicle nonetheless.
- ✔ You are a small vehicle that is not easily seen by operators of motor vehicles.

Follow these rules to help ensure your safety and enjoyment on the road:

- ✔ **Never ride without your helmet or protective eyewear.**
- ✔ **Ensure that everything you're carrying with you is secured in your saddle bag or fits tightly in a pocket of a jersey or jacket and won't bounce out.**
- ✔ **Wear bright clothing with reflective materials, if possible.** Do not ride in the dusk or dark if you can prevent it. Be especially aware of what you're wearing on cloudy days or when you're driving on heavily shaded roads. Sun glare and shade can make you virtually invisible to drivers. Make sure you stand out.
- ✔ **Ride defensively.** Drivers can be preoccupied; don't assume everyone will see you or stop for you. And drivers may not have a good sense of just how fast you're going.
- ✔ **Obey all traffic laws.** You're a vehicle on the road. If you want respect from other drivers, show respect for traffic laws. Make left turns from left lanes. Stop at red lights and stop signs — don't run them.
- ✔ **When stopping at a red light, keep your position in the line of cars.** Don't squeeze between the cars and the curb to get to the front of the line and make everyone wait for you to cross the intersection.
- ✔ **Get in the left lane when making a left turn.** Stay in the center of the lane, not off to the right where someone can pass you.
- ✔ **Keep your line when riding on roads where cars are parallel parked.** Don't duck in toward the curb and pull back out when you encounter a car. Drivers will not be able to predict your movements.
- ✔ **Be aware if you're to the right of a vehicle at a traffic light.** The driver may make a right turn, even if you don't see the blinker.
- ✔ **When passing parked cars, keep a look out for someone to open a door or to pull out in front of you.**
- ✔ **As you approach an intersection and a car is on your left, know there is a chance that it'll turn right in front of you.** Be prepared.
- ✔ **When you're approaching a car coming out of a side street, know that the driver may pull out in front of you either because he expects that you should stop or because he isn't estimating your speed accurately.**

If you're uncertain of the driver's intentions, make him certain of yours. Signal by pointing straight ahead or use your voice loudly to let the driver know you're going to keep moving straight.

✔ **Use hand signals for turns, lane changes, and stops to let drivers and other cyclists know where you're going.** Don't worry about the old hand signals you may have learned as a child. Most drivers won't know them. Use a clear and easy sign: Point in the direction you plan to turn. To turn right, stretch your right arm out straight and point right (see the top photo in Figure 6-5). To turn left, stretch your left arm out straight and point left (see the middle photo in Figure 6-5). To indicate a stop, drop your left arm down, palm facing backward (see the bottom photo in Figure 6-5).

✔ **Make eye contact.** If you need to signal your intention to a driver, don't assume the driver sees you. Make eye contact, signal, or speak, and wait for acknowledgment.

✔ **Look for hazards.** Be aware of road obstacles and scan for them as you ride, always looking ahead, not directly down at the ground. If you're riding in a group, point out hazards to the riders behind you or call them out loudly. In groups, you'll also want to call out cars that are approaching from behind ("car back") or from the front ("car up" or "car front") to let other cyclists know to stay to the right side of the road.

✔ **Ride on the right side, with the traffic.** If you're pedaling 15 mph and a car is coming up behind you at 30 mph, the car is closing on you at only 15 mph. If you are pedaling at the same 15 mph on the wrong side of the road facing traffic, that same car moving at 30 mph is closing in on you at 45 mph. If the operator of the car is inattentively talking on a cellphone, he has much less time to see you and avoid you.

✔ **Ride no more than a foot to the left of the painted line, which marks the outer edge of the road.** This allows overtaking motor vehicles space to pass you.

✔ **When riding in a group, ride single file.** In most states, you're permitted to ride two abreast, but only do that on rural roads with very little traffic. If a car approaches from behind, return to single file.

✔ **Avoid slick surfaces.** When roads are wet, white lines can be slick, causing you to slip. Also, avoid manholes and gravel, and use caution when turning on wet roads.

✔ **Use caution when riding over railroad tracks or grated bridges. Cross perpendicular to railroad tracks.** And don't pedal across bridges. Stay straight and secure on your bike. Or dismount and walk your bike across the bridge.

✔ **Be courteous.** At some point, you're bound to encounter a driver who foolishly endangers you with his driving. You may be yelled at. Don't yell or gesture. You have a right to be on the road, but you won't win a battle against a 3,000-pound vehicle.

Figure 6-5:
Signal your
intentions
clearly by
outstretch-
ing your arm
and pointing
in the direc-
tion you
plan to turn
or dropping
your arm,
palm facing
out, to indi-
cate a stop.

Photo by Kathy Johnson Brown

Training for the Bike

When starting out with your bike training, set a goal of three rides per week. Start with 5-milers two days a week and a 7½-mile ride for your long ride. Add 10 percent each week to your distances until your short rides are 10 miles and your long ride is 30 miles. Having the days off in between rides lets your body recover.

Depending on the distance of your event, you can continue to add miles or begin to work on speed or strength on the hills. The majority of these miles are best traveled on roads. Sometimes, though, you'll need to find alternate ways to train depending on the weather or daylight.

Spinning inside

When you need to take your cycling training indoors, you can add a "living-room loop" to your workouts. You don't need to purchase a stationary bike for your living room. You can set up your bike on a *wind trainer,* which creates a stationary bike from your road bike. You attach your back wheel to a roller, and the pressure of your tire against the roller and the gear you choose creates resistance. Training DVDs, such as *Spinnervals* (www. spinnervals.com), are available to keep you focused and motivated and if it gets a little too quiet, recruit your family members to yell an occasional, "Hey, get off the road."

An entry-level wind trainer costs between $150 and $300. You don't *need* a wind trainer, but it provides a great advantage when you want to train during bad weather. It also helps you get comfortable with shifting and clipping into and unclipping from your pedals if you're new to using clipless pedals.

If you have a gym membership, stationary bikes can help you work on your endurance during darkness or a rainy day. Many gyms offer spin classes — they're a great way to maintain your aerobic fitness during the winter months.

Although these classes and a stationary bike help to maintain your endurance, you still need to spend time on the road to be comfortable climbing hills, staying steady in winds, and cornering.

Giving drills a try

After you've established your base miles, you can try drills to add strength and speed to your legs.

Single-leg drills

Single-leg drills help you add strength because you learn to use both legs to complete the full circle of a spin (pushing down and pulling up equally with both legs). The more you practice, the more natural the movement becomes.

You'll find this drill easier to do (and safer) on your wind trainer or a stationary bike.

Here's the drill:

1. **Ride your trainer or stationary bike for 20 minutes to warm up.**

2. **Remove the foot of your dominant leg (usually right, if you're right-handed) from the pedal (unclipping or pulling out of the toe clip).**

3. **Place that foot on the center of the stationary bike or move it forward out of the way on your trainer.**

   You can rest it on a stool or chair pulled closed to your bike.

4. **Pedal with the other leg using a low gear (big cog on the rear), concentrating on the full circle with each pedal stroke. Pedal with that one leg for 30 seconds, aiming for 80 to 90 rpm.**

5. **Switch and pedal with the other leg for 30 seconds.**

6. **Spin with both legs for one minute.**

7. **Repeat the sequence for 15 minutes and continue to spin using both legs for 30 to 60 minutes.**

If you're outside on your bike and you don't have access to a stationary bike or wind trainer, find a flat stretch of road. Switch to a low gear. Do not remove one foot from your pedal or clip, but focus on using the other leg only to move you forward for 30 seconds. Switch your focus to the other leg and repeat. Spin for one minute between each set of legs and repeat for 15 minutes. Then continue your ride.

Spinning

Shift to a low gear (big ring) and pedal at 100 to 110 rpm, focusing on pedal stroke and using all the major muscles of the legs through the entire "circle" of the pedal stroke. Concentrate on not bouncing in the saddle as you pedal. Keep your upper body relaxed with little movement, using just your leg muscles. Do this drill as a way to practice perfecting your complete spin or as an active recovery workout after a long bike ride.

You also can try this spinning drill if you're riding in a group and some riders are falling behind. Shifting into a lower gear compromises power, so even though you're pedaling at 100 rpm, you won't jump ahead. You can focus on your full pedal rotation, giving riders behind you a chance to catch up.

Hill repeats

Hill repeats help you master your climbing techniques and build strength for your ascents. Don't try hill repeats, though, until you feel comfortable with gear and climbing. Pick a hill that you've climbed before.

After a 10- to 15-minute warm-up, head for the hill and climb for 2 minutes. As you approach the hill, set your gears to keep your cadence high and climb for two minutes. At the two-minute mark, stop, turn around, and spin down the hill. Repeat this drill five to ten times, depending on your fitness level.

Big-gear drills

Save the big-gear drills for after you've developed a fitness base on your bike and a level of comfort. When you're ready, use this drill to help develop muscular strength and endurance. Think of it as strength training on your bike.

Warm up for 10 to 15 minutes, and then shift into a higher gear (small ring on the back). Lower your cadence and concentrate on your pedal stroke. Focus on using your quadriceps, hamstrings, and glutes to complete the circle as you pedal. Maintain this drill for two minutes. Shift into a higher gear (smaller ring) and spin for one minute at a 100-rpm cadence. Repeat the cycle for 15 to 20 minutes.

Chapter 7

Run: Finding Your Stride

In this chapter, you rediscover how to run as we all did when we were kids — relaxed and comfortably. You learn what keeps runners on the roads, addicted to the positive emotional and physical effects of running.

After reviewing the many benefits of running, if you're still not sure you can actually enjoy a run, you find a section on the mechanics of good form and how to let your body fall naturally into a comfortable rhythm.

When you're ready to start your running program, we offer up a beginner's guide to building a base of 20 minutes of running, which you can work toward in just ten weeks. You find out where to run and the benefits and hazards of each surface, as well as how to keep yourself safe wherever you run. And from there, you find three types of runs — short, long, and brick — and two drills to help you build on your speed and your distance.

Catching Up with the Benefits of Running

You may have heard people refer to a "runner's high" — and you may have wondered if they were kidding. You won't see many runners on the roads with big smiles on their faces. Road running is hard, no doubt about it. But running does bring to your body and mind great benefits. If you can get past that first mile and learn to let your body relax and run naturally, you can experience that runner's high — confidence, happiness, and feeling as if you can run forever.

If you're new to running

Of the three events in a triathlon, swimming seems to cause the most anxiety, but for many triathletes, running is their hardest — and least favorite — of the sports. Part of that is because the run comes after the swim and bike legs, so you're already tired when you start your run. Mostly, though, it's because running, the sport that seems most natural to our bodies, is hard.

There are many more people who take up running and quit shortly after than there are people who fall in life-long love with the sport. Don't let this be you.

And don't make the same mistakes eager triathletes make when starting out — beginning too fast and going too far. Be patient and take it slow. More so than the other two sports, it takes time for your body to adapt to running. Start out with a run/walk program, gradually building up to 20 minutes of jogging. Don't get caught up with distance, targeting a certain number of miles in your daily runs. Train by time. Commit to getting on the road for 20 minutes, and when you're there, walk, skip, run — whatever it takes to do 20 minutes without stopping movement. And do it with a positive attitude. If you think you can, you can.

Remember: You don't have to run to complete a triathlon. You'll see plenty of participants at your event who will walk part or all of the running leg. But give it a shot — you'll be glad you did. And you *can* do it!

Exercise of all types relieves stress, but running has long been associated with this high. Completing a run can put you in a better mindset. Plus, as you run and find a rhythm, all the worries of the day disappear. You let your mind wander, or you can focus on something specific — like your breathing or, well, your pain — and everything else melts away.

Whether you're enjoying the runner's high or struggling through a painful low, your body is still reaping the rewards of your efforts, and when it's all done, running leaves you with a feeling of satisfaction. It can bring perspective and peace that stays with you all day long.

Here are more of our favorite reasons to run, selected from a long list of the many benefits of running:

✔ **Running is inexpensive.** We list this first because it's a nice change from all the equipment and resources you need for cycling and swimming. For running, you need you, the road, and a good pair of shoes. It's simple. It's visceral. It's cheap.

✔ **Running is flexible and fast.** You can run just about anywhere at any time. Put your running shoes on and hit the road or the trails. No tires to pump and no equipment to check. And after 30 minutes of running, you'll return feeling refreshed, energized, and clear-headed. So, why wouldn't you run? (Okay, we'll get to that in a bit.) And when you travel, running is easy to fit into your schedule — and your suitcase. Just bring your running clothes and your shoes and enjoy the new surroundings.

- ✔ **Running brings you cardiovascular fitness faster than any of the triathlon sports.** And few sports burn as many calories as quickly as a good run.

- ✔ **Running helps you maintain bone density.** And bone density matters. Even if you're *not* training for a triathlon, you should include weight-bearing exercises in your fitness routine. It's that important. During a weight-bearing exercise such as running, walking, or any sport where you're on your feet, you support your body weight while exercising, which in turn maintains and can even increase your bone density, reducing your risk of bone breaks or osteoporosis later in life.

- ✔ **Running lets you see the world.** Well, the part you're in, anyway. Running gets you out on the road or into the woods, where you experience your surroundings in a new way, catching sights and smells you may have missed while driving quickly in a car. And running gets you on roads you may never be on during your daily commute or drive to the grocery store.

- ✔ **Running lets you meet new people.** Running clubs are everywhere — you can find them online or ask other runners or triathletes if they belong to them. Club runs are a great way to train with other people at your level or to improve by running with slightly more experienced or faster runners.

- ✔ **Running makes your legs strong and your lungs healthy, giving you more strength and stamina for cycling.**

Mastering the Mechanics

You ran just fine as a child without thinking much about mechanics — why start now? Because sometime between second grade and adulthood, many people forget how to run. Running should come naturally, but stress and pressure to pound the pavement can strip the joy and ease from the sport.

Even your choice in running shoes can affect your running style. Running shoes with heavy cushioning and hi-tech shock absorption, while reducing stress to your joints and spine, promote heavy heel striking. When you lead with your heel and it's the first part of your foot to hit the ground, you must then roll to the front of your foot and push from your toes.

All this takes time and sacrifices momentum. But cushioned shoes greatly improve your ability to run for longer distances comfortably, as long as you practice running like a child — easy and light and striking with your mid or forefoot.

Before you begin your training, take a minute to run just for the sheer joy of it. Kick off your shoes and chase your child across the grass. Toss your flip-flops and run hard for the surf the way you did as a child. Remind yourself that running is fun!

Running can feel good if you relax your body and enjoy it. In this section, we take a look at the basics of proper form when running. Use these as guidelines to find the style that works comfortably and efficiently for you.

Foot strike

Your *foot strike* is where your foot first lands on the ground as you run. Runners who cover long distances tend to land on their heels or midfoot first, and then roll to the toes and propel forward from there. Sprinters tend to run on their toes for speed — but running on the fronts of your feet for long distances can drain your energy and cause shin pain and tight calves.

As a first-time triathlete, don't be too concerned about foot strike unless you run on your toes. If you do, you'll want to focus on landing on your midsole so that you'll be able to cover more ground comfortably.

Most people naturally land on their heels and roll up to push off their toes. Make sure your knee is slightly bent to absorb some of the impact when your foot lands.

Concentrate on running "lightly," as if you were running on eggshells or hot coals. Keep it light and fast. If you can hear your foot slap the ground with every step, try to lighten your steps.

When you run, each time your foot hits the ground, the impact on your lower body is twice your body weight. This impact is absorbed from your foot up your body and your spine all the way to your neck and head. That's why cushioning in sneakers is important for long-distance running.

Stride

Your *stride* is the distance between each step. You may think it's best to strive for as long a stride as possible, to cover the most ground with each step. But doing so can waste energy and create more impact as you land, increasing the potential for injury.

Instead focus on your cadence, moving your feet from one step to the next as quickly as possible.

Keeping your stride short will help you to decrease the impact of each strike. Shorter strides create an energy-efficient movement. Think about running uphill. Your body naturally adjusts to shorter strides to make your ascent easier.

Run in a straight line, making sure your feet move directly out in front of you and not side to side.

Also, concentrate on moving forward, rather than up and down. Bouncing as you run will drain your energy faster. Use all your motion to propel you ahead.

Posture

Your upper body form is easier to adjust than anything happening below your waist, but it affects your running almost as much as what you do with your lower body.

Remember when you were a kid and you'd be running so fast and leaning so far forward that you actually would trip over your own feet? That was the weight of your upper body falling forward. Although you do want to run like you did as a child, embracing that joy and freedom, you also want to skip the skinned knees: A slight lean forward is good, but don't lean too far forward as you run.

Practice good posture daily, not just when you're running. Then when you do run, you'll find it easier to remember to run tall, keeping your head up, your back straight, and your shoulders slightly back and relaxed.

Relax. Bend your elbows, but don't lock them in place. Swing your arms forward and back, not side to side across your body, with your hands brushing just slightly below your hip bones near your waistband. Don't clench your fists. Hold your hands as if you were holding something delicate in each one, touching the tip of your middle finger to your thumb. Keep your shoulders down and comfortable, not scrunched up near your ears, which causes tension and steals energy. Figure 7-1 shows the proper running form.

Breathing and pacing

You breathe throughout your day without even thinking about it. Set out for a run, though, when your body needs the extra oxygen the most, and suddenly you may forget to breathe or how to breathe.

Your muscles need oxygen, and if you don't breathe, they can't get it. Then you have no choice but to walk because your legs are out of "air" and don't move you forward quickly.

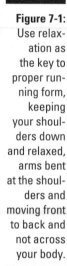

Figure 7-1:
Use relax-
ation as
the key to
proper run-
ning form,
keeping
your shoul-
ders down
and relaxed,
arms bent
at the shoul-
ders and
moving front
to back and
not across
your body.

Photo by Kathy Johnson Brown

Your breathing will naturally become labored during your run. Don't panic. And don't worry that you're not doing it right. Just breathe. Let your breaths be relaxed.

The only way to prevent labored breathing during a run is to slow down. Follow the "talk test" to determine the appropriateness of your pace: Talk to your running partner — or to yourself if you're alone. If you can't find the breath to hold a conversation, even if it's one-sided, slow your pace.

If you're just starting a running program, you need to build up a base of fit-ness, which you can achieve by running at a pace that's comfortable for you, and then gradually increasing your mileage.

Where to Run

The beauty of running is that you can do it anywhere: local roads, trails, beaches, tracks, or even in your house. In this section, we discuss the risks and rewards of each surface.

Vary the surfaces on which you train to give your legs relief from the pound-ing of the hard surfaces of the roads or the flat routine of a treadmill.

Roads

Distance runners generally divide themselves into two groups — road runners and trail runners. Roads are the easiest and most common places to find runners, and they're where you'll probably do most of your training.

Obvious hazards of the road include traffic, debris, and uneven surfaces (such as storm drains on the shoulders).

Trails

Head to the trails for a soft surface. Trail running is fun! You can't help but smile as you jump logs and splash through puddles. You run slower on trails, because the softer surface absorbs some of your forward momentum and you're watching your footing for roots and rocks. Trail running doesn't do much for your speed on the roads, but the side-to-side motions and jumping work your leg muscles in a way that the straight motion of the roads does not. You build muscle and endurance on the trails.

Some trails, such as towpaths, can be hard-packed gravel and easy to run; others can be rocky surfaces on which an ankle roll can ruin your run. Hazards include the very elements that make trails fun: rocks, roots, water crossings, and slippery leaves.

Add some tick repellent to your sunscreen routine and keep an eye out for poison ivy or sticker bushes.

Beaches

Sand is an ideal surface on which to run to strengthen your legs. A beach run is slower and harder than running on the roads, but the rewards of the surroundings make it worth the effort.

Avoid running where sand might angle sharply toward the water. Running on an angle can be hard on your ankles, knees, and hips.

Track

Track running offers routine and simplicity. Here, you won't need to worry about hazards — other than boredom. You can count laps or just run yourself in circles for an allotted time. A track is also a great place to run if you want to time yourself or do interval workouts. Running on tracks is also easier on your joints, as the material used to pave tracks is softer than the roads.

Treadmill

Some runners consider treadmill training a necessary evil, if not a punishment. But when the weather is bad or you just can't get outside, treadmills can be a training lifesaver. If work or family commitments keep you in the dark when it's time to run, hit the treadmill.

Especially as a beginning runner, you may enjoy the controlled environment and timing of a treadmill. You can enter your pace and stay at that pace. Some treadmills incline so that you can get a small hill workout (without the downhill pressure on your knees). Adding periodic inclines also varies your stride and reduces your chances of an injury. A treadmill offers a soft, consistent surface (which some people find boring). If you're a multitasker, you can run on the treadmill while you catch your favorite show or listen to a podcast or some high-energy tunes.

If most of your training runs need to be on a treadmill, be sure to schedule some time as you approach your event to get your feet on the road. You'll want to be sure you're comfortable navigating hills and adjusting to the climate. You'll also want to experience running on the same surface you'll encounter at your event.

Staying Safe

Common sense will take you safely across many miles of running. Trust your gut and your intuitions when you're on the road, and follow these basic rules of the road to help keep yourself safe:

- ✔ **When running on roads, be sure to run against the traffic — the traffic should be coming toward you.** You don't want to be running with cars coming up behind you where you can't see them. Running against the traffic allows you to see what's coming so that you can make adjustments in your pace or where you're running if necessary. You may need to step off the road at times if cars appear to be driving fast or erratically. Pay attention and be prepared.

- ✔ **Plan your routes.** Choose roads that are traveled so that you're not alone, but not so heavily traveled at high speeds that you're at risk of being hit or need to stop every block or so to let cars pass so that you can cross safely. You need enough space on the shoulder to run, and the road should be wide enough for cars to safely pass.

- ✔ **Watch for turning cars.** If you're approaching an intersection, pay attention to any cars in front of you. They may be turning right, across your path. Do not run alongside them toward or into the intersection — the drivers may not see you. Stay behind the cars until they turn.

If a car is stopped next to you at an intersection, don't cross the intersection until you make eye contact with the driver and signal your intention. More often than not, drivers will wave you on before they turn, but never assume a driver sees you.

✔ **Make yourself visible.** If you have to run at night or early in the morning, wear a reflective vest and bright colors. Or purchase inexpensive clip-on flashing lights and attach them to your clothing, one in front and one on your back.

✔ **Run with a group.** Running with other people gives you added motivation, as well as increased visibility on the road. Avoid running alone in unpopulated or unfamiliar areas or wooded trails.

✔ **Let someone know the route you plan to run and what time to expect you back.** If you live alone, leave your route map or cue sheet at your home or with a friend or trusted neighbor.

✔ **Vary your routes and the times you run.** Being less predictable can help keep you safe.

✔ **Carry identification with you with your name, phone number, and emergency contact name and number.** Check out RoadID (`www.roadid.com`) for a variety of ID tags for runners and cyclists. Some runners choose to carry their cellphones with them in case they get lost or injured (or just plain exhausted) on a run. If you do, enter an emergency contact on your phone as ICE (short for, *in case of emergency*).

✔ **Carry pepper spray or take a self-defense class.** It's unfortunate that we have to list this one, but it's the reality in many places, and you're better off prepared. Also, we're not concerned solely about fending off human attackers — pepper spray can work on a dog that's chasing you as well.

✔ **Listen up.** You'll see people on the roads wearing headphones or earbuds. Yes, music can amp a workout. But listening while on the roads makes you vulnerable. You can't hear traffic, dogs, people, or even cyclists approaching from behind. Save the tunes for your treadmill runs.

Training for the Run

In this section, you find a training plan to help you build a base of comfortably running for 20 minutes if you're new to running. After you've established your base (or if you're already a runner), you can add the drills to your workouts to improve your strength and speed.

If you're new to any cardiovascular exercise other than running out to the mailbox once a day, begin your running training with two to three weeks of walking at a faster pace than a leisurely stroll, for 30 minutes three times a week. Then you can add running in intervals of a few minutes at a time, taking walking breaks in between. By following the run/walk program outlined in this section, you'll gradually lengthen your running times, while decreasing your resting periods. Perform this interval program for ten weeks before you begin the training schedule in Chapter 10.

If you've built a base of cardiovascular fitness through another aerobic sport but you haven't added running to your repertoire, give yourself ten weeks of a run/walk program before you start your triathlon-training program. The run/walk program outlined in this section will help get you running 20 minutes without walking breaks, as well as prepare you to move on to a training schedule (see Chapter 10).

Starting with a run/walk

In this section, we show you how to work up to a 20-minute run, so that you can get ready to train for your triathlon (see Table 7-1).

The brisk five-minute walk at the beginning of each workout isn't a stroll — pick up your pace to get your heart rate up. Use this same pace for your recovery walks between runs. The last walk segment of each workout should be done as a cool-down. Finally, all the running should be done at a moderate pace — fast enough that your breathing is labored, but not so fast that you can't carry on a conversation.

Don't run and ride or swim on the same days yet. Wait until you've established your running program to double up your workouts.

Table 7-1	Run/Walk Schedule
Week 1	
Day	**Workout**
Day 1	Walk briskly for 5 minutes. Then run 60 seconds and walk 90 seconds, repeating this run/walk pattern for 20 minutes.
Day 2	Rest, bike, or swim.
Day 3	Walk briskly for 5 minutes. Then run 60 seconds and walk 90 seconds, repeating this run/walk pattern for 20 minutes.
Day 4	Rest, bike, or swim.
Day 5	Walk briskly for 5 minutes. Then run 60 seconds and walk 90 seconds, repeating this run/walk pattern for 20 minutes.
Day 6	Rest, bike, or swim.
Day 7	Rest, bike, or swim.

Week 2	
Day	**Workout**
Day 1	Walk briskly for 5 minutes. Then run 90 seconds and walk 90 seconds, repeating this run/walk pattern for 20 minutes.
Day 2	Rest, bike, or swim.
Day 3	Walk briskly for 5 minutes. Then run 90 seconds and walk 90 seconds, repeating this run/walk pattern for 20 minutes.
Day 4	Rest, bike, or swim.
Day 5	Walk briskly for 5 minutes. Then run 90 seconds and walk 90 seconds, repeating this run/walk pattern for 20 minutes.
Day 6	Rest, bike, or swim.
Day 7	Rest, bike, or swim.
Week 3	
Day	**Workout**
Day 1	Walk briskly for 5 minutes. Then run 2 minutes and walk 3 minutes, repeating this run/walk pattern for 20 minutes.
Day 2	Rest, bike, or swim.
Day 3	Walk briskly for 5 minutes. Then run 2 minutes and walk 3 minutes, repeating this run/walk pattern for 20 minutes.
Day 4	Rest, bike, or swim.
Day 5	Walk briskly for 5 minutes. Then run 2 minutes and walk 3 minutes, repeating this run/walk pattern for 20 minutes.
Day 6	Rest, bike, or swim.
Day 7	Rest, bike, or swim.
Week 4	
Day	**Workout**
Day 1	Walk briskly for 5 minutes. Then run 3 minutes, walk 90 seconds, run 5 minutes, walk 3 minutes, run 3 minutes, walk 90 seconds, run 5 minutes, and walk 3 minutes.
Day 2	Rest, bike, or swim.
Day 3	Walk briskly for 5 minutes. Then run 3 minutes, walk 90 seconds, run 5 minutes, walk 3 minutes, run 3 minutes, walk 90 seconds, run 5 minutes, and walk 3 minutes.
Day 4	Rest, bike, or swim.
Day 5	Walk briskly for 5 minutes. Then run 3 minutes, walk 90 seconds, run 5 minutes, walk 3 minutes, run 3 minutes, walk 90 seconds, run 5 minutes, and walk 3 minutes.
Day 6	Rest, bike, or swim.
Day 7	Rest, bike, or swim.

Week 5	
Day	**Workout**
Day 1	Walk briskly for 5 minutes. Then run 6 minutes, walk 4 minutes, run 6 minutes, walk 4 minutes, run 3 minutes, and walk 3 minutes.
Day 2	Rest, bike, or swim.
Day 3	Walk briskly for 5 minutes. Then run 6 minutes, walk 4 minutes, run 6 minutes, walk 4 minutes, run 3 minutes, and walk 3 minutes.
Day 4	Rest, bike, or swim.
Day 5	Walk briskly for 5 minutes. Then run 6 minutes, walk 4 minutes, run 6 minutes, walk 4 minutes, run 3 minutes, and walk 3 minutes.
Day 6	Rest, bike, or swim.
Day 7	Rest, bike, or swim.
Week 6	
Day	**Workout**
Day 1	Walk briskly for 5 minutes. Then run 5 minutes, walk 3 minutes, run 8 minutes, walk 3 minutes, run 5 minutes, and walk 3 minutes.
Day 2	Rest, bike, or swim.
Day 3	Walk briskly for 5 minutes. Then run 5 minutes, walk 3 minutes, run 8 minutes, walk 3 minutes, run 5 minutes, and walk 3 minutes.
Day 4	Rest, bike, or swim.
Day 5	Walk briskly for 5 minutes. Then run 5 minutes, walk 3 minutes, run 8 minutes, walk 3 minutes, run 5 minutes, and walk 3 minutes.
Day 6	Rest, bike, or swim.
Day 7	Rest, bike, or swim.
Week 7	
Day	**Workout**
Day 1	Walk briskly for 5 minutes. Then run 10 minutes, walk 3 minutes, run 10 minutes, and walk 3 minutes.
Day 2	Rest, bike, or swim.
Day 3	Walk briskly for 5 minutes. Then run 10 minutes, walk 3 minutes, run 10 minutes, and walk 3 minutes.
Day 4	Rest, bike, or swim.
Day 5	Walk briskly for 5 minutes. Then run 10 minutes, walk 3 minutes, run 10 minutes, and walk 3 minutes.
Day 6	Rest, bike, or swim.
Day 7	Rest, bike, or swim.

Week 8	
Day	**Workout**
Day 1	Walk briskly for 5 minutes. Then run 15 minutes, walk 3 minutes, run 10 minutes, and walk 5 minutes.
Day 2	Rest, bike, or swim.
Day 3	Walk briskly for 5 minutes. Then run 15 minutes, walk 3 minutes, run 10 minutes, and walk 5 minutes.
Day 4	Rest, bike, or swim.
Day 5	Walk briskly for 5 minutes. Then run 15 minutes, walk 3 minutes, run 10 minutes, and walk 5 minutes.
Day 6	Rest, bike, or swim.
Day 7	Rest, bike, or swim.
Week 9	
Day	**Workout**
Day 1	Walk briskly for 5 minutes. Then run 18 minutes and walk 5 minutes.
Day 2	Rest, bike, or swim.
Day 3	Walk briskly for 5 minutes. Then run 18 minutes and walk 5 minutes.
Day 4	Rest, bike, or swim.
Day 5	Walk briskly for 5 minutes. Then run 18 minutes and walk 5 minutes.
Day 6	Rest, bike, or swim.
Day 7	Rest, bike, or swim.
Week 10	
Day	**Workout**
Day 1	Walk briskly for 5 minutes. Then run 20 minutes and walk 5 minutes.
Day 2	Rest, bike, or swim.
Day 3	Walk briskly for 5 minutes. Then run 20 minutes and walk 5 minutes.
Day 4	Rest, bike, or swim.
Day 5	Walk briskly for 5 minutes. Then run 20 minutes and walk 5 minutes.
Day 6	Rest, bike, or swim.
Day 7	Rest, bike, or swim.

Now you're ready to start your triathlon training. For efficiency, break your running training into three runs: a short run, a long run, and an every-other-week *brick* (a bike ride immediately followed by a run).

Going on short runs

Use your short run as your basic weekly training run. From this run, you'll build your distance or your strength on hills.

For your first triathlon, and especially if you're new to running, your goal will most likely be simply to finish the running leg still running.

If you're already comfortable with running, though, and think you can build on your strength in this sport to shave some seconds from your time, you can add speed workouts to your short runs.

Speed training can be strenuous and can result in injuries if you aren't physically fit or if you don't allow yourself adequate rest. Be sure to have a comfortable base or be at least four weeks into your triathlon training before you add speed training to your short runs.

You don't need to train for speed for your event. If you're not ready for speed training, you shouldn't do it, and you don't need it to finish a triathlon.

You can train for speed in your workouts using fartleks, tempo runs, or intervals:

- **Fartleks:** Go ahead and laugh. That's appropriate, because even experienced runners snicker when they say "fartlek." And the word fits the activity. Fartleks add fun to your run.

  A *fartlek* is an increase in speed for a set time or distance. The pickup is not a sprint but just a slight increase in the speed for a set amount of time or distance. Then you return to your regular pace for a recovery period and repeat the fartlek throughout your run.

  For a fartlek training run, warm up for at least ten minutes and find a comfortable running pace. Decide between designating timed fartleks (such as a two-minute increased pace followed by a five-minute regular pace) or distance-based fartlek runs (designating landmarks along your route such as alternating your pickups and regular pace between telephone poles, mailboxes, or street signs). You also can just pick it up when you feel like it, and slow it down the same way. What's fun about fartleks is you can do whatever you want and make it something different each time you go out to add variety to your runs.

- **Tempo runs:** A *tempo run* is a warm-up, a run slightly faster than your training pace, and a cool-down. Similar to a fartlek, you increase your speed, but for tempo runs you maintain that speed for a longer period of time. Tempo runs should feel comfortably hard — but they aren't sprints.

Set a time for which you want to perform the tempo portion of your run before you go out. Like everything else, start slow and work your way up. For example, after your warm-up, start with ten minutes of your regular pace followed by a five-minute pickup and a ten-minute cool-down. Add to the tempo time as you feel stronger on your tempo runs.

✔ **Intervals:** Head to a track for your interval training, during which you warm up for 10 to 15 minutes, then perform five hard and fast sprints with short recovery jogs in between each sprint. Of the three speed-training options, your interval sprints are the hardest and fastest. To start, you'll want to keep the speed intervals short and increase them as you progress. Work toward a set of five one-minute sprints followed by one- to two-minute recovery jogs. Listen to your body — if you need more recovery in between the sprints, take it.

If you dislike running on tracks or don't live near one, you also can perform intervals on a treadmill. A treadmill allows you to program your sprint intervals. Because the treadmill is adjusting the speed for you, it's easier to stay motivated to continue to run hard for the set time period.

Going the distance: Long runs

Long is a relative term. If your base or short run is 20 minutes, a long run may be only 30 minutes. Anything that takes you beyond your current base qualifies as your long run. Long runs build endurance and are great for helping you work up to running the entire distance of your event. Add to your distance slowly, adding no more than 30 percent to your current time during a week (as you're building your base) or to your current comfortable long-run time or distance.

Biking then running: Bricks

A *brick* is a bike/run workout in which you go for a run immediately after a bike ride. These back-to-back workouts teach your legs to go from one sport to the next, making your transition on event day easier and preparing you for that heavy-legged feeling you'll have when you start running after a bike ride.

You can do bricks in a series of short intervals, such as a 5-mile bike ride, followed by a 1-mile run, repeated three or four times.

While you're building leg strength, you're also practicing your transitions as you get off your bike, change your shoes, grab some hydration or nutrition, and start to run.

Drills to try when you're not running

Running drills are exercises you can do at the ends of your short runs or after a five- to ten-minute warm-up. Drills can help to increase your speed. They're easy to do, and they deliver big rewards. Here are two we recommend:

- **Butt kicks:** Start running. After a few steps, try to kick up your heels behind you and kick your butt. You won't be moving forward as you do these butt kicks — stay in place. Do ten butt kicks on each side, repeating the movement as quickly as you comfortably can. Then return to a run for 30 seconds and repeat.

  You don't have to reach your butt with your heels for this drill to be effective. You'll be learning to move your feet quickly, which will help your *turnover* (the speed with which you place your foot on the ground, push off, pick it up, and place it again).

- **Knee-ups:** Knee-ups are the reverse of butt kicks. Start running and, after a few steps, start lifting your knees in front of you to just below your hips. While performing knee-ups, you move slightly forward. Do ten knee-ups on each side, repeating them as quickly as you can while staying in control of your movements.

Chapter 8

Putting It All Together

*T*ri means "three," so maybe triathlon is a misnomer, because you actually need to train for four elements of your event: the three sports and the transitions. Transitions get you from one sport to the next and, believe it or not, they can make a significant difference in your triathlon time. We're not talking margins of seconds — we're talking minutes or tens of minutes. Mess up your transition, and you can find yourself out of the race entirely.

But don't worry. Transition training is easy. In this chapter, we tell you how to practice your transitions and why you only need to put two of your three sports back-to-back at a time during training. Here, you find tips on the most important aspects of transitions, setting up your gear, arriving prepared, keeping your transition simple, and saving time. We help you remember where you racked your bike (these tips may even come in handy the next time you park your car!) and how to get on and off your bike quickly.

If the thought crosses your mind that you can save yourself some time during your training sessions by not worrying about setting up your transition areas or practicing transitions, know that the minutes you save during a training session can cost you *double* that on race day. Being comfortable moving from one sport to the next and efficiently getting your gear on and off makes you more relaxed, confident, and comfortable — and it's one of the easiest ways to cut minutes from your overall race time.

In this chapter, we cover transitions in depth. But we start by helping you focus your training, balancing all three sports and the transition to set yourself up for the best possible race.

Knowing Where to Focus Your Training

Focus first on fun. If you're enjoying your training, you'll be eager to get back out for the next session. And when you're meeting all your training goals, you'll cross the finish line of your event with a smile on your face.

Although we're all talk about how you should be having fun, we're sure there's a sport you're absolutely dreading. And we know most people tend to avoid training for the sport they like least. Before you start your training program, spend some time focusing on the sport you like the least or that makes you feel the least confident. During this pre-training period, your main focus will be on the sport you *don't* like.

If the swim causes you anxiety, then get in the water as much as possible and enlist the help of an experienced swim coach. You'll be pleasantly surprised by how much easier swimming is when it's done correctly, using proper form.

If it's running you dread, begin with an alternating schedule of walking and running. Gradually increase the time you spend running, with shorter recovery walks in between until you're comfortable running for 20 minutes without walking. Then begin your training program.

If you aren't comfortable riding on the roads and are putting off your cycling training, join a beginner's cycling group or ask a friend to lead you on a few rides on quiet roads to help get you more comfortable.

Continue focusing on your least favorite or your weakest sport throughout your training program. If you're an experienced cyclist and you have to choose between a cycling workout and a swim, choose the swim.

Adding Dual Workouts: Why You Need to Combine Two Sports in Training

Your event day is the time to pull all the pieces together, going from one sport to the next. The key to successful triathlon training is balancing the time and intensity you spend on each sport, not on all three together.

On your event day, though, you (and your muscles) will need to know how to get from one sport to the next. You'll do this by combining two sports in back-to-back workouts during your training weeks. Doing so will help you:

- ✔ Practice your swim-to-bike and bike-to-run gear transitions
- ✔ Get your muscles accustomed to moving from one sport to another with little or no time in between for rest

If you're following the training schedules in Chapter 11, some days you'll swim and bike or bike and run. These days are your dual-workout days, and they'll get your muscles comfortable going from one sport to the next and help you to improve your endurance. Treat your dual-workout days as opportunities to practice what you'll need to do in the transition area as well.

Practicing the transition from the swim to the bike leg will help you get comfortable changing clothes or removing your wetsuit, and then getting your shoes and gear on and getting ready for the bike leg. There's a lot to remember in this transition, and you need to practice to get your mind used to all that has to be done.

Your muscles will learn to adapt quickly when you go from swimming to spinning. For this reason, you don't need to do back-to-back workouts for every training session — just enough to make the process smooth and easy. Dual-sport workouts are as much about getting comfortable with quickly shedding the clothing or gear for one sport and getting started on the next one as they are about getting your muscles accustomed to the challenge.

The transition from swimming to spinning is the harder of the two transitions because there's more gear involved, so mimicking this transition often during your training will help to prepare you for coming out of the water, running to the transition area, cleaning off your wet (and maybe sandy) feet before slipping them into your shoes, and jumping on your bike for your ride.

But because most of your swim training will be done in a pool, setting up a realistic transition for your dual-workout days will take a little creativity. Whether you swim in a pool indoors or outside, you can set up a transition area and run from the pool to your bike set up nearby. You can even add a wetsuit to your transition practice by putting on your wetsuit over your tri suit to practice training in your gear and for your transition:

1. **Find a parking space near the pool in which you can set up your cycling gear.**

2. **Lay out your gear.**

3. **For your swim, wear your tri suit underneath your wetsuit.**

4. **After your swim, run from the building or the pool to the transition area you set up.**

5. **Remove your wetsuit.**

6. **Put on your cycling shoes, helmet, sunglasses, and gloves.**

7. **Head out for your training ride, leaving everything in the pool parking lot or in your car.**

If you can't easily secure your wetsuit and other belongings before your ride, ask a friend or family member to help by gathering your belongings for you to keep them secure.

You'll find it easier and more realistic to practice your swim-to-bike transitions during your open-water swim training. Simulate an actual race scenario as much as possible by finding a place in which you can lay out your transition area. Go for your swim. When you exit the water, run to your transition area, get on your cycling gear as quickly as possible, and head out for your training ride.

You'll also want to add dual-sport training days to combine your cycling and running workouts. Although the transition from the bike to the run is easier than the swim-to-bike transition in terms of changing gear, the challenge to your muscles is just as great.

The bike-to-run workout is called a *brick,* mostly because that's what your legs feel like when you get off a bike after 45 minutes and then try to run.

The more you combine cycling and running workouts, the easier it'll be to run through this feeling of having awkward, heavy legs. To help your muscles prepare to go from spinning to running, as you approach the end of your cycling route where you've set up your transition area, downshift to a lower gear to reduce the resistance and spin without further fatiguing your muscles.

When you first start to run after cycling, your legs will feel uncooperative. After some time, they'll begin to feel normal again — as normal as they'll ever feel after swimming and biking first.

Because back-to-back workouts are strenuous, don't plan more than one of these every other week.

Becoming a Quick-Change Artist: Planning Your Transitions

You need to know exactly what you'll do when you arrive at your transition areas during your event. It's easy to think through the steps in your head and assume you'll have no problems. But when you actually go through the process at your triathlon, you may find that your system doesn't work so well. Race day is not the time to make this discovery.

Plan to practice setting up your transition area and creating mock workouts to get from one event to the next. Transition practice is different from your dual-sport workout days, which will be full workouts.

Transition practice can be as simple as getting some fellow triathletes together to set up a mock transition area in a driveway or parking lot, and then taking turns timing each other getting out of your wetsuits and onto your bikes or off your bikes and into your running shoes. On warm days, you can spray a hose to wet the triathlete coming from the "swim" to the bike, just to make it as realistic as possible.

You don't need to rush through your transitions. Yes, you need to get through the changes quickly, but just like the rest of the race, your technique is more important than your speed.

Transition 1: Swim to bike

In your event, the swim-to-bike transition is called T1. This transition is your first and will be more time-consuming then the transition from the bike to the run.

To keep your transition time to a minimum, keep the process simple. The more clothes you have to take on or off, or the more fiddling you do with straps, zippers, or laces, the longer your transition time will be.

The most experienced athletes simply grab their helmets and sunglasses and run out with their bikes, with their shoes already attached to the pedals. For your first event, though, plan to take it slowly and don't do more than you have to in the transition area.

Here are the steps to plan for and consider in the transition area:

1. **Find your bike and gear.**

   See the nearby sidebar, "Like a needle in a haystack: Finding your bike," for more information.

2. **Remove your wetsuit, cap, and goggles.**

   If you're not wearing a wetsuit when you leave the water, you shouldn't have to remove any clothing.

3. **Remove sand or grit from your feet and dry them.**

4. **Put on your socks (if you're going to wear them) and shoes.**

5. **Put on your bike helmet.**

6. **Put on your sunglasses.**

7. **Put on your bike gloves (if you're going to wear them).**

8. **Guide your bike to the transition exit and begin riding.**

Here's how to save time getting in and out of the crowded transition area:

- Push your bike along on your right side so that the chain ring is away from your body.

- Mount your bike at the appropriate mark outside the transition area. You may be able to place your left foot on the pedal, push off with your right foot, and then swing your right leg over the saddle and clip in. Practice this move often before your event.

- Be sure to have water or a sports drink ready to go on your bike. To save time, hydrate after you start riding, instead of while you're standing in your transition area.

Like a needle in a haystack: Finding your bike

When you're practicing your transitions, you'll leave the pool or water, and your bike will be right there where you left it (assuming you locked it, of course, or that someone is watching it for you). Because of this, it's easy to fall into a false sense of security — when you leave the transition area on race day with your towel and equipment all neatly arranged, you may assume that you'll easily spot your bike after your swim. After all, you spent so much time with it during training, you'd know it anywhere, right?

Chances are, when you arrive on race day for your first triathlon, you'll be one of the first people in the transition area. It'd be nice to think that when you return after your swim, you'd be one of the first, as well. But it's more likely that, when you return, what you remember as a neat and orderly transition area will now be a mess of black cycling shoes and a blur of spokes and shining metal. Unless you prepare before you leave the transition area, you may not have any idea where your bike is.

Where you rack your bike and how easily you find it can add minutes to your transition time, or help you cut time. Here are ways to save time when searching for your bike:

✔ **Arrive early to get the best spot available near the entrance or exit of the transition area.** If your transition area is first-come, first-served, try to position yourself at the end of the rack.

✔ **If permitted by the race organizers, mark your bike with a flag or other identifier.** (See Chapter 18 for specific tips on ways to mark your bike and area.)

✔ **Create a mental path to the entrance and exit of the transition area, so that you know where you need to go when you leave with your bike and when you return for your run.**

✔ **Instead of relying only on your race number, count the number of rows your bike is from the exit and the entrance of the transition area; also count the number of spaces (or estimate whether you're halfway down the row, a quarter of the way down, and so on).** If the transition area is organized by race number, knowing your number is the first step. But when you're tired after your swim and you're your facing down row after row of bikes with little signs that offer a range of numbers, you may feel like a child at a library. Suddenly, you can't even count, and all the rows look the same.

Transition 2: Bike to run

The bike-to-run transition is your second transition in your event, so it's called T2. This transition is easier because you'll have less to do. You'll also be tired, as well as excited, because you're entering the last leg of your event.

To prepare for T2, you need to:

✔ **Know where you enter the transition area when you return on your bike.**

✔ **Get familiar with where you have to dismount your bike.** You can't ride into the transition area; you'll need to get off your bike early and walk it into the transition area.

✔ **Remember where your bike belongs so that you can re-rack it and get the rest of your equipment.**

At T2, you'll follow these steps:

1. **Remove your cycling gloves and cycling shoes (if you're wearing them).**

2. **Put on your running shoes and tie them (or use elastic-style laces that don't need to be tied).**

3. **Put on your hat, if you're wearing one.**

4. **Get to the transition exit and start running.**

Saving Time: Making Your Transitions Smoother

Your triathlon transitions can make or break your event times. If you're well-prepared and you've practiced transitions, it's easier to cut minutes from your overall time during transitions than it is to save time during your swim, bike, or run. With practice, you may be able to enter a transition area full of dozens of people who are getting ready for their rides or runs, and leave them all there still fumbling with their shoes as you head out again.

You can save time and maintain your cool with practice — and a few insider tips:

- ✔ **Have a plan.** Create a setup system for your transition area. How you lay out your gear depends on what works best for you. Think through your steps and do what comes most naturally and quickly for you. For example, you may always put your helmet on when you're getting ready for a bike ride, then your sunglasses, and then shoes — set up your transition area in that way and try it out.

- ✔ **Slow down.** Yes, we said slow down — to save time. If you're rushed and nervous, you can cost yourself time dropping gear or fumbling with shoelaces. Try to relax and approach the transition methodically.

- ✔ **Practice doing more than one task at a time.** Take off your goggles and cap in one movement as you run to the transition area. Start removing your wetsuit as you approach, too. Or put on your hat after you've already started running.

  If you're wearing a long-sleeved wetsuit, hold your cap and goggles in one hand. As you pull off the arms of your wetsuit inside out, release the cap and goggles inside the sleeve to keep them together.

- ✔ **Dry-run it.** Walk yourself through the process without actually putting on the gear. Think, "I'll put my shoes on first. Where are they? What will I need next?"

- ✔ **After you have the timing chip on, never, ever, *ever* take it off, until you're across the finish line.** If you put it under a wetsuit, the wetsuit will come off over it just fine. If you take it off after your swim to get your wetsuit off, you'll lose minutes getting it back on and risk leaving it behind entirely.

- ✔ **Sprinkle some talc powder in your shoes or socks so that you'll have an easier time sliding your wet feet into them.**

- ✔ **Roll your socks halfway down to what would be the ball of your foot.** When you put your toes into the rolled socks, you can then easily roll the heel and ankle part across your foot.

- ✔ **Tape nutrition packets onto the top tube or handlebars of your bike.** Open the packets, too. Or use a gummy nutrition cube and stick the cube itself right onto the top tube of your bike.

- ✔ **Leave the change of clothes behind.** Don't lose time by trying to change or put on a new shirt or shorts over your bathing suit.

- ✔ **Relax.** Unless you were planning to win the first triathlon you enter, concentrate on relaxing through the transition period so that you're calm and focused when you get on your bike or head out for your run.

Part III
Training for Your Triathlon

In this part . . .

You find out what it means to live like an athlete. Even if you're new to all three sports, if you're training for a multi-sport event, you're an athlete.

Chapter 9 discusses eating for energy. Here, you find out why you need to stay hydrated before, during, and after your training and how snacking on the go and refueling during your peak recovery period after training can help you improve your performance moving forward.

Chapter 10 provides training schedules for every event and tells you how to schedule your training for efficiency. In Chapter 11, you find out how to supplement your training with stretching and strength training.

Chapter 12 covers potential injuries and possible causes. Here, you discover what you can to do prevent or relieve pain and identify when you need to give yourself time to heal. We provide information on the most common swimming-, cycling-, and running-related injuries and tell you how to treat them. We also share tips and cautions for training in hot, humid weather or in temperatures below freezing.

Chapter 9

Living like an Athlete

*T*raining for a triathlon will give you a new appreciation for your body — how it works and what it can do for you. You'll push yourself beyond limits you ever thought possible. And in the process, you'll gain a new appreciation for the food you eat. At some point during your training program, as you prepare a meal or raise a forkful of a greasy favorite, you'll stop and think, "How will this power my workout?"

If you're paying attention, it'll take you only a few intense training sessions to recognize the difference between fueling your body with sugar and caffeine and powering your muscles with a balance of carbohydrates, proteins, and fats.

In this chapter, you find the basic tools to help you make the food choices that give you the most energy for your training, to maintain that energy throughout your workouts, and to fuel your body for quick recovery so that you're ready to do it again the next day.

You won't find specific meal plans here, because every triathlete has a list of personal favorite foods. Bananas and whole-grain bread may be a great way to start your morning exercise — or a banana may remind you for your entire workout that you ate it. Start taking notes now, and you'll quickly find the foods that fuel you.

If you go out one morning and you're feeling fast and fit, think about what you ate and drank the day before your workout, especially one or two hours before. If you're feeling sluggish, as if there are dumbbells where your hands used to be, and you're certain your shoes weigh 10 pounds more than the day before, check the octane of the fuel you put in your tank.

A food diary can help. Keep track of what you eat before, during, and after your workouts. Remember to use those foods to fuel your hard training sessions — and maybe even your race day performance.

You may be hoping someone will hand you a daily menu for your 12 to 30 weeks of training. After all, you have a training schedule — why not an eating schedule, too? But there isn't one magic menu that works for everyone. In this chapter, we give you guidelines to help you develop your *own* nutrition plan that will get you moving and keep you moving.

Eating for Energy Every Day

If you're new to endurance sports, you may have approached meals by counting calories to figure out only how to reduce them or burn them off. For tri-athetes, it isn't so much about how to get *rid* of calories as it's about how to get them *in* — in the form that will best fuel your workouts.

Approximately 70 percent to 80 percent of the calories you ingest supply energy to your heart and lungs, just for your basic survival. How quickly you burn off the rest of your caloric intake in a day depends on your *metabolic rate* (the rate at which you burn calories) and your activity level.

When you're training for a triathlon, you need to think of calories as your fuel. A basic understanding of what fuels your body can help you select the foods that work best for you. Your energy (or your calories) will come from carbohydrates, fats, and proteins, while water, vitamins, and minerals will help maintain your health and energy levels.

We give you the basics in this chapter, but if you want even more information on nutrition, check out *Nutrition For Dummies,* 4th Edition, by Carol Ann Rinzler (Wiley).

Carbohydrates

Carbohydrates are your primary energy source for endurance training. Training for a triathlon is not the time to go low-carb. Just the same, getting the green light on carbs doesn't mean you should load a large plate with spaghetti every night.

To determine how many grams of carbohydrates you need per day for training, multiply your body weight by 3.2. For example, if you weigh 130 pounds, your diet should include 416 grams of carbohydrates. An alternate way to count your carbs for endurance training is to consume approximately 60 percent of your total calories as carbs.

Your body will use carbohydrates that are stored in the form of glucose in your muscles. You have a limited supply of glucose, and when you run out during a workout, you're empty. (This is called *bonking,* and it doesn't feel good. When you bonk, you can't keep your muscles moving.) Unfortunately, you can't simply tap into your reserve tank (your stored fat). The only way to get past bonking is to refuel your body with more carbohydrates. To avoid bonking during a training session, you need to be aware of the quantity and quality of the carbs you put into your body before you exercise and during your exercise.

Avoid refined, or simple, carbohydrates — such as the kind you get in white breads, pastries, cookies, sugary cereals, crackers, or pastas. They give you a quick boost of energy, but that boost is followed by a drop in energy. Often the refined-carb foods also pack in some extra fat content — another reason to take a pass on refined carbs.

Instead, you want to aim for unrefined, or complex, carbohydrates. They contain a high vitamin and mineral content and take longer to be absorbed by the body than their refined cousins — which means the fuel they provide will get you farther. Aim to get your carbs from whole-grain products (bagels, breads, or cereals), baked potatoes (skip the butter and sour cream) or other starchy veggies, fresh fruit, green leafy vegetables, and low-fat dairy products.

Fat

Don't fear the fat. Your body needs a certain amount of fat for its natural processes, including storing energy and absorbing essential vitamins. You body's fat is actually stored energy. If you aren't exerting a lot of energy, your fat stores grow.

Fat contains more calories than carbs or protein — 9 calories per gram versus just 4 calories for a gram of carbohydrate or a gram of protein. It may seem, then, that you'd get more energy from fat. Unfortunately for ice-cream lovers, that's not the case. You can't effectively fuel your workout on high-fat snacks or greasy breakfasts — that's like putting dirty gas into your car: It'll slow you down or, at a minimum, cause you to rattle along the way. High-fat foods can also give you stomach trouble and throw off your training. If your diet is not balanced and most of your calories are coming from fats, your body may even have to break down muscle mass for fuel.

Your *long-term* fuel is in your fat stores. Whenever you exercise, you tap your carbohydrates and your fat stores, but not at the same rate. High-intensity short bursts will draw from your carb reserves. Long workouts at easy or moderate paces draw from your fat stores. Although a long, slow workout will require fat fuel, the short, intense workouts also raise your metabolism and help you burn fat all day long — you need both kinds of workouts and both kinds of energy stores.

Getting enough fat into your body to fuel a workout is not usually the problem. The trick is knowing how much is enough and how to find the best fat.

Just because you need fat for sustained energy during long workouts doesn't give you license to chow down on cookies, cakes, and pie. You want to avoid partially hydrogenated fats — called *trans fats* — which are common in these foods.

Instead, consume unsaturated fats and limit your daily intake to about 25 percent of your calories. Good choices include olive oil, nuts (such as almonds and walnuts), olives, and fish.

Protein

Protein is essential for muscle-tissue building, repair, and recovery, and it can be used as an energy source when carbohydrate levels are low during more intense exercise sessions, such as speed training or hill repeats. Aim to get 15 percent of your calories from protein sources. To determine the correct amount in grams, multiply your weight by 0.6. So, a 130-pound triathlete would need 7.8 grams of protein per day.

After a long workout or maybe an intense dual-sport training session, you may think it'll be easy to justify a cheeseburger. But don't make a habit of refueling with high-fat protein sources.

Instead, choose lean beef, skinless chicken or turkey, fish, peanut butter, beans, whole-grain breads, and low-fat milk, yogurt, and cheese for your protein sources.

Finding protein sources can present an extra challenge for vegan or vegetarian triathletes, but a little creativity can fill the gaps left by meat. For tips on vegetarian nutrition, check out *Being Vegetarian For Dummies* and *Vegetarian Cooking For Dummies,* both by Suzanne Havala, MS, RD (Wiley).

Water

Water accounts for 60 percent to 75 percent of your body weight. Throughout the day, you lose approximately 40 ounces of water simply by breathing, perspiring, and excreting wastes. You need to replace this water and whatever you lose when you exercise. Maintaining a correct balance of water is essential to maintaining body temperature, carrying nutrients to muscles and organs, and carrying waste away from cells. Drink at least eight glasses of water each day, in addition to the fluids you take in during exercise.

Vitamins

Vitamins are essential to normal bodily functions. Although they're not an energy source, vitamins can contribute to your recovery and to keeping you healthy during your training. There's nothing worse than being sidelined with a cold or falling victim to a chronic illness. A well-balanced diet rich in variety and color can provide ample supplies of vitamins including A, B complex, C, D, E, and K. But vitamin supplements are an acceptable backup to a balanced nutritional plan.

There's no proof that vitamin-loading will make you a super-triathlete. Your best bet is to get your vitamins from the foods you eat, rather than from chemical sources. Although taking a daily multivitamin does have studied health benefits, popping pills is not a substitute for a well-balanced diet.

Minerals

Minerals are not an energy source, but they are essential elements in your body's functions and can only be obtained from foods. Calcium helps to keep your bones strong. Iron helps to transport oxygen to muscles to keep them working. Sodium and potassium are important in maintaining fluid and electrolyte balance and should be an essential part of your training nutritional plan.

If you're eating a well-balanced diet and taking a vitamin supplement with minerals, your body should take care of the rest.

Sussing Out Supplements

Some athletes also reach for sports supplements — man-made products that claim to boost performance, not just provide fuel for a workout. Three of the most common supplements are caffeine (which is loaded into energy drinks), creatine, and protein powders.

Caffeine

There's no disputing the pick-me-up of a morning cup of coffee. But there is great debate on whether caffeine's jolt has more harmful long-term effects than it does short-term benefit. Caffeine occurs naturally in coffee, tea, and chocolate, and many sodas and energy drinks are loaded with caffeine.

Caffeine stimulates the central nervous system and can reduce the feeling of tiredness. For athletes, studies have shown that caffeine has been shown to reduce fatigue in long-duration exercise sessions and also to lower athletes' perceptions of how hard they're working.

But caffeine also is a diuretic, which can compromise your ability to stay properly hydrated.

Drinking a cup of coffee in the morning with a well-balanced breakfast may help you get started in the morning, but if you're struggling to find the energy to start or complete a workout or feel you need a caffeine boost during a workout, it's time to consider a day of rest or reevaluate what you're eating and how you're sleeping, instead of resorting to high-sugar, high-caffeine energy drinks. Caffeine is not the answer to low energy during a workout.

Creatine

Creatine is a naturally occurring amino acid made in the body by the liver; it's also found in meat and fish. Body builders often rely on creatine supplements to increase the intensity of their workouts, enabling them to build muscle strength.

Amid the great controversy about the benefits and side effects of creatine, research has shown that the substance does not provide any benefit to endurance athletes (that's you). And long-term use can lead to short-term health complications, such as dehydration and cramping, and chronic complications including high blood pressure.

Protein powder

You should be getting about 0.05 to 0.06 grams of protein per pound of body weight per day — an amount that's easy to attain with proper nutrition. Still, protein shakes and smoothies have gained popularity as ways to fuel your body quickly before a workout without needing up to two hours to digest a high-protein meal. Vegetarians who may not be consuming enough protein-rich foods can benefit from these supplements as well.

Still, protein powder is not a miracle food. Don't plan to add powder to your meals expecting to magically build muscle.

Some supplements claim to do everything but make you leap tall buildings in a single bound. As the saying goes: If it *sounds* too good to be true, it *is*. Don't get caught up in all the hype; there is no substitute for training and eating properly.

Fueling Your Workouts and Your Race

What, when, and how much you should eat and drink depends on what, when, and how much you're planning to exercise. You should be preparing for training sessions every day by eating foods that contain a balance of carbs, protein, and fats.

Eating with training in mind

One factor to consider when you're eating for a training session is what time of day you'll be training. Your biggest challenge may be morning workouts. If you only have an hour from the time you get up until you have to be getting ready for work or getting the kids out to school, and your training schedule calls for a 60-minute workout, when do you eat?

Eating too much or too soon before a workout can leave you feeling sluggish, as your body works to digest the food. You may also feel full or bloated, or you may have an upset stomach or diarrhea. On the flip side, the wrong choice in fuel or skipping a meal entirely can cause a drop in your blood-sugar level, resulting in a feeling of lightheadedness. If you feel lightheaded, stop your workout and get a snack and a drink.

Most athletes need about two hours to digest a meal before being able to work out comfortably. If you're planning to start training at 5:30 a.m., you have to be up for breakfast at 3:30 a.m. We're with you — that's not happening. To fuel your body for a morning workout, plan to have a high-protein snack later the evening before and a high-carb snack during the hour before you get started in the morning. This rule depends greatly on the type and intensity of your exercise — for example, running tends to be harder on your stomach than cycling.

Your choice of pre-exercise foods is highly personal, and it may take some trial and error to find out what works best and tastes best for you. But here are guidelines that may help you in your planning:

- ✓ **Don't wait until the day before an event or a long training session to eat well.** You should be eating well-balanced, high-carbohydrate meals every day.

- ✓ **If you'll be exercising longer than 90 minutes, eat an easily digestible light meal with protein and lots of carbohydrates one hour or more before exercising.**

- ✓ **Allow two hours to digest a full meal before heading out for an intense workout.**

- ✓ **If your training session will last less than one hour, eat a light carbohydrate snack or sports energy bar within an hour of your workout.**

Hydrating for peak performance

Don't underestimate the power of water. It can make or break your workout and your event-day performance. If you start a workout dehydrated, you'll feel heavy and low in energy. If you push through a tough workout without adequate fluids, you'll put yourself at great health risk.

Water *does* make a difference. In addition to replacing fluids *after* you exercise, you need to drink well *before* the session. How much you should drink before your workout is dependent on your size, the length of your training or event, and the weather, all of which are factors in your fluid loss, but you can start with these guidelines:

- ✓ Drink caffeine-free and low-sugar fluids throughout the day.

- ✓ Drink 8 to 16 ounces of water two hours before your exercise.

- ✓ Drink another 8 ounces of water 15 minutes before you begin to exercise.

Planning your race day meals

Eating a daily diet high in carbohydrates, low in fat, and balanced with adequate protein, vitamins, and minerals is essential for both training and racing. You don't need to eat huge amounts of carbohydrates the night before an endurance event. If you're following your training schedule and tapering properly, you only need to maintain the same diet you've been following during your training. As you exercise less, tapering as you approach your event day, but still maintaining the same intake of carbohydrates, your muscles will be storing the unused calories as extra fuel.

If you know you'll have a hard time eating on the morning of your event due to nerves, eat well the day before and have a snack before bedtime.

 Plan ahead by experimenting with liquid nutrition so that the morning of your race you can fuel up with your favorite protein shake or smoothie. Play around with a simple blend of frozen fruits, such as blueberries or strawberries, a banana, ¾ cup of nonfat vanilla yogurt, a splash of low-fat milk or water, and a tablespoon or two of protein powder.

Make sure you know exactly what you'll eat before, during, and after your event well before you go. All your trial and error should be figured out during training, not at a race. And if you have a favorite food that gives you "super powers," make sure you plan to eat it on race day or pack it to bring with you.

 Avoid caffeine on race day if you aren't used to caffeinated drinks or supplements. You can find yourself with stomach cramps or even diarrhea.

Maintaining Your Energy

For some of your more intense or long-distance workouts, you'll find that no matter how well you fueled and hydrated before you started out, you'll still be struggling to maintain your momentum. There's a trick to going long — fueling on the go.

To maintain your energy during your training sessions, you need to find foods and drinks you can take with you, especially on the bike (because this is where you'll spend the most time during any one workout).

Are you drinking enough fluids?

There are a number of ways to determine how much water you lose during exercise. Weighing yourself before and after exercise is one way to gauge how much sweat you lost and, in turn, how much you need to replace. For every pound you lose, drink 16 ounces of water.

You can also observe the quantity and quality of your urine. If your urine is dark in color (such as the color of Mountain Dew or darker) and there's not much of it, you need to drink more fluids. You can also determine your hydration level by the way you feel. Headaches, muscle cramps, fatigue, and lightheadedness are all signs that you haven't replaced an adequate amount of fluids lost during exercise.

Staying hydrated: Energy drinks and water

Unfortunately, the majority of endurance athletes do not consume enough water. If you start a race or training session dehydrated, you'll finish dehydrated — and deplete your energy stores much quicker.

Thirst is not an adequate indicator of your hydration level. If you're thirsty, you're already dehydrated. Drink twice as much water as you think you need to quench that feeling of thirst. Being tired is one of the first signs of dehydration.

Drinking water, by sipping it throughout the day, is the optimal way to remain hydrated. By the same token, drinking small amounts of water throughout your training or event, ideally every 15 minutes, as opposed to guzzling large amounts at one time, is the best way to prevent dehydration.

Water is important to drink daily and during shorter races or workouts. But for longer workouts, you'll need to reach for sports drinks as well. Alternate between drinking sports drinks and plain water during exercise sessions.

If you're training or racing for longer than 90 minutes, you want to look for replacement fluids that contain small amounts of carbohydrates and sodium, which will give your muscles the added fuel needed to boost your body's water absorption.

With so many sports-drink brands and varieties on the market, you may find it difficult to determine what's best. But there is no "best" — only what works for you. Avoid caffeinated energy or sugar-loaded sweet drinks (such as straight Gatorade or Powerade) and stick to sports drinks with electrolytes and a good taste (such as Gatorade Endurance, Gu2O, Cytomax, Heed,

Accelerade, Infinit). Taste is important. If you don't like the taste of your drink or it disagrees with your stomach, you won't drink enough. And if it affects your stomach, such as causing stomach cramps, that won't do much for enhancing your workout either.

Ideally, your sports drink will have approximately 60 grams of carbohydrates and anywhere from 300mg to 1,000mg of sodium per 32 ounces of fluid.

Snacking on the go: Bars, gels, and natural foods

You should be able to get through a workout of fewer than 60 to 90 minutes without needing extra nutrition. If you're working out for more than 90 minutes, plan to consume 100 to 300 calories (in the form of carbohydrates) per hour. Some triathletes take all those calories at once each hour; others do better popping some nutrition into their mouths every 15 minutes.

Some of these calories may come from your sports drink, but you may also find yourself reaching for a snack. Natural foods can travel well if you have a favorite fuel, such as bananas or good old-fashioned raisins and peanuts (GORP).

You'll also find a variety of bars, blocks, gels, and gooey substances that promise power. Try a few different brands and flavors to find what works for you. Some triathletes can't stomach anything syrupy; others can't bring themselves to chew through an energy bar.

Energy bars and gels contain carbohydrates, sodium, potassium, protein, vitamins, minerals, and fat in different amounts. Check the ingredients and calculate how your choice — and how many you eat during your workout — fits with your overall nutrition plan.

Read the ingredients before you purchase bars, gels, or blocks. Some may contain caffeine or other ingredients that you may want to limit.

Energy bars and gels are not a substitute for proper nutrition. If you're reaching for a bar during a one-hour exercise or regularly before you begin your workout, take a look at why you're not fueling your body with whole foods and make changes in your nutritional plan to get more of your nutrients from whole foods and natural sources.

Regardless of the energy source you choose, be sure to drink plenty of water with each. The general rule is to drink 8 ounces of water for each energy bar or gel packet.

Gels and gummy blocks

Gels and gummy blocks digest faster than solids, so they can be a good choice for fast energy, especially during a race.

Gels come in small "shot" packages, basically portioned for easy consumption. They can be hard to tolerate and tend to be a little like trying to swallow a spoonful of peanut butter without anything to help wash it down. But they provide concentrated and quick energy.

Gummy blocks are easier to get down (after a little chewing). The flavors and texture generally are more appetizing, but one block doesn't offer the same energy punch as one packet of gel. You'll need to pop a few blocks into your mouth for the same benefit.

You can find gels at your local cycling or running store or online. Gel packs and gummy blocks cost from $1 to $2 per package. When you find a flavor you like, you can purchase bulk packages for less than $1 per package.

Bars

One trip to the grocery store can leave you overwhelmed by the number of sports bars on the shelf all claiming to do the same thing. Try as many as you like to decide which brand and flavor tastes best and which your stomach can tolerate while you're training.

It's surprising how delicious these bars can be after a 50-mile bike ride and how utterly dry and awful they seem if you're thinking you just might need a non-workout snack.

When you really need one, energy bars can be more appetizing than a gel shot. Some bars are made with nuts, peanut butter, dried fruits, and even chocolate. The chocolate ones usually taste great, but think about how well they'll travel on a hot day — the chocolate will probably melt.

Read the ingredient list and choose the bar that is best for your workout. High-carbohydrate bars are best for short workouts. Bars high in protein are best for long training sessions.

You can buy bars in running and cycling stores and even in your local grocery store or discount store. Look for frequent sales on bars, even at local grocery stores, and stock up. They cost from $1 to $2.50 each. Also, check prices at Amazon.com. With Amazon's Subscribe & Save feature, you can buy Clif Bars, PowerBars, Balance Bars, and more, and get an additional 15 percent discount off the Amazon.com price (which is already typically lower than the list price). Go to `www.amazon.com/gp/subscribe-and-save/details/index.html` for more information.

Some popular bars are Cliff Builder Bars and PowerBar Performance Energy Bars.

Natural foods

Bars and gels are convenient and easy to carry, but they can be expensive. You can get the same nutritional value from old-fashioned granola bars, cereal bars, or fruit. Some alternatives to sports bars are raisins, fig cookies, pretzels, bananas, and breakfast bars.

Because you'll be eating on the go, either while cycling or running, look for foods that are easy to transport in a small pack or in a pocket of your cycling jersey. Also look for foods that are high in carbohydrates without being overly high in fat.

Experiment with a variety of energy sources while training to see what works best for your taste buds and digestive system and is easily portable.

Recovering Quickly

You've made it through your workout and arrive back home with empty energy-bar wrappers and water bottles. You're not done, yet.

Recovering from training, especially more intense training and racing, requires additional refueling — more eating and drinking. Sounds like a good reward for a workout, no?

Your first priority should be to replace the fluids lost during exercise. The best replacement for shorter bouts of exercise is always water. When you finish your workout, drink 8 to 16 ounces within one hour.

For any exercise longer than 90 minutes, choose drinks high in carbohydrates and electrolytes, such as sports drinks or natural fruit juices. Avoid sodas or other products containing caffeine — caffeine is a diuretic and can contribute to fluid depletion.

After your workout, replacing the glycogen stores in your muscles by eating foods high in carbohydrates and protein will help your body recover quickly and prepare you for your next workout. The sooner you eat the carbohydrates after exercise, the better it is for your muscles. Aim for 30 to 60 grams of carbs within a half-hour of an intense training session.

Muscles absorb these nutrients better immediately after exercise than they do if you wait for your next regular meal. An energy bar can come in handy, but fruit, beans, or whole-grain breads are better choices. One of Donna's favorites is peanut butter on a bagel.

Chapter 10

Training Schedules: From Super Sprint to Ironman

In This Chapter

▶ Working training for a triathlon into your life

▶ Finding training plans for every distance

*A*fter you get over the initial thrill of deciding to do a triathlon, you'll probably be faced with a very scary reality: actually finishing the event. You really *can* finish a triathlon, and the key is to take it one day at a time, training in a way that's right for the distance of your event. In this chapter, we provide training schedules you can follow to build your endurance and finish your race — and if you're new to endurance training and triathlon racing, finishing, not winning, should be your initial goal.

After you develop a good aerobic base and have completed a number of triathlons, you'll be ready to move on to more competitive training — or you may be comfortable and enjoy the experience and be happy to continue on with moderate training. Either way, the training plans in this chapter are a great place to start.

But first you have to find the time to train. And in this chapter, we offer concrete tips for uncovering hidden minutes for training.

Finding the Time to Train

Ask people what they want more of and you'll find "time for fitness" high on the list. Yet, our daily schedules don't always reflect this priority. It's easy to fill up your day with chores and tasks and look back at the end of the day and think, "There was just no time." We're here to tell you there *is* — if you know where to look. And when you make fitness a priority, even if you can uncover only 20 minutes a few times a week, you'll be pleasantly surprised to find that this time expands to fit your training goals.

Heart-rate training simplified

You can monitor your heart rate to determine the intensity of your workouts. Knowing your target heart-rate zone helps you make the most of your workouts, especially important if you're tight on time.

The best way to monitor your heart rate during training is to use a heart-rate monitor. You'll find heart-rate monitors in many styles and price ranges — from a simple watch-and-chest-strap system for $100, to a more complicated model that allows you to upload your training data to a computer log for as much as $350. For your training, you most likely won't need the expensive level of equipment. A basic heart-rate monitor, which is all you need, costs $45 to $50 and is available in most sporting-goods stores.

Look for a basic monitor. As a beginning triathlete, you just need one that tells you your heart-rate reading as you're training.

The majority of your training — other than tempo, fartlek, or interval run training and hill workouts — should be at a Z1 (65 percent to 74 percent) or Z2 (75 percent to 84 percent) to help you increase your endurance. To figure out what your Z1 and Z2 ranges are, subtract your age from 220, and then multiply by the corresponding percentages. For example, if you're 40 years old, your maximum heart rate is 180 (220 − 40 = 180). The low end of your Z1 is 180 × 0.65 = 117, and the high end of your Z1 is 180 × 0.74 = 133.2. (You can do the same for your Z2.)

Remember: Don't go all out on every workout — pushing yourself will only cause injuries, and you'll never get to the starting line healthy.

Here are some tips for finding the extra hours in your day that you can use for triathlon training:

- **If training is truly your priority, do it first.** Get your clothes ready the night before and get up 20 minutes early. When you get accustomed to rising earlier, set your clock to give you another 10 minutes, and 10 minutes after that. Get your training done before your day fills with deadlines and obligations. You'll enjoy the positive focus and energized spirit you'll have at the end of your training session all day.

- **Make an appointment with yourself.** The first step in finding the time is adding it to your schedule. Write it on your calendar. Enter it in your BlackBerry or iPhone. Make it a lunch date — and give it the same respect you would any other appointment.

- **Give up just one TV show each week.** That'll free up 30 to 60 minutes of time. Sure, it may be difficult to go without *Grey's Anatomy* the first few weeks. You're tired and you want your quiet time. But exercise will give you more energy, and you'll look forward to that time to rejuvenate your body and clear your mind.

✔ **Stay close to home.** Skip the gym workouts and set out for a run right from your house. You'll be surprised at how much time you save when you don't have to pack up your gear, drive to the gym, find a spot, and hope to find an open treadmill or spin cycle.

✔ **Make it a chore.** Well, not really — but instead of driving to the store for a small purchase or to return a video, do your errands on your bike or in your running shoes. You'll be killing two birds with one stone.

✔ **Be flexible.** Although it's much more fun to cycle outside, it isn't always necessary — nor is it always possible. If you have a project due at work, you need to read briefs for an afternoon meeting, or your kids are home from school, hop on a stationary bike instead of hitting the road — you can read (or make sure the kids aren't getting into trouble) and get in a workout at the same time. If you can't do your long runs or rides on the weekends, find the days that are quiet for you and do them then.

Training for Your Event

Follow the training plan in this chapter that corresponds to the event distance you've chosen.

Before you begin, look at the first week's training schedule for your distance and be confident that you can complete it comfortably before you start in on the entire program. If you can't complete the first week's training without extreme fatigue, work on building your endurance in the sport(s) that you find to be the biggest challenge.

Your weekly training schedule will include the following workouts:

✔ **Swim:** Your swim workout will include a warm-up, a drill set, a swim set, and a cool-down.

It doesn't matter whether you're training in a 25-yard pool or a 25m one. Just follow the schedule, whether you're doing yards or meters. For example, if the schedule says, "Warm up 100," you swim four lengths of the pool — whether it's a 25-yard pool or a 25m pool. No math required. For all training plans, plan on incorporating a number of swims in open water. These should be close to the distance you will be swimming for your triathlon so that you can be more familiar with swimming a straight distance without stopping and also to practice sighting.

For the swim set of the workout, sometimes you'll swim your set as one distance without rest, and other times you'll do a combination of laps with a rest period between them. For example, a set identified as "100@10" is one set of 100 yards or meters, followed by 10 seconds of rest; "2x200@20" is two sets of 200 yards or meters with a 20-second rest after each 200.

Some training programs you'll find elsewhere use timed swim workouts. We prefer laps for swimming for two reasons: (1) Timed swims, in which you just go back and forth for a set time, are even more boring than they sound; and (2) as you tire, your technique may suffer — and laps in which you spend time and energy using poor form will not help your triathlon performance.

✔ **Bike:** The bike workouts are based on time, not distance. You'll want to pedal at a cadence of 80 rpm to 100 rpm with a heart rate in the Z1 to Z2 range (see the nearby sidebar, "Heart-rate training simplified").

If you live in a hilly area, you'll find that your heart rate goes up as you do — that's okay. Spin down the other side, continuing to pedal, and then get back into the correct gear for your cadence and bring your heart rate back to Z2. An added bonus: Hill work will help strengthen your legs.

✔ **Run:** Your run workouts are also based on time, not distance. If you're training in the correct heart-rate zone and train for the designated time, you'll comfortably get to the correct number of miles using these training plans.

As you improve your fitness, you'll add speed training, using tempo or interval runs or fartleks, on your short-distance days to help you run the distance faster. Always warm up for 10 to 15 minutes before adding one of these trainings into your run, and cool down for 10 to 15 minutes when you're finished.

The most important runs in your triathlon training are your long ones. Long runs are where you train your cardiovascular system and improve your endurance. If you miss a long-distance training day, try to schedule it for another day that week.

When you ride your bike, dismount, throw on your sneakers, and set off for a run, your legs will object. These bike-run workouts, or *bricks* (aptly named, because bricks are just what your legs will feel like), are an important part of your training. At first, you'll feel as though your legs are trying to go in the wrong direction as you run. But as you train, your muscles will be accustomed to the transition, and these workouts will get easier. Bricks also give you the chance to practice laying out your gear for your bike-to-run transition.

You can also practice your transition-area setup when you go from a swim to a ride. Set up your gear in your driveway or wherever you'll be returning to after your workout. Practice changing quickly to prepare for the run and go right out as soon as you're ready. Try to limit these transition times as much as possible so that you're fully prepared on race day and know exactly where everything will be set up and in what order you'll be changing for each leg of the race.

Each of the training schedules in this chapter builds on the previous plan. In other words, you need to be comfortable with Sprint/Super Sprint training before you move on to the Olympic. Don't jump from a Sprint to an Ironman and definitely don't make an Ironman your first triathlon.

We list the training schedules by day number (Day 1, Day 2, and so on), instead of by day of the week (Monday, Tuesday, Wednesday . . .). To figure out which day of the week should be your "Day 1," look at what day your triathlon is on, and build backward from there. For example, if your triathlon is on a Saturday, your first day of training should be a Sunday.

You may want to photocopy the training schedule you're following and write the exact dates on the schedule so that you don't lose track of where you are.

Training for a Sprint or Super Sprint in 12 weeks

Before you start this 12-week program (see Table 10-1), you should be able to swim, bike, and run the amount of time specified in the first week of training relatively easily. If you aren't able to do this, concentrate on building your endurance in each of them separately, and then return to the 12-week program.

This is not a couch potato-to-sprint-in-12-weeks training program. There's no such schedule. Spend some time getting comfortable with the sport(s) that may be new for you, and then start your training.

Follow the program to the best of your ability. Sometimes, life can get in the way of training plans. Don't worry. If you miss a day, move the schedule up a day or skip it all together. Skipping one or two occasional training days over the course of 12 weeks won't hurt — in fact, sometimes it's just what you need to come back refreshed and stronger. That said, skipping five to ten training days may make your event difficult to complete.

If you have to miss a training day, try not to miss a long cycling or running one. These training days are important to help you build endurance.

Include two rest days in your weekly training. Rest and recovery are as important as swimming, cycling, and running are. You'll need to give your muscles time to recover to prevent injuries and avoid burnout.

Table 10-1	A 12-Week Sprint or Super Sprint Training Schedule		
Week 1	**Swim**	**Bike**	**Run**
Day 1	Warm up 100, drill 100, swim 200, cool down 100	None	20 minutes
Day 2	*Rest*	*Rest*	*Rest*
Day 3	None	35 minutes	None
Day 4	None	None	20 minutes
Day 5	Warm up 100, drill 100, swim 200, cool down 100	20 minutes	None
Day 6	*Rest*	*Rest*	*Rest*
Day 7	None	35 minutes	None
Week 2	**Swim**	**Bike**	**Run**
Day 1	Warm up 100, drill 150, swim 250, cool down 100	None	20 minutes
Day 2	*Rest*	*Rest*	*Rest*
Day 3	None	40 minutes	10 minutes
Day 4	None	None	22 minutes
Day 5	Warm up 100, drill 150, swim 250, cool down 100	None	None
Day 6	*Rest*	*Rest*	*Rest*
Day 7	None	40 minutes	None
Week 3	**Swim**	**Bike**	**Run**
Day 1	Warm up 100, drill 150, swim 300, cool down 100	None	20 minutes
Day 2	*Rest*	*Rest*	*Rest*
Day 3	None	45 minutes	None
Day 4	None	None	24 minutes
Day 5	Warm up 100, drill 150, swim 300, cool down 100	20 minutes	None
Day 6	*Rest*	*Rest*	*Rest*
Day 7	None	45 minutes	None

Week 4	Swim	Bike	Run
Day 1	Warm up 100, drill 150, swim 350, cool down 100	None	20 minutes
Day 2	*Rest*	*Rest*	*Rest*
Day 3	None	45 minutes	10 minutes
Day 4	None	None	27 minutes
Day 5	Warm up 100, drill 150, swim 350, cool down 100	None	None
Day 6	*Rest*	*Rest*	*Rest*
Day 7	None	40 minutes	None
Week 5	**Swim**	**Bike**	**Run**
Day 1	Warm up 100, drill 150, swim 2x200@15, cool down 100	None	20 minutes
Day 2	*Rest*	*Rest*	*Rest*
Day 3	None	45 minutes	None
Day 4	None	None	30 minutes
Day 5	Warm up 100, drill 150, swim 2x200@15, cool down 100	None	None
Day 6	*Rest*	*Rest*	*Rest*
Day 7	None	50 minutes	None
Week 6	**Swim**	**Bike**	**Run**
Day 1	Warm up 100, drill 150, swim 3x100@10 and 3x50@10, cool down 100	None	20 minutes
Day 2	*Rest*	*Rest*	*Rest*
Day 3	None	45 minutes	15 minutes
Day 4	None	None	35 minutes
Day 5	Warm up 100, drill 150, swim 3x100@10 and 3x50@10, cool down 100	None	None
Day 6	*Rest*	*Rest*	*Rest*
Day 7	None	60 minutes	None

Week 7	Swim	Bike	Run
Day 1	Warm up 100, drill 150, swim 2x250@20, cool down 100	None	20 minutes
Day 2	*Rest*	*Rest*	*Rest*
Day 3	None	45 minutes	None
Day 4	None	None	40 minutes
Day 5	Warm up 100, drill 150, swim 2x250@20, cool down 100	20 minutes	None
Day 6	*Rest*	*Rest*	*Rest*
Day 7	None	65 minutes	None
Week 8	Swim	Bike	Run
Day 1	Warm up 100; drill 150; swim 300@20, 200@15, and 100@10; cool down 100	None	20 minutes
Day 2	*Rest*	*Rest*	*Rest*
Day 3	None	45 minutes	15 minutes
Day 4	None	None	45 minutes
Day 5	Warm up 100; drill 150; swim 300@20, 200@15, and 100@10; cool down 100	None	None
Day 6	*Rest*	*Rest*	*Rest*
Day 7	None	70 minutes	None
Week 9	Swim	Bike	Run
Day 1	Warm up 100, drill 150, swim 2x300@30, cool down 100	None	20 minutes
Day 2	*Rest*	*Rest*	*Rest*
Day 3	None	45 minutes	None
Day 4	None	None	50 minutes
Day 5	Warm up 100, drill 150, swim 2x300@30, cool down 100	20 minutes	None
Day 6	*Rest*	*Rest*	*Rest*
Day 7	None	75 minutes	None

Week 10	Swim	Bike	Run
Day 1	Warm up 100; drill 150; swim 300@20, 200@15, and 100@10; cool down 100	None	20 minutes
Day 2	*Rest*	*Rest*	*Rest*
Day 3	None	45 minutes	15 minutes
Day 4	None	None	50 minutes
Day 5	Warm up 100, drill 150, swim 800, cool down 100	None	None
Day 6	*Rest*	*Rest*	*Rest*
Day 7	None	80 minutes	None
Week 11	**Swim**	**Bike**	**Run**
Day 1	Warm up 100, drill 150, swim 2x350@30, cool down 100	None	20 minutes
Day 2	*Rest*	*Rest*	*Rest*
Day 3	None	45 minutes	None
Day 4	None	None	50 minutes
Day 5	Warm up 100, drill 150, swim 2x350@30, cool down 100	None	None
Day 6	*Rest*	*Rest*	*Rest*
Day 7	None	75 minutes	None
Week 12	**Swim**	**Bike**	**Run**
Day 1	Warm up 100, drill 150, swim 300, cool down 100	None	20 minutes
Day 2	*Rest*	*Rest*	*Rest*
Day 3	None	30 minutes	None
Day 4	None	None	15 minutes
Day 5	Warm up 100, drill 150, swim 300, cool down 100	None	None
Day 6	*Rest*	*Rest*	*Rest*
Day 7	RACE DAY	RACE DAY	RACE DAY

Training for an Olympic in 20 weeks

If you're looking at 20 weeks to an Olympic-distance event (see Table 10-2), you've either trained for and comfortably completed a Sprint-distance triathlon or you just like to read ahead in a book. Because an Olympic-distance triathlon is close to twice the distance of a Sprint, expect to put in twice the time in training. You'll also want to start this training with a solid fitness base. The first week of training shouldn't feel overwhelming to you.

If you feel comfortable adding speed training into your runs, use the Monday run workout for this and throw in interval or tempo training or fartleks (see Chapter 5). If you do, move the swim training to every other Wednesday when you don't already have a brick workout scheduled.

Table 10-2	A 20-Week Olympic Training Schedule		
Week 1	**Swim**	**Bike**	**Run**
Day 1	Warm up 100; drill 100; swim 300@30 and 200@20; cool down 100	None	22 minutes
Day 2	*Rest*	*Rest*	*Rest*
Day 3	None	45 minutes	15 minutes
Day 4	None	None	50 minutes
Day 5	Warm up 100; drill 100; swim 300@30 and 200@20; cool down 100	None	None
Day 6	*Rest*	*Rest*	*Rest*
Day 7	None	80 minutes	None
Week 2	**Swim**	**Bike**	**Run**
Day 1	Warm up 100, drill 200, swim 6x100@15, cool down 100	None	24 minutes
Day 2	*Rest*	*Rest*	*Rest*
Day 3	None	50 minutes	None
Day 4	None	None	55 minutes
Day 5	Warm up 100, drill 200, swim 6x100@15, cool down 100	60	None
Day 6	*Rest*	*Rest*	*Rest*
Day 7	None	88 minutes	None

Week 3	Swim	Bike	Run
Day 1	Warm up 200; drill 150; swim 300@30 and 200@15; cool down 100	None	26 minutes
Day 2	Rest	Rest	Rest
Day 3	None	45 minutes	15 minutes
Day 4	None	None	60 minutes
Day 5	Warm up 200; drill 150; swim 300@30 and 200@15; cool down 100	None	None
Day 6	Rest	Rest	Rest
Day 7	None	96 minutes	None
Week 4	**Swim**	**Bike**	**Run**
Day 1	Warm up 100, drill 150, swim 5x100@15, cool down 100	None	20 minutes
Day 2	Rest	Rest	Rest
Day 3	None	45 minutes	None
Day 4	None	None	50 minutes
Day 5	Warm up 100, drill 150, swim 5x100@15, cool down 100	60	None
Day 6	Rest	Rest	Rest
Day 7	None	80 minutes	None
Week 5	**Swim**	**Bike**	**Run**
Day 1	Warm up 200; drill 200; swim 400@30 and 200@15; cool down 100	None	26 minutes
Day 2	Rest	Rest	Rest
Day 3	None	45 minutes	15 minutes
Day 4	None	None	60 minutes
Day 5	Warm up 200; drill 200; swim 400@30 and 200@15; cool down 100	None	None
Day 6	Rest	Rest	Rest
Day 7	None	96 minutes	None

Week 6	Swim	Bike	Run
Day 1	Warm up 200; drill 200; swim 5x100@15 and 3x50@10; cool down 100	None	28 minutes
Day 2	Rest	Rest	Rest
Day 3	None	50 minutes	None
Day 4	None	None	66 minutes
Day 5	Warm up 200; drill 200; swim 5x100@15 and 3x50@10; cool down 100	60	None
Day 6	Rest	Rest	Rest
Day 7	None	105 minutes	None
Week 7	Swim	Bike	Run
Day 1	Warm up 200; drill 200; swim 400@40 and 300@30; cool down 100	None	30 minutes
Day 2	Rest	Rest	Rest
Day 3	None	45 minutes	15 minutes
Day 4	None	None	72 minutes
Day 5	Warm up 200; drill 200; swim 400@40 and 300@30; cool down 100	None	None
Day 6	Rest	Rest	Rest
Day 7	None	115 minutes	None
Week 8	Swim	Bike	Run
Day 1	Warm up 100; drill 150; swim 300@20, 200@15, and 100@10; cool down 100	None	20 minutes
Day 2	Rest	Rest	Rest
Day 3	None	45 minutes	None
Day 4	None	None	50 minutes
Day 5	Warm up 100; drill 150; swim 300@20, 200@15, and 100@10; cool down 100	60	None
Day 6	Rest	Rest	Rest
Day 7	None	80 minutes	None

Week 9	Swim	Bike	Run
Day 1	Warm up 200; drill 200; swim 400@40 and 300@30; cool down 100	None	30 minutes
Day 2	Rest	Rest	Rest
Day 3	None	45 minutes	15 minutes
Day 4	None	None	72 minutes
Day 5	Warm up 200; drill 200; swim 400@40 and 300@30; cool down 100	20 minutes	None
Day 6	Rest	Rest	Rest
Day 7	None	155 minutes	None
Week 10	Swim	Bike	Run
Day 1	Warm up 200; drill 200; swim 3x200@20 and 150@15; cool down 100	None	33 minutes
Day 2	Rest	Rest	Rest
Day 3	None	55 minutes	None
Day 4	None	None	80 minutes
Day 5	Warm up 200; drill 200; swim 3x200@20 and 150@15; cool down 100	60	None
Day 6	Rest	Rest	Rest
Day 7	None	126 minutes	None
Week 11	Swim	Bike	Run
Day 1	Warn up 200, drill 200, swim 2x400@40, cool down 100	None	36 minutes
Day 2	Rest	Rest	Rest
Day 3	None	45 minutes	15 minutes
Day 4	None	None	88 minutes
Day 5	Warm up 200, drill 200, swim 2x400@40, cool down 100	None	None
Day 6	Rest	Rest	Rest
Day 7	None	138 minutes	None

Week 12	Swim	Bike	Run
Day 1	Warm up 200, drill 200, swim 4x100@15, cool down 100	None	22 minutes
Day 2	Rest	Rest	Rest
Day 3	None	45 minutes	None
Day 4	None	None	55 minutes
Day 5	Warm up 200, drill 200, swim 4x100@15, cool down 100	60 minutes	None
Day 6	Rest	Rest	Rest
Day 7	None	85 minutes	None
Week 13	Swim	Bike	Run
Day 1	Warm up 200, drill 200, swim 2x400@40, cool down 100	None	36 minutes
Day 2	Rest	Rest	Rest
Day 3	None	45 minutes	15 minutes
Day 4	None	None	88 minutes
Day 5	Warm up 200, drill 200, swim 2x400@40, cool down 100	None	None
Day 6	Rest	Rest	Rest
Day 7	None	138 minutes	None
Week 14	Swim	Bike	Run
Day 1	Warm up 200; drill 200; swim 50@15, 100@15, 150@15, 200@15, 150@15, 100@15, 50@15; cool down 150	None	40 minutes
Day 2	Rest	Rest	Rest
Day 3	None	60 minutes	None
Day 4	None	None	96 minutes
Day 5	Warm up 200; drill 200; swim 50@15, 100@15, 150@15, 200@15, 150@15, 100@15, 50@15; cool down 150	60 minutes	None
Day 6	Rest	Rest	Rest
Day 7	None	152 minutes	None

Week 15	Swim	Bike	Run
Day 1	Warm up 200, drill 200, swim 2x400@40, cool down 200	None	44 minutes
Day 2	Rest	Rest	Rest
Day 3	None	45 minutes	15 minutes
Day 4	None	None	105 minutes
Day 5	Warm up 200, drill 200, swim 2x400@40, cool down 200	None	None
Day 6	Rest	Rest	Rest
Day 7	None	168 minutes	None
Week 16	Swim	Bike	Run
Day 1	Warm up 200, drill 200, swim 2x250@20, cool down 200	None	27 minutes
Day 2	Rest	Rest	Rest
Day 3	None	45 minutes	None
Day 4	None	None	63 minutes
Day 5	Warm up 200, drill 200, swim 2x250@20, cool down 200	60 minutes	None
Day 6	Rest	Rest	Rest
Day 7	None	100 minutes	None
Week 17	Swim	Bike	Run
Day 1	Warm up 200, drill 200, swim 3x300@30, cool down 200	None	36 minutes
Day 2	Rest	Rest	Rest
Day 3	None	45 minutes	15 minutes
Day 4	None	None	88 minutes
Day 5	Warm up 200, drill 200, swim 3x300@30, cool down 200	None	None
Day 6	Rest	Rest	Rest
Day 7	None	138 minutes	None

Week 18	Swim	Bike	Run
Day 1	Warm up 200, drill 200, swim 2x500@45, cool down 200	None	40 minutes
Day 2	Rest	Rest	Rest
Day 3	None	60 minutes	None
Day 4	None	None	96 minutes
Day 5	Warm up 200, swim 1200, cool down 200	None	None
Day 6	Rest	Rest	Rest
Day 7	None	151 minutes	None
Week 19	Swim	Bike	Run
Day 1	Warm up 200, drill 200, swim 2x400@30, cool down 200	None	27 minutes
Day 2	Rest	Rest	Rest
Day 3	None	45 minutes	15 minutes
Day 4	None	None	63 minutes
Day 5	Warm up 200, drill 200, 2x400@30, cool down 200	None	None
Day 6	Rest	Rest	Rest
Day 7	None	120 minutes	None
Week 20	Swim	Bike	Run
Day 1	Warm up 200, drill 200, swim 2x200@20, cool down 200	None	35 minutes
Day 2	Rest	Rest	Rest
Day 3	None	45 minutes	15 minutes
Day 4	None	None	60 minutes
Day 5	Warm up 200, drill 200, swim 2x200@20, cool down 200	None	None
Day 6	Rest	Rest	Rest
Day 7	RACE DAY	RACE DAY	RACE DAY

Training for a Half-Iron in 24 weeks

Now it's time to get serious. Of course, you were serious about your Sprint or Olympic training, but as you move toward the Half-Iron and Ironman, you need to be prepared for the increase in training time and intensity. You'll add one more day per week of training and incorporate speed training into runs, and speed and hill training into your cycling (see Table 10-3).

Train for and participate in *more than one* Sprint- and Olympic-distance event to ensure you have the aerobic base to start this training program.

Do your long workouts for this distance back to back and then take a rest day. You can move your long workouts to other days but keep them on back-to-back days with a day's rest after.

During your first four weeks of training, concentrate on being in the Z2 heart-rate zone to increase your aerobic base and prepare for longer workouts. This training schedule allows for recovery every fourth week, and then goes back to building again.

On the short runs indicated as speed workouts in the schedule, add fartleks or interval or tempo training. (For more on fartleks, intervals, or tempo training, see Chapter 7.)

For your hill-workout cycling training (see Week 6, Day 4), you can simply ride a hilly course that day or perform hill repeats, in which you select a hill to ride up for two minutes, turn around and spin down, and then ride up again. Repeat this five times and build up to ten repeats as you progress in your training. Be sure to warm up for 15 minutes before hill repeats and cool down for another 15 minutes after them. Hill repeats are challenging and should only be done periodically.

Do your speed, hill, and brick workouts on alternate weeks to avoid overtraining or injury.

Know as much as you can about your event's course to help you plan for hills. Even if you find out you're riding a flat course, you'll still want to train on hills, because the power needed to get you to the top will strengthen your legs.

Table 10-3	A 24-Week Half-Iron Training Schedule		
Week 1	*Swim*	*Bike*	*Run*
Day 1	*Rest*	*Rest*	*Rest*
Day 2	Warm up 200; drill 200; swim 400@30 and 200@15; cool down 100	None	25 minutes
Day 3	None	30 minutes	15 minutes
Day 4	Warm up 200; drill 200; swim 400@30 and 200@15; cool down 100	45 minutes	None
Day 5	None	None	25 minutes
Day 6	None	60 minutes	None
Day 7	None	None	45 minutes
Week 2	*Swim*	*Bike*	*Run*
Day 1	*Rest*	*Rest*	*Rest*
Day 2	Warm up 200, drill 200, swim 6x100@15, cool down 100	None	28 minutes
Day 3	None	30 minutes	15 minutes
Day 4	Warm up 200, drill 200, swim 6x100@15, cool down 100	50 minutes	None
Day 5	None	None	28 minutes
Day 6	None	70 minutes	None
Day 7	None	None	50 minutes
Week 3	*Swim*	*Bike*	*Run*
Day 1	*Rest*	*Rest*	*Rest*
Day 2	Warm up 300, drill 200, swim 3x200@20, cool down 100	None	31 minutes
Day 3	None	30 minutes	15 minutes
Day 4	Warm up 300, drill 200, swim 1x600, cool down 100	55 minutes	None
Day 5	None	None	31 minutes
Day 6	None	80 minutes	None
Day 7	None	None	55 minutes

Week 4	Swim	Bike	Run
Day 1	*Rest*	*Rest*	*Rest*
Day 2	Warm up 200; drill 200; swim 400@30 and 200@15; cool down 100	None	25 minutes
Day 3	None	30 minutes	15 minutes
Day 4	Swim 1,000 at moderate pace	45 minutes	None
Day 5	None	None	25 minutes
Day 6	None	60 minutes	None
Day 7	None	None	45 minutes
Week 5	**Swim**	**Bike**	**Run**
Day 1	*Rest*	*Rest*	*Rest*
Day 2	Warm up 300, drill 200, swim 2x350@30, cool down 100	None	28 minutes fartlek
Day 3	None	30 minutes	15 minutes
Day 4	Warm up 300, drill 200, swim 2x350@30, cool down 100	50 minutes	None
Day 5	None	None	28 minutes
Day 6	None	90 minutes	None
Day 7	None	None	60 minutes
Week 6	**Swim**	**Bike**	**Run**
Day 1	*Rest*	*Rest*	*Rest*
Day 2	Warm up 200; drill 200; swim 200@20, 300@20, and 200@20; cool down 100	None	32 minutes
Day 3	None	30 minutes	15 minutes
Day 4	Warm up 200; drill 200; swim 200@20, 300@20, 200@20; cool down 100	55 minutes hills	None
Day 5	None	None	32 minutes
Day 6	None	100 minutes	None
Day 7	None	None	70 minutes

Week 7	Swim	Bike	Run
Day 1	Rest	Rest	Rest
Day 2	Warm up 300; drill 200; swim 6x100@15 and 6x50@10; cool down 100	None	35 minutes tempo
Day 3	None	30 minutes	15 minutes
Day 4	Warm up 300; drill 200; swim 6x100@15 and 6x50@10; cool down 100	60 minutes	None
Day 5	None	None	35 minutes
Day 6	None	110 minutes	None
Day 7	None	None	80 minutes
Week 8	Swim	Bike	Run
Day 1	Rest	Rest	Rest
Day 2	War up 300; drill 200; swim 400@30 and 200@15; cool down 100	None	28 minutes
Day 3	None	30 minutes	15 minutes
Day 4	Swim 1,400 at moderate pace	45 minutes	None
Day 5	None	None	28 minutes
Day 6	None	90 minutes	None
Day 7	None	None	60 minutes
Week 9	Swim	Bike	Run
Day 1	Rest	Rest	Rest
Day 2	Warm up 300, drill 200, swim 2x400@40, cool down 100	None	35 minutes interval
Day 3	None	45 minutes	15 minutes
Day 4	Warm up 300, drill 200, swim 4x200@20, cool down 100	60 minutes	None
Day 5	None	None	35 minutes
Day 6	None	110 minutes	None
Day 7	None	None	80 minutes

Week 10	Swim	Bike	Run
Day 1	*Rest*	*Rest*	*Rest*
Day 2	Warm up 300; drill 200; swim 600@60 and 2x200@15; cool down 200	None	40 minutes
Day 3	None	45 minutes	15 minutes
Day 4	Warm up 300; drill 200; swim 600@60 and 2x200@15; cool down 200	65 minutes hills	None
Day 5	None	None	40 minutes
Day 6	None	120 minutes	None
Day 7	None	None	90 minutes
Week 11	Swim	Bike	Run
Day 1	*Rest*	*Rest*	*Rest*
Day 2	Warm up 300; drill 200; swim 400@30, 300@20, and 200@15; cool down 200	None	45 minutes
Day 3	None	45 minutes	15 minutes
Day 4	Warm up 300; drill 200; swim 400@30, 300@20, and 200@15; cool down 200	70 minutes	None
Day 5	None	None	45 minutes
Day 6	None	140 minutes	None
Day 7	None	None	100 minutes
Week 12	Swim	Bike	Run
Day 1	*Rest*	*Rest*	*Rest*
Day 2	Warm up 300, drill 200, swim 2x400@40, cool down 200	None	35 minutes
Day 3	None	45 minutes	15 minutes
Day 4	Swim 1,500 at moderate pace	60 minutes	None
Day 5	None	None	35 minutes
Day 6	None	110 minutes	None
Day 7	None	None	80 minutes

Week 13	Swim	Bike	Run
Day 1	Rest	Rest	Rest
Day 2	Warm up 300; drill 200; swim 3x300@30 and 4x50@10; cool down 200	None	45 minutes fartlek
Day 3	None	45 minutes	15 minutes
Day 4	Warm up 300; drill 200; swim 3x300@30 and 4x50@10; cool down 200	70 minutes	None
Day 5	None	None	45 minutes
Day 6	None	140 minutes	None
Day 7	None	None	100 minutes
Week 14	Swim	Bike	Run
Day 1	Rest	Rest	Rest
Day 2	Warm up 300; drill 200; swim 400@40, 300@30, 200@20, and 2x100@15; cool down 200	None	50 minutes
Day 3	None	45 minutes	15 minutes
Day 4	Warm up 300; drill 200; swim 400@40, 300@30, 200@20, 2x100@15; cool down 200	70 minutes	None
Day 5	None	None	50 minutes
Day 6	None	160 minutes	None
Day 7	None	None	110 minutes
Week 15	Swim	Bike	Run
Day 1	Rest	Rest	Rest
Day 2	Warm up 300; drill 200; swim 600@60 and 500@50; cool down 200	None	55 minutes
Day 3	None	45 minutes	15 minutes
Day 4	Warm up 300; drill 200; swim 600@60 and 500@50; cool down 200	75 minutes	None
Day 5	None	None	55 minutes
Day 6	None	180 minutes	None
Day 7	None	None	120 minutes

Week 16	Swim	Bike	Run
Day 1	*Rest*	*Rest*	*Rest*
Day 2	Warm up 300; drill 200; swim 3x300@30 and 4x50@10; cool down 200	None	45 minutes
Day 3	None	45 minutes	15 minutes
Day 4	Swim 1,600 at moderate pace	70 minutes	None
Day 5	None	None	45 minutes
Day 6	None	140 minutes	None
Day 7	None	None	100 minutes
Week 17	Swim	Bike	Run
Day 1	*Rest*	*Rest*	*Rest*
Day 2	Warm up 300; drill 200; swim 400@40, 300@40, 200@40, and 100@40; cool down 300	None	55 minutes
Day 3	None	45 minutes	15 minutes
Day 4	Warm up 300; drill 200; swim 400@40, 300@40, 200@40, and 100@40; cool down 300	75 minutes	None
Day 5	None	None	55 minutes
Day 6	None	180 minutes	None
Day 7	None	None	120 minutes
Week 18	Swim	Bike	Run
Day 1	*Rest*	*Rest*	*Rest*
Day 2	Warm up 300, drill 200, swim 2x550@45, cool down 300	None	60 minutes
Day 3	None	45 minutes	15 minutes
Day 4	Warm up 300, drill 200, swim 2x550@45, cool down 300	75 minutes hills	None
Day 5	None	None	60 minutes
Day 6	None	200 minutes	None
Day 7	None	None	130 minutes

Week 19	Swim	Bike	Run
Day 1	Rest	Rest	Rest
Day 2	Warm up 300; drill 200; swim 400@40, 300@30, 200@20, 100@15, and 2x50@10; cool down 300	None	60 minutes
Day 3	None	45 minutes	15 minutes
Day 4	Warm up 300; drill 200; swim 400@40, 300@30, 200@20, 100@15, and 2x50@10; cool down 300	75 minutes	None
Day 5	None	None	60 minutes
Day 6	None	220 minutes	None
Day 7	None	None	140 minutes
Week 20	Swim	Bike	Run
Day 1	Rest	Rest	Rest
Day 2	War up 300; drill 200; swim 400@40, 300@40, 200@40, and 100@40; cool down 300	None	55 minutes
Day 3	None	45 minutes	15 minutes
Day 4	Swim 1,700 at moderate pace	75 minutes	None
Day 5	None	None	55 minutes
Day 6	None	180 minutes	None
Day 7	None	None	120 minutes
Week 21	Swim	Bike	Run
Day 1	Rest	Rest	Rest
Day 2	Warm up 300, drill 200, swim 2x600@60, cool down 300	None	60 minutes
Day 3	None	45 minutes	15 minutes
Day 4	Warm up 300, drill 200, swim 2x600@60, cool down 300	75 minutes	None
Day 5	None	None	60 minutes
Day 6	None	220 minutes	None
Day 7	None	None	140 minutes

Week 22	Swim	Bike	Run
Day 1	Rest	Rest	Rest
Day 2	Warm up 300, drill 200, swim 2x400@40, cool down 200	None	45 minutes
Day 3	None	30 minutes	15 minutes
Day 4	Warm up 200, swim 1600, cool down 200	60 minutes	None
Day 5	None	None	45 minutes
Day 6	None	175 minutes	None
Day 7	None	None	100 minutes
Week 23	Swim	Bike	Run
Day 1	Rest	Rest	Rest
Day 2	Warm up 300, drill 200, swim 2x400@40, cool down 200	None	45 minutes
Day 3	None	30 minutes	15 minutes
Day 4	Warm up 300, drill 200, swim 2x400@40, cool down 200	60 minutes	None
Day 5	None	None	45 minutes
Day 6	None	175 minutes	None
Day 7	None	None	100 minutes
Week 24	Swim	Bike	Run
Day 1	Rest	Rest	Rest
Day 2	Warm up 200; drill 200; swim 400@30 and 200@15; cool down 300	None	30 minutes
Day 3	None	30 minutes	15 minutes
Day 4	Warm up 200; drill 200; swim 400@30 and 200@15; cool down 300	45 minutes	None
Day 5	None	None	30 minutes easy
Day 6	Rest	Rest	Rest
Day 7	RACE DAY	RACE DAY	RACE DAY

Training for an Ironman in 30 weeks

You don't have to be made of iron to complete this distance, but you do have to be prepared.

Some people would wince at *driving* 140.6 miles, never mind swimming, cycling, and running that distance! An Ironman is no walk in the park (or drive through it). Donna equates training for and competing in a triathlon to pregnancy and childbirth: You sign up for both, close to a year in advance; your body goes through experiences you're not sure it was meant to; you worry the entire time; if it's your first, you have no idea what to expect; you try hard not to listen to the horror stories; while you're waiting for the event you feel sick to your stomach; you think you'll never finish; it's painful; and when you finally finish, you can't believe you've done it, and you call everyone you know to tell them how great you feel, even though you feel as if you've been trampled over repeatedly.

Still in? Great. But first, be sure you've trained for and participated in triathlons of other distances or endurance events in each individual sport. This is a *serious* time commitment. The schedule in Table 10-4 will prepare you, as long as you have a solid base from which to start, in 30 weeks.

You can and should rest during your Ironman training. Don't eliminate your rest days — they're just as important as your training days.

This training plan is meant as a guideline. If you're ready — physically and mentally — to train for an Ironman, consider hiring a coach to make the best use of your time and workouts.

Table 10-4	A 30-Week Ironman Training Schedule		
Week 1	**Swim**	**Bike**	**Run**
Day 1	*Rest*	*Rest*	*Rest*
Day 2	Warm up 400, drill 400, swim 2x500@45, cool down 100	None	30 minutes
Day 3	None	30 minutes	15 minutes
Day 4	Warm up 400, drill 400, swim 2x500@45, cool down 100	50 minutes	None
Day 5	None	None	30 minutes
Day 6	None	90 minutes	None
Day 7	None	None	60 minutes

Week 2	Swim	Bike	Run
Day 1	Rest	Rest	Rest
Day 2	Warm up 400, drill 400, swim 5x200@20, cool down 200	None	35 minutes
Day 3	None	30 minutes	15 minutes
Day 4	Warm up 400, drill 400, swim 5x200@20, cool down 200	55 minutes	None
Day 5	None	None	35 minutes
Day 6	None	100 minutes	None
Day 7	None	None	65 minutes
Week 3	Swim	Bike	Run
Day 1	Rest	Rest	Rest
Day 2	Warm up 400, drill 400, swim 5x200@20, cool down 200	None	40 minutes
Day 3	None	30 minutes	15 minutes
Day 4	Warm up 400, drill 400, swim 5x200@20, cool down 200	60 minutes	None
Day 5	None	None	40 minutes
Day 6	None	110 minutes	None
Day 7	None	None	70 minutes
Week 4	Swim	Bike	Run
Day 1	Rest	Rest	Rest
Day 2	Warm up 400, drill 400, swim 10x100@20, cool down 200	None	35 minutes
Day 3	None	30 minutes	15 minutes
Day 4	Warm up 400, drill 400, swim 10x100@20, cool down 200	55 minutes	None
Day 5	None	None	35 minutes
Day 6	None	100 minutes	None
Day 7	None	None	65 minutes
Week 5	Swim	Bike	Run
Day 1	Rest	Rest	Rest
Day 2	Warm up 400; drill 400; swim 2x300@30 and 2x200@20; cool down 200	None	40 minutes

Day 3	None	35 minutes	15 minutes
Day 4	Warm up 400; drill 400; swim 2x300@30 and 2x200@20; cool down 200	60 minutes	None
Day 5	None	None	40 minutes
Day 6	None	120 minutes	None
Day 7	None	None	75 minutes
Week 6	**Swim**	**Bike**	**Run**
Day 1	*Rest*	*Rest*	*Rest*
Day 2	Warm up 400; drill 400; swim 2x300@30, 2x200@20, and 2x100@10; cool down 200	None	45 minutes fartlek
Day 3	None	40 minutes	15 minutes
Day 4	Warm up 400; drill 400; swim 2x300@30, 2x200@20, and 2x100@10; cool down 200	70 minutes	None
Day 5	None	None	45 minutes
Day 6	None	140 minutes	None
Day 7	None	None	80 minutes
Week 7	**Swim**	**Bike**	**Run**
Day 1	*Rest*	*Rest*	*Rest*
Day 2	Warm up 400; drill 400; swim 500@30, 400@30, 300@30, and 200@30; cool down 200	None	50 minutes
Day 3	None	45 minutes	15 minutes
Day 4	Warm up 400; drill 400; swim 500@30, 400@30, 300@30, and 200@30; cool down 200	80 minutes hills	None
Day 5	None	None	50 minutes
Day 6	None	160 minutes	None
Day 7	None	None	85 minutes
Week 8	**Swim**	**Bike**	**Run**
Day 1	*Rest*	*Rest*	*Rest*
Day 2	Warm up 400; drill 400; swim 2x300@30, 2x200@20, and 2x100@10; cool down 200	None	45 minutes
Day 3	None	40 minutes	15 minutes

Day 4	Warm up 400; drill 400; swim 2x300@30, 2x200@20, and 2x100@10; cool down 200	70 minutes	None
Day 5	None	None	45 minutes
Day 6	None	140 minutes	None
Day 7	None	None	80 minutes
Week 9	*Swim*	*Bike*	*Run*
Day 1	*Rest*	*Rest*	*Rest*
Day 2	Warm up 400, drill 400, swim 3x500@50, cool down 200	None	55 minutes
Day 3	None	45 minutes	15 minutes
Day 4	Warm up 400, drill 400, swim 3x500@50, cool down 200	75 minutes	None
Day 5	None	None	55 minutes
Day 6	None	160 minutes	None
Day 7	None	None	90 minutes
Week 10	*Swim*	*Bike*	*Run*
Day 1	*Rest*	*Rest*	*Rest*
Day 2	Warm up 400, drill 400, swim 6x250@20, cool down 200	None	60 minutes tempo
Day 3	None	45 minutes	15 minutes
Day 4	Warm up 400, drill 400, swim 6x250@20, cool down 200	75 minutes	None
Day 5	None	None	60 minutes
Day 6	None	180 minutes	None
Day 7	None	None	95 minutes
Week 11	*Swim*	*Bike*	*Run*
Day 1	*Rest*	*Rest*	*Rest*
Day 2	Warm up 400, drill 400, swim 6x250@20, cool down 200	None	60 minutes
Day 3	None	45 minutes	15 minutes
Day 4	Warm up 400, drill 400, swim 6x250@20, cool down 200	75 minutes hills	None
Day 5	None	None	60 minutes
Day 6	None	200 minutes	None
Day 7	None	None	100 minutes

Week 12	Swim	Bike	Run
Day 1	Rest	Rest	Rest
Day 2	Warm up 400, drill 400, swim 6x250@20, cool down 200	None	60 minutes
Day 3	None	45 minutes	15 minutes
Day 4	Warm up 400, drill 400, swim 6x250@20, cool down 200	75 minutes	None
Day 5	None	None	60 minutes
Day 6	None	180 minutes	None
Day 7	None	None	95 minutes
Week 13	Swim	Bike	Run
Day 1	Rest	Rest	Rest
Day 2	Warm up 400; drill 400; swim 3x400@40 and 3x200@20; cool down 200	None	60 minutes interval
Day 3	None	45 minutes	15 minutes
Day 4	Warm up 400; drill 400; swim 3x400@40 and 3x200@20; cool down 200	75 minutes	None
Day 5	None	None	60 minutes
Day 6	None	200 minutes	None
Day 7	None	None	100 minutes
Week 14	Swim	Bike	Run
Day 1	Rest	Rest	Rest
Day 2	Warm up 400; drill 400; swim 3x400@40 and 3x200@20; cool down 200	None	60 minutes
Day 3	None	45 minutes	15 minutes
Day 4	Warm up 400; drill 400; swim 3x400@40 and 3x200@20; cool down 200	80 minutes hills	None
Day 5	None	None	60 minutes
Day 6	None	220 minutes	None
Day 7	None	None	110 minutes

Week 15	Swim	Bike	Run
Day 1	Rest	Rest	Rest
Day 2	Warm up 400; drill 400; swim 600@45, 500@45, 400@45, and 300@45; cool down 200	None	60 minutes
Day 3	None	45 minutes	15 minutes
Day 4	Warm up 400; drill 400; swim 600@45, 500@45, 400@45, and 300@45; cool down 200	85 minutes	None
Day 5	None	None	60 minutes
Day 6	None	245 minutes	30 minutes
Day 7	None	None	120 minutes
Week 16	**Swim**	**Bike**	**Run**
Day 1	Rest	Rest	Rest
Day 2	Warm up 400; drill 400; swim 3x400@40 and 3x200@20; cool down 200	None	60 minutes
Day 3	None	45 minutes	15 minutes
Day 4	Warm up 400; drill 400; swim 3x400@40 and 3x200@20; cool down 200	80 minutes	None
Day 5	None	None	60 minutes
Day 6	None	220 minutes	None
Day 7	None	None	110 minutes
Week 17	**Swim**	**Bike**	**Run**
Day 1	Rest	Rest	Rest
Day 2	Warm up 400; drill 400; swim 600@45, 500@45, 400@45, and 300@45; cool down 200	None	60 minutes fartlek
Day 3	None	45 minutes	15 minutes
Day 4	Warm up 400; drill 400; swim 600@45, 500@45, 400@45, and 300@45; cool down 200	80 minutes	None
Day 5	None	None	60 minutes
Day 6	None	250 minutes	30 minutes
Day 7	None	None	120 minutes

Week 18	Swim	Bike	Run
Day 1	*Rest*	*Rest*	*Rest*
Day 2	Warm up 400; drill 400; swim 600@45, 500@45, 400@45, and 300@45; cool down 200	None	60 minutes
Day 3	None	45 minutes	15 minutes
Day 4	Warm up 400; drill 400; swim 600@45, 500@45, 400@45, and 300@45; cool down 200	80 minutes hills	None
Day 5	None	None	60 minutes
Day 6	None	275 minutes	None
Day 7	None	None	135 minutes
Week 19	**Swim**	**Bike**	**Run**
Day 1	*Rest*	*Rest*	*Rest*
Day 2	Warm up 400; drill 400; swim 600@45, 500@45, 400@45, and 300@45; cool down 200	None	60 minutes tempo
Day 3	None	45 minutes	15 minutes
Day 4	Warm up 400; drill 400; swim 600@45, 500@45, 400@45, and 300@45; cool down 200	80 minutes	None
Day 5	None	None	60 minutes
Day 6	None	305 minutes	30 minutes
Day 7	None	None	150 minutes
Week 20	**Swim**	**Bike**	**Run**
Day 1	*Rest*	*Rest*	*Rest*
Day 2	Warm up 400; drill 400; swim 600@45, 500@45, 400@45, and 300@45; cool down 200	None	60 minutes
Day 3	None	45 minutes	15 minutes
Day 4	Warm up 400; drill 400; swim 600@45, 500@45, 400@45, and 300@45; cool down 200	80 minutes	None
Day 5	Warm up 400; drill 400; swim 600@45, 500@45, 400@45, and 300@45; cool down 200	None	60 minutes
Day 6	None	275 minutes	None
Day 7	None	None	130 minutes

Week 21	Swim	Bike	Run
Day 1	*Rest*	*Rest*	*Rest*
Day 2	Warm up 400; drill 400; swim 2x500@50 and 3x400@40; cool down 200	None	60 minutes
Day 3	None	45 minutes	15 minutes
Day 4	Warm up 400; drill 400; swim 2x500@50 and 3x400@40; cool down 200	80 minutes	None
Day 5	Warm up 400; drill 400; swim 2x500@50 and 3x400@40; cool down 200	None	60 minutes
Day 6	None	330 minutes	30 minutes
Day 7	None	None	145 minutes
Week 22	Swim	Bike	Run
Day 1	*Rest*	*Rest*	*Rest*
Day 2	Warm up 400; drill 400; swim 2x500@50, 2x400@40, and 2x300@30; cool down 200	None	60 minutes
Day 3	None	45 minutes	15 minutes
Day 4	Warm up 400; drill 400; swim 2x500@50, 2x400@40, and 2x300@30; cool down 200	80 minutes hills	None
Day 5	Warm up 400; drill 400; swim 2x500@50, 2x400@40, and 2x300@30; cool down 200	None	60 minutes
Day 6	None	360 minutes	None
Day 7	None	None	160 minutes
Week 23	Swim	Bike	Run
Day 1	*Rest*	*Rest*	*Rest*
Day 2	Warm up 400; drill 400; swim 2x500@50, 2x400@40, and 2x300@30; cool down 200	None	60 minutes interval
Day 3	None	45 minutes	15 minutes
Day 4	Warm up 400; drill 400; swim 2x500@50, 2x400@40, and 2x300@30; cool down 200	80 minutes	None
Day 5	None	None	60 minutes
Day 6	None	400 minutes	30 minutes
Day 7	None	None	170 minutes

Week 24	Swim	Bike	Run
Day 1	Rest	Rest	Rest
Day 2	Warm up 400; drill 400; swim 2x500@50, 2x400@40, and 2x300@30; cool down 200	None	60 minutes
Day 3	None	45 minutes	15 minutes
Day 4	Warm up 400; drill 400; swim 2x500@50, 2x400@40, and 2x300@30; cool down 200	80 minutes hills	None
Day 5	Warm up 400; drill 400; swim 2x500@50, 2x400@40, and 2x300@30; cool down 200	None	60 minutes
Day 6	None	360 minutes	None
Day 7	None	None	180 minutes
Week 25	Swim	Bike	Run
Day 1	Rest	Rest	Rest
Day 2	Warm up 400; drill 400; swim 3x500@60, 3x300@30, and 200@20; cool down 200	None	60 minutes
Day 3	None	45 minutes	15 minutes
Day 4	Warm up 400; drill 400; swim 3x500@60, 3x300@30, and 200@20; cool down 200	80 minutes	None
Day 5	Warm up 400; drill 400; swim 3x500@60, 3x300@30, and 200@20; cool down 200	None	60 minutes
Day 6	None	370 minutes	30 minutes
Day 7	None	None	180 minutes
Week 26	Swim	Bike	Run
Day 1	Rest	Rest	Rest
Day 2	Warm up 400; drill 400; swim 2x600@60, 2x500@50, and 2x200@20; cool down 200	None	60 minutes
Day 3	None	45 minutes	15 minutes

	Swim	Bike	Run
Day 4	Warm up 400; drill 400; swim 2x600@60, 2x500@50, and 2x200@20; cool down 200	80 minutes	None
Day 5	Warm up 400; drill 400; swim 2x600@60, 2x500@50, and 2x200@20; cool down 200	None	60 minutes
Day 6	None	380 minutes	None
Day 7	None	None	160 minutes
Week 27	*Swim*	*Bike*	*Run*
Day 1	*Rest*	*Rest*	*Rest*
Day 2	Warm up 400; drill 400; swim 2x800@75 and 2x500@50; cool down 200	None	60 minutes fartlek
Day 3	None	45 minutes	15 minutes
Day 4	Warm up 400; drill 400; swim 2x800@75 and 2x500@50; cool down 200	80 minutes	None
Day 5	Warm up 400; drill 400; swim 2x800@75 and 2x500@50; cool down 200	None	60 minutes
Day 6	None	400 minutes	30 minutes
Day 7	None	None	180 minutes
Week 28	*Swim*	*Bike*	*Run*
Day 1	*Rest*	*Rest*	*Rest*
Day 2	Warm up 400; drill 400; swim 10x100@15, 10x50@10, and 20x25@5; cool down 200	None	45 minutes
Day 3	None	30 minutes	15 minutes
Day 4	Warm up 400; drill 400; swim 10x100@15, 10x50@10, and 20x25@5; cool down 200	60 minutes	None
Day 5	Warm up 400; drill 400; swim 10x100@15, 10x50@10, and 20x25@5; cool down 200	None	45 minutes
Day 6	None	300 minutes	None
Day 7	None	None	120 minutes

Week 29	Swim	Bike	Run
Day 1	Rest	Rest	Rest
Day 2	Warm up 400, drill 400, swim 3x500@50, cool down 200	None	45 minutes
Day 3	None	30 minutes	15 minutes
Day 4	Warm up 400; drill 400; swim 3x500@50; cool down 200	60 minutes	None
Day 5	None	None	45 minutes
Day 6	None	200 minutes	None
Day 7	None	None	60 minutes
Week 30	Swim	Bike	Run
Day 1	Rest	Rest	Rest
Day 2	Warm up 400, drill 400, swim 2x500@50, cool down 200	None	30 minutes
Day 3	None	30 minutes	15 minutes
Day 4	None	45 minutes	None
Day 5	Swim 1,000 easy	None	30 minutes easy
Day 6	Rest	Rest	Rest
Day 7	RACE DAY	RACE DAY	RACE DAY

Chapter 11

Strength Training and Stretching

In This Chapter

▶ Lifting weights to improve your performance

▶ Starting with the basics — equipment and exercises

▶ Stretching and relaxing after a workout

*Y*ou're busy swimming, riding, and running — and practicing how to transition from one to the next. Now you're supposed to find time for lifting and stretching, too?

It's true that triathlon training improves your overall fitness — cardiovascular and aerobic endurance, muscle strength, and flexibility. So you may be wondering why we're suggesting that you lift weights and stretch as well. Simply put, you'll perform better and reduce your risk of injury.

Swimming, cycling, and running don't isolate specific muscles. For example, when you're swimming, you use all your major muscle groups. The muscles in your upper and lower body work together and share the load. By targeting specific muscles, you can build their strength and endurance to help you finish faster or stronger.

We know you're already cramming three sports into your busy schedule. Before you decide you'll never find time for lifting or stretching, read this chapter to discover the benefits of adding weights to your workouts and how to fit it in. You'll also find out what equipment you'll need for a basic weight-training workout. And in this chapter, we pull together 12 basic exercises you can do in 15 to 20 minutes and 13 stretches to cool you down in 5 to 10 minutes.

Adding Weights to Your Workout

When you add weights to your workouts, you're performing strength training. *Strength training* isolates a muscle and works it repetitively in a focused manner to make it stronger. By directing the intensity of your workout to a specific muscle group, you develop these muscles' ability to work together longer before fatigue sets in.

Strong muscles take you that extra mile when you think you've got nothing left. They help you slice through choppy waters or climb a hill. And strong muscles help you maintain your form for efficiency. Improving your core strength (your abdominal and back muscles) prevents muscle fatigue during long workouts that can cause you to slouch into poor form. Maintaining proper form throughout your workouts keeps your swimming, cycling, and running efficient and reduces your chance of injury.

To strength train, you can use hand weights (also called free weights or dumbbells), large rubber bands (called *resistance bands*), or sophisticated weight machines at your local fitness center.

Identifying the benefits of strength training

Strength training brings benefits beyond strong leg muscles that will help you go faster and farther. For example, think about your upper body during cycling. Your neck, shoulder, abdominals, and lower-back muscles are all working to support your weight and keep you balanced. If these muscles are weak, they'll fatigue quickly, affecting your form on the bike, as well as your performance on the run.

And even after you've crossed the finish line, your strength training will still impact your life. Lifting weights:

- Makes you stronger, so everyday tasks are easier
- Improves bone density, which can prevent osteoporosis
- Improves your endurance by increasing your muscle tolerance of lactic acid, which causes that burning feeling in your legs as you climb a big hill
- Reduces your risk of injuries
- Gives you an all-over toned, athletic look
- Boosts your metabolism, which helps you burn more calories, even when you're not working out

So, with all these benefits, why wouldn't you want to strength train? Some athletes fear lifting weights will cause them to add bulk. Women may fear looking masculine. Men may fear that added weight will slow them down.

The exercises in this chapter won't add bulk. When you feel how strength training makes hills easier and laps faster, you'll be hooked.

Fitting in your workouts with weights

The number of strength-training workouts you incorporate into your week will depend on the time you have available. You can train and complete a triathlon without adding weight workouts, but these basic exercises can deliver big bonuses. Allow 30 minutes twice a week or 15 minutes four times a week for your strength-training workouts.

If you can't work on a muscle group at least twice a week consistently, you won't experience much benefit at all. If you're that pressed for time, focus on your running, swimming, and cycling instead.

Ideally, you should do weight workouts for specific muscle groups giving yourself 48 hours between workouts, to allow your muscles time to rest and heal. Here are tips for finding time to lift weights and deciding when to skip a workout:

- ✔ Break up your workouts into focused sessions of one or two muscle groups and fit those ten-minute workouts into your daily routine.

- ✔ Combine your workouts. Jump on your bike and ride or run to the gym, train with weights, and then ride or run home.

- ✔ Do your strength training on the days you're at your gym anyway for your swim training.

Don't give up a swimming, cycling, or running workout for a strength-training session. Lunges alone won't get you through any one leg of your race, so the triathlon training should take priority.

Learning the ropes

If you ask ten different people the best way to strength train, you'll undoubtedly get ten different answers. Ask the Arnold wannabe, and he'll tell you to focus on high load, fewer reps, and many sets. Ask a woman who fears a bulked-up body, and she'll tell you to do one set of many reps using light weights.

Reps, sets, loads. . . . What are they talking about? Here's a rundown:

- ✔ **Reps:** Short for *repetitions,* reps are the number of times you repeat an individual exercise. For example, if you hold a dumbbell in your hand with your arm down at your side, bend your elbow until your hand is close to your shoulder, and then return to the starting position, that's one repetition of a bicep curl.

✔ **Set:** A *set* is a group of 10 to 12 repetitions of a specific exercise. We recommend performing two to three sets of each exercise during a workout. Rest between each set for approximately 30 seconds.

✔ **Load:** *Load* is the amount of weight you use for each rep. Your load is individual and will depend on where you are in your strength-training program. If you're new to strength training, you'll want to start with light weights — light enough that you can perform a set of 10 to 12 reps without fatiguing your muscles to exhaustion. Work with a weight for at least two weeks before increasing. *Note:* For an exercise such as push-ups, your load is your body weight.

If you can't complete at least 10 reps, the weight is too heavy. If you can do more than 12 reps, the weight you're lifting is too light. The only way to really determine what weight is right for you when you start out is through trial and error. If you're a woman, start with a 5-pound load for working on the upper arms; move up to 8 pounds for chest presses and 10 pounds for lunges and leg work, and see how you feel. If you're a man, you can probably start with more weight — 10 to 15 pounds for biceps if you're new to strength training, 20 to 30 pounds for chest presses and lunges.

Keeping it in balance

To get the maximum benefit from your strength training for a triathlon, you'll want to focus on your major muscle groups:

✔ Biceps and triceps (arms)

✔ Quadriceps and hamstrings (legs)

✔ Pectorals (chest)

✔ Deltoids (upper back)

✔ Core muscles — your various abdominal muscles and lower-back muscles

Muscle balance is an important component of a strength-training program. Muscle imbalance, caused by overusing one muscle and not developing the supporting muscle, can lead to injury.

If you work one muscle, you need to work the opposing muscle as well. In other words, if you work your biceps (the muscles you use to bend your elbow), you have to train your triceps (the muscles you use to straighten your elbow). If you work your abdominals, you have to work your back muscles.

We've grouped the exercises in this chapter by muscle group, to make it easy to remember to work these groups together for the best workout in the least amount of time.

Choosing the right equipment

If you have a gym membership, everything you need to complete a strength-training workout will be within arm's reach. But you can get an equally effective workout just as easily with basic equipment at home. You can re-create almost every exercise done on a machine with hand weights, resistance bands, and a bench or stability ball. The advantage of a gym membership is that you have a lot more equipment available to use — but a disadvantage (aside from the cost) is that you'll have to allow for the time to get there. If you have equipment at home, you can fit in your workout at any time during the day or night — and even work out in those ratty old sweatpants you love so much.

If you plan to strength train at home, consider purchasing some or all of the following equipment:

- ✓ **Free weights:** Free weights are individual, hand-held dumbbells or plates that you put on a barbell. We recommended starting with dumbbells. You'll find them sold individually or in sets in weight increments from 2 pounds, 3 pounds, and 5 pounds up to 30 pounds. Buy a range of weights — you'll need light weights for triceps exercises, heavier weights for legs.

  We don't recommend purchasing barbells with various plates. Because you're likely pressed for time, you won't want to stop to unscrew a washer, slide off the weights on either side, and then rebuild the set with new weights.

  You can choose between metal and plastic-coated dumbbells — select the dumbbells that feel good in your hands. Expect to pay around $3 for an individual 3-pound dumbbell and up to $100 for a set of two dumbbells in three different weights. Weight systems that allow you to select a setting on the dumbbell to change the weight save space and time, but they won't save you money. Expect to pay from $150 for a set to more than $300.

- ✓ **Resistance bands:** Resistance bands are circles or lengths of latex much like overgrown rubber bands. They come in varying resistance (light, medium, or heavy), colors, and sizes. Pilates-style bands are sold in sets of three for less than $20. Bands that feature handles cost around $13 to $15 apiece.

  If you decide to use bands instead of dumbbells, we recommend purchasing a set of three bands in light, medium, and heavy resistance. Feel the band before you purchase it and look for comfortable padded handles. As with dumbbells, avoid bands that require that you switch the handles to use a different resistance band.

  Bands are often sold with a booklet or DVD telling you how you can convert common dumbbell exercises for various muscle groups to band training. Take the time to review these exercises.

- **Platform:** Remember step aerobics? Those great heart-working, gut-busting classes are no longer the favorites at gyms, but the steps stuck around and are being used for a variety of workouts. A bench or platform that you can adjust by making it lower or higher is a great addition to a home gym. You'll find benches for as little as $40 and as much as $200.

  Platforms are nice to have, but they aren't necessary for your home gym. You can do some of the exercises on the bottom stair of your house, on the floor, on a chair, or on a stability ball.

- **Stability ball:** Basically, stability balls are good, old-fashioned children's fun, marketed as exercise equipment — but they really work! When you sit or lie on a ball to perform your exercises, you engage your core muscles for balance, thus increasing the effectiveness of your workout. Stability balls come in a variety of sizes from around 50 to 120 centimeters (20 to 47 inches) in diameter. (The diameters are typically listed in centimeters, not inches.) Prices vary considerably, starting at only $20; a good-quality foam plastic ball can cost as much as $200. Different size balls work best for different size bodies. For example, if you're under 5'3", a 55cm ball will work well for you. If you're under 5'11", look for a 65cm ball, and if you are taller than 5'11", use a 75cm to 105cm ball. Stability balls feature size recommendations on the packaging. When you're seated on the inflated ball with your legs bent and feet flat on the floor, your thighs should be almost parallel to the floor.

Choosing free weights versus machines

You may not have the option of using weight machines if you don't belong to a gym or can't join one. Lucky for you, it's one less decision you have to make. Grab your free weights or resistance bands and get to work. Consider purchasing a DVD on weight training or hiring a personal trainer to get you started.

If you're trying to decide which option (free weights or machines) will work best for you, welcome to the fitness debate of the past 30-plus years. Some fitness professionals believe free weights require more balance and coordination to perform, so you recruit more muscle groups for each exercise, enhancing your benefit. Free weights also offer a greater range of motion than machines for more variety in your workout and better muscle isolation. Free weights are inexpensive compared to gym memberships and home machines.

Fitness professionals urge caution, though. When you use free weights at home, you'll be unsupervised and at risk of injury if you consistently use incorrect form. This is why many fitness experts recommend machines for beginners — they keep your body in the appropriate alignment for that exercise (of course, many people in gyms are using the machines or free weights incorrectly as well). Machines effectively isolate the muscle you're working on, and eliminate the possibility that you could use other muscles to take some of the load.

Decide what works best for you with the time and budget you have for your strength training, and focus on making the best and safest use of that choice.

Strength training 101: Exercises to try

You're ready to hit the weights. In this section, we provide twelve exercises that will get you started and provide a good foundation for your strength-training workout.

We focus on exercises you can do at home. If you belong to a gym, start with these exercises for the largest muscle groups, and then seek out a personal trainer or staff member at your gym if you want to know more about translating these movements to machines.

You can't assume that the buff body next to you on a weight machine knows the proper form and use of the machine. Don't watch and learn. And don't be shy about asking for help at your gym. You won't have to pay a personal-training fee just to learn the correct use of the machine. The staff at your gym will *want* you to know how to use the machines safely, so they'll be happy to help you set the seats at the correct heights and help you select the appropriate weights. Ask for their help and guidance.

Before you begin your strength-training workout, complete one set of each exercise with a lighter weight to warm up. As you perform each exercise, keep the following tips in mind for safety and maximum benefit:

- **Maintain proper form.** There's a reason gym walls are adorned with mirrors. Don't be embarrassed to watch yourself to be sure you're performing the exercise correctly. And don't worry about the seriously large and intense body builders — they're too busy watching themselves to notice what you're doing. At home, get a full-length mirror to set up in your exercise area so that you can check your form. Even the reflection in a window will do.

- **Use a full range of motion.** Don't skimp here. Use full flex and full extension for the maximum benefit of each repetition.

- **Use slow and controlled movements.** Think about the muscles you're using, and focus on how they feel. Don't rush through your strength training. Swinging your arms, hips, or back to get through your workout faster can cause injury or make your workout ineffective. The basic rule of thumb is a two-count on the exertion phase and a four-count on the down, recovery phase. For example, on a bicep curl, as you lift the weight up to your shoulder, slowly count to two; as you lower the weight, slowly count to four. On four, you should be back to your starting position.

- **Breathe!** Exhale on the *work phase* (the part of the exercise that feels hardest); inhale on the *recovery* (the part that's easiest). If in doubt, just breathe — don't hold your breath.

- **Know when to increase your weight.** When you can complete 12 reps easily, increase the weight for your next workout by 5 percent to 10 percent (but no more than that). You'll likely find that you need to go back to doing only eight repetitions with the new weight, until your muscles get stronger.

When you first start a weight-training program, use light weights to avoid pushing your muscles to the point of failure and being so sore the next day that you'll have difficulty completing a swim, bike, or run. *Remember:* Your focus is on training in the three sports. You don't want to lift so much that you can't move your muscles the next day.

✔ **Lift, rest, repeat.** Ideally, you'll want to perform two to three sets of 10 to 12 repetitions for each exercise. If you're short on time, cut out a set or complete one set of reps using a heavier weight.

✔ **Allow 48 hours rest before working the same muscle group again.**

Loving those legs

The **basic squat** strengthens your quadriceps, the muscles at the tops of your legs (essentially, your thighs) and works your hamstrings and *gluteus maximus* (your rear). Here's how to do it:

1. **Stand with your feet shoulder-width apart, toes slightly turned out, knees over your toes (see Figure 11-1a).**

   Keep you hands free at your sides, straight out in front, or on your waist, or add a dumbbell in each hand for extra resistance.

   Keep your spine in the neutral position by keeping your head straight, in line with your spine.

Figure 11-1:
Squats strengthen the muscles used in running and cycling.

Photo by Kathy Johnson Brown

2. **Bend your knees and lower your rear end as if you were sitting in a chair (see Figure 11-1b), and descend until your knees and hips are at a 90-degree angle.**

   Make sure your knees don't push forward over your toes. Don't lean forward. Keep most of your weight centered on your feet or slightly back on your heels.

3. **Return to the starting position, maintaining a neutral spine and keeping your head up.**

Lunges work your hamstrings and quadriceps for a strong leg that makes hill climbs easier and helps you pull out a good kick as you run to the finish line. Here are the steps to a great lunge:

1. **Stand with your feet shoulder-width apart, toes straight (see Figure 11-2a).**

   If you want, you can place your hands on your hips to aid your balance or hold dumbbells in each hand, starting with light weights until you feel comfortable with the movement.

2. **Starting with your dominant leg, step forward, placing your foot about a stride's width away and keeping the other leg in place.**

   Keep your head and shoulders up and your back straight.

Figure 11-2:
When performing lunges, reach with the front leg only so far as to stretch — not so far that you'll compromise your balance.

Photo by Kathy Johnson Brown

3. **Bend the knee of the leg in front, lowering your body, raising your heel on the back leg and bending the knee of that leg until it almost touches the floor (see Figure 11-2b).**

   Be sure your front knee is in alignment with your toes and not pushing past them.

4. **Push up and back on your front leg to return to the starting position, and repeat with the other leg.**

Focusing on the chest and upper back

Chest presses isolate the pectoral muscles. Here's how to do them:

1. **Pick up light-weight dumbbells or a barbell, and lie on your back on a bench or elevated platform, with your feet flat on the floor.**

   If you prefer, you can use a stability ball instead of a bench.

2. ***If you're using a barbell,* position your hands on the bar slightly more than shoulder-width apart and bend your elbows so that the barbell is just above your chest. *If you're using dumbbells,* hold them slightly more than shoulder-width apart just above the chest level (see Figure 11-3a).**

3. **Straighten your elbows and raise the bar or dumbbells toward the ceiling, keeping it straight up over your chest (see Figure 11-3b).**

4. **Return to the starting position.**

Nothing beats a **push-up** to strengthen your entire upper body. This no-equipment exercise can be done anywhere and uses your body weight as the load.

1. **Place your hands on the floor just slightly more than shoulder-width apart, arms extended, fingers pointing forward.**

2. **Stretch your body out straight behind you, balancing on your toes (see Figure 11-4a).**

   If you're just starting out, you can balance on your knees with your feet up and crossed at the heels.

   Keep your back and knees straight and parallel to the floor.

3. **Slowly bend your elbows and lower your body to the floor, until your nose and chest are almost in contact with the floor (see Figure 11-4b).**

4. **Push up with your arms and return to the starting position.**

Figure 11-3:
Perform
chest
presses
on a flat
bench or
stability ball.

Photo by Kathy Johnson Brown

Figure 11-4:
When performing push-ups, be sure to keep your back straight. Don't drop or lift your rear end.

Photo by Kathy Johnson Brown

TIP

If you find it too difficult to perform a set of push-ups (or even a single push-up) while maintaining proper form, start out doing your push-ups against a wall. Stand at arm's length from the wall. Position your hands flat against the wall at shoulder height. Keeping your feet in place and heels down, bend your elbows and let your body move toward the wall until your face is a few inches from the wall. Push back with your arms to the starting position. From there, you can move to push-ups on a solid hand rail that puts you closer to parallel to the floor than the wall. After you've mastered these push-ups, move to the floor.

The **seated reverse fly** works the latisimus dorsi muscle of the upper back, as well as the rear shoulders. Here's how you do it:

1. **Pick up a set of light-weight dumbbells, one in each hand.**

2. **Sit at the edge of a flat bench or on a stability ball with your feet flat on the ground and lean forward at your waist, keeping your back straight and your abdominals tight. Position your hands above the outside of each ankle, palms facing each other (see Figure 11-5a).**

3. **Bend your elbows and pull the weights up until your upper arms are parallel to the floor, keeping your elbows slightly bent (see Figure 11-5b).**

4. **Return to the starting position.**

Figure 11-5: The seated reverse fly works your upper back.

Photo by Ed Pagliarini

The **one-arm dumbbell row** works the upper back and biceps. Here's how you do it:

1. **Pick up a light-weight dumbbell in one hand.**

2. **Place your free hand at the top of a bench and your knee on the bench toward the back. Drop your hand with the weight straight down, palm facing in.**

   Keep your back straight and your head in a neutral position in line with your spine (see Figure 11-6a).

3. **Keeping your abdominals tight, bend your elbow and lift the weight straight up to about waist height (see Figure 11-6b).**

4. **Return the arm to the start position and repeat.**

Figure 11-6:
The one-arm
dumbbell
row works
your upper
back.

Photo by Ed Pagliarini

Building strong arms

The **tricep kickback** builds the smaller of the arm's two largest muscles, the tricep, which is located at the back of your arm. Here's how to do it:

1. **Pick up a lightweight dumbbell.**

2. **Place your free hand at the top of a bench and your knee toward the back of the bench.**

3. **Raise the dumbbell to your waist, with your elbow bent at about 90 degrees (see Figure 11-7a).**

   Keep your back straight and your head in a neutral position in line with your spine.

4. **Straighten the lower part of your arm holding the dumbbell out behind you, keeping the upper arm still (see Figure 11-7b).**

5. **Return to the starting position.**

Seated alternating dumbbell curls isolate the biceps. Here are the steps:

1. **Sit on a bench, at the edge of a chair, or on your stability ball, with your feet flat on the floor, your knees bent, and your abdominal muscles tight.**

2. **Hold a dumbbell in each hand, palms facing in and at your sides (see Figure 11-8a).**

3. **Slowly curl the dumbbell in your right hand up to your shoulder, keeping your elbow tucked in at your side. As you're curling, turn your palm up toward the ceiling (see Figure 11-8b).**

4. **Hold the position at the top, squeezing the bicep for two counts, and then return slowly to the starting position.**

5. **Repeat with the other arm to complete one repetition.**

Shaping your shoulders

Working your shoulders adds strength to your swim and will reduce aches and fatigue when riding long distances and when running. The **seated dumbbell shoulder press** works your deltoids, or the front, back and tops of your shoulders. Here are the steps:

1. **Sit on a chair or on your stability ball with your back straight, head up, and abdominals tight.**

2. **With a dumbbell in each hand, bend your elbows and position your hands just outside of each shoulder with your palms facing forward (see Figure 11-9a).**

3. **Raise both dumbbells over your head, pushing them toward each other at the top of the motion (see Figure 11-9b).**

4. **Return to the starting position, just outside of each shoulder, and repeat.**

Figure 11-7:
One way
to work
the triceps
is using
dumbbells
to perform
the tricep
kickback.

Photo by Kathy Johnson Brown

Figure 11-8:
Seated
alternating
dumbbell
curls work
your biceps.

Photo by Kathy Johnson Brown

Figure 11-9:
Build strong
shoulders to
benefit your
swim and
to reduce
fatigue on
the bike
and during
the run.

Photo by Kathy Johnson Brown

Lateral raises work your deltoids. You'll also feel the benefit to your *trapezius,* the muscle that runs along the back of your shoulder to your neck. Here's how to do them:

1. **Hold a dumbbell in each hand and drop your hands to your sides (see Figure 11-10a).**

2. **Slowly raise your arms out to the side, keeping them straight, palms facing down, until your arms are parallel to the floor and your hands are slightly above your shoulder level (see Figure 11-10b).**

3. **Slowly return to the starting position and repeat.**

Figure 11-10: Lateral raises work the muscles of your shoulders for a strong upper body and to reduce shoulder and neck fatigue.

Photo by Kathy Johnson Brown

Knowing what's at the core

Creating a **plank,** sometimes called a *bridge,* helps you to tone and strengthen your core muscles — the muscles of your abdomen and lower back. Here's how to do it:

1. **Put yourself in the push-up position, legs straight, toes down, hands just below your shoulders.**

2. **Bend your elbows and lower yourself onto your forearms, with your hands facing forward (see Figure 11-11).**

   Keep your back straight and concentrate on not lifting your rear end or arching your back. Keep your neck in alignment with your back.

3. **Hold the position for 30 seconds, working up to 1 minute and increasing by 30 seconds as you get stronger.**

Figure 11-11:
Perform the plank to strengthen the muscles at your core — your abdominals and your lower back.

Photo by Ed Pagliarini

The **bug** puts the focus on your abdominals by removing the possibility that you might pull on your neck or shoulders as people often do when performing crunches or traditional sit-ups. Here are the steps:

1. **Lie on your back on the floor, bend your knees, and place your feet flat on the floor.**

2. **Lift your arms straight up over your chest, palms facing in, and press your shoulders into the floor (see Figure 11-12a).**

3. **Raise your right knee until it's at a right angle from your hip. Then lift your left knee in the same manner.**

   Hold the position for 30 seconds.

4. **Extend your left leg straight out at the same level as your right knee, and extend your right arm straight over your head slightly above the ground (see Figure 11-12b).**

   Hold for 30 seconds.

5. **Bring your right leg and left arm back to the starting position and repeat with the left leg and right arm for 30 seconds (see Figure 11-12c).**

6. **Come back to the starting position with your knees up and arms over your chest, hold for 30 seconds, and relax.**

Figure 11-12:
The bug isolates the abdominal muscles, building your core strength and stability and contributing to better form and posture.

Photo by Ed Pagliarini

Stretching Your Limits

Stretching takes only five to ten minutes but enhances your muscle balance and flexibility, which improves your overall performance and can change the way you feel for the entire day. But stretching is the "chore" most athletes never find time for, unless they feel sore or are tending to an injury.

The best time to stretch is *before* you feel sore — and stretching can help to *prevent* injuries.

While you're working one muscle training in the water, on your bike, or by running, you'll be stretching the opposing muscle. Swimming freestyle, for example, tends to tighten the chest muscles while stretching out the back muscles. If you don't stretch your chest muscles, you'll end up with tight muscles and poor posture, which contributes to bad form.

Never stretch cold muscles and never bounce. Stretch after your workout session when your muscles are warm. Give yourself five minutes to cool down, and then stretch all the muscles you just worked, as well as the opposing muscle groups.

Recognizing the benefits of stretching

Stretching helps you to become more flexible and improves your muscle balance. With increased flexibility, you have an enhanced range of motion, making it more comfortable to reach forward or tuck for better aerodynamics when you're cycling.

Stretching also improves circulation and promotes good posture and form, reducing your chance of injury. Plus, a good stretching session just *feels* good, and it can help you to relax and relieve stress.

Stretching 101: Stretches to try

The best way to determine how to stretch a muscle is to think about how you worked it and do the opposite. For example, to *work* the quadriceps, you perform leg extensions. So, to *stretch* your quadriceps, you do leg curls, bending your knee and bringing your foot toward your rear end. It's easy to tell if you're doing the right exercise for the muscle you want to work — just focus on that muscle and feel the stretch.

In this section are stretches for each of the major muscles. Perform the stretches below by holding each one for 20 to 30 seconds.

Quadriceps

Your quadriceps are four large muscles at the front of your thigh. Follow these steps to stretch these muscles:

1. **Stand with your right hand holding onto a fixed object for support.**

2. **Bend your left knee, moving your foot toward your rear end and reach for your left foot with your left hand.**

3. **Gently pull your heel toward your butt, keeping your left knee pointing to the floor and in line with your right knee (see Figure 11-13).**

   Stand tall as you hold the stretch.

4. **Return to standing and repeat with the opposite leg.**

Figure 11-13:
Do this simple stretch for your quadriceps.

Photo by Kathy Johnson Brown

Hamstrings

Your hamstrings are a set of three muscles that run from the pelvis down the back of the thigh. Tight hamstrings can contribute to lower-back pain. Try this simple stretch for this muscle group:

1. **Lie on your back on the floor, extending one leg straight out on the floor and the other up toward the ceiling.**

2. **Wrap a towel around the arch of your foot.**

3. **Press your heel toward the ceiling as you gently pull down on both sides of the towel to increase the stretch (see Figure 11-14).**

4. **Return your leg to the floor and repeat with the opposite leg.**

Photo by Ed Pagliarini

Figure 11-14:
Stretch your hamstring to avoid injuries to this easily pulled muscle.

Calves

Two muscles make up your calves — the gastrocnemius and soleus — and this series of steps stretches both:

1. **Stand straight and place your hands on your hips.**

2. **Place your right foot behind you, keeping the right knee straight and bending the left knee.**

3. **Press your right heel to the ground (see Figure 11-15a).**

4. **Hold the stretch.**

5. **From the same position, bend your right knee toward the ground until you feel a stretch in your lower calf closer to your ankle (see Figure 11-15b).**

6. **Relax and repeat both stretches on the opposite leg.**

If you prefer, you can do this stretch facing a wall, with your hands pressed against the wall for support.

Photo by Ed Pagliarini

Figure 11-15: This exercise stretches both major muscles in the calf.

Hips

Stretching your hips helps to prevent pain and injury. Try this easy stretch to loosen your hips:

1. **Lie on your back on the floor with your shoulders flat against the floor and your back relaxed.**

2. **Bend your right knee and lay it across your left knee (see Figure 11-16a).**

3. **Drop both knees to the right (see Figure 11-16b), and gently press on the right knee to increase the stretch.**

   Try to keep both shoulders flat on the ground as you roll to the side to increase the stretch in your hip and lower back.

4. **Return to the starting position, relax, and repeat with the left leg, stretching to the right.**

Hip flexors

Stretching your hips can help to prevent running and cycling injuries. Try this simple stretch to open your hip flexors:

1. **Stand with your feet together and your hands on your hips.**

2. **Step forward with your right foot as if performing a lunge (see Figure 11-17a).**

Figure 11-16:
Keep your
shoulders
flat against
the floor to
increase the
stretch in
your hip.

Photo by Ed Pagliarini

3. **Drop the left knee to the ground, making sure your right knee is in alignment with your right foot and not moving beyond your toes (see Figure 11-17b).**

4. **Gently pull your hips forward to feel the stretch at the top of your left thigh.**

5. **Relax and repeat with the left leg.**

Figure 11-17:
Gently stretch-ing your hip flexors can help to reduce running and cycling injuries.

Photo by Ed Pagliarini

Inner thighs

Stretching your inner thighs is especially important to prevent running injuries. This stretch works the inner thighs, as well as the lower back:

1. **Sit on the floor and bring the soles of your feet together, pulling them toward you with your hands until you feel the stretch in your inner thighs (see Figure 11-18).**

   Sit tall, back straight, shoulders back.

2. **Gently push your pelvis toward your feet to increase the stretch.**

   Don't bounce your knees or lean forward and press on them.

3. **Relax and repeat.**

Figure 11-18:
Don't
bounce
or press
on your
legs when
stretch-
ing your
inner-thigh
muscles.

Photo by Ed Pagliarini

Lower back

Many triathletes feel pain in their lower backs after running or cycling. Try this stretch to loosen the lower back and prevent pain and injury:

1. **Position yourself on your hands and knees on the floor.**

   Your hands should be shoulder-width apart and directly under your shoulders; your knees, hip distance apart and directly under your hips (see Figure 11-19a).

   Keep the elbows soft and don't lock the joint.

2. **While exhaling, gently round your back, starting with your lower back and moving through to your shoulders, and press your chin to your chest (see Figure 11-19b).**

3. **Relax and repeat.**

Figure 11-19:
A lower-
back stretch
feels great
after a
workout.

Photo by Ed Pagliarini

Chest

The pectoral muscles are the large muscles that fan across the front of the chest. Try this simple stretch for the chest muscles:

1. **Stand with your right side facing a wall or a chair, arm's length away.**

2. **Place your right hand on the wall or chair, with your right arm fully extended.**

3. **Gently twist your left shoulder and hip away from the wall or chair until you feel a stretch in the right side of the chest (see Figure 11-20).**

4. **Relax and repeat on the left side.**

Figure 11-20: Try this gentle stretch for your pectoral muscles.

Photo by Ed Pagliarini

Shoulders

Stretching the muscles of your shoulders, including the large deltoid muscle, can help relieve tension and pain. Try this easy stretch:

1. **In a standing or seated position, lift your left arm and extend it across your chest.**

2. **Take your right hand and gently press it against your left elbow, bringing the left arm closer to your chest (see Figure 11-21).**

3. **Relax and repeat with the right arm and shoulder.**

Figure 11-21: This stretch can help to relieve tension across the tops of your shoulders and your neck.

Photo by Ed Pagliarini

Triceps

The tricep muscles run across the backs of your arms. Follow these steps for a feel-good stretch:

1. **Raise your right arm over your head, with your upper arm close to your ear.**

2. **Bend your elbow and drop your hand toward the middle of your back, palm facing your back as if you were going to scratch it.**

3. **With your left hand, grab your right elbow, gently pressing it back toward the middle of the back of your head until you feel a stretch in your tricep (see Figure 11-22).**

4. **Relax and repeat with the left arm.**

Photo by Ed Pagliarini

Figure 11-22:
You'll feel this stretch across the length of the back of your arm.

Biceps

The biceps are the large muscle group at the front of your arm. Try this easy stretch for your arms:

1. **Extend your right arm straight out in front of you at shoulder height with your palm facing the sky.**

2. **Take your left hand and gently press down on your right fingers, bending at the wrist.**

3. **Press up slightly on your bicep to increase the stretch (see Figure 11-23).**

4. **Relax and repeat with the left arm.**

After you stretch your triceps, always stretch your biceps, the opposing muscles.

Photo by Ed Pagliarini

Neck

After a long workout, especially a bike ride or a run, you may feel tension in your neck. A simple stretch can help to relieve that, as well as feelings of fatigue. Try this quick stretch for your neck:

1. **Tilt your head to the right side with your ear moving toward your shoulder.**

2. **Reach over the top of your head with your right hand, and gently press on the left side of your head, pressing it toward your right shoulder (see Figure 11-24a).**

3. **Bring your head back to the center and press your chin to your chest (see Figure 11-24b).**

4. **Relax, bringing your head back to the center, and repeat on the left side.**

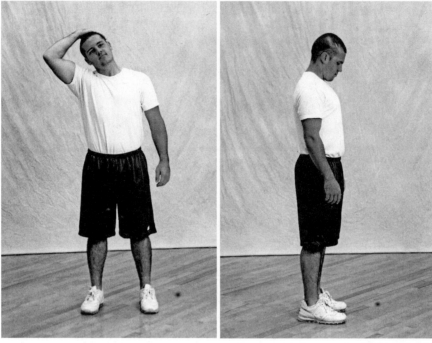

Figure 11-24:
Stretching
your neck
will feel
especially
good after
a long
bike ride.

Photo by Ed Pagliarini

The best stretch

When you're finished with your stretches, take a moment to lie flat and stretch your body "long" from head to toe. This is a relaxing stretch that melts away tension.

1. **Lie on your back on a soft, flat surface and extend both arms over your head onto the surface behind you, reaching as high as you can.**

2. **Stretch both legs out in the opposite direction and point your toes (see Figure 11-25).**

3. **Hold the stretch and inhale.**

4. **Exhale and relax.**

5. **Close your eyes and relax your entire body, breathing out as you feel yourself melt into the surface beneath you.**

   Picture yourself somewhere serene, perhaps on a beach in Hawaii (nowhere near an Ironman) sipping a piña colada.

Figure 11-25:
This stretch, popular with athletes and people who practice yoga, relaxes the whole body.

Photo by Ed Pagliarini

Chapter 12

Coping with Injuries

. . . .

In This Chapter

▶ Training without injury

▶ Knowing when and why you should rest

▶ Recognizing common symptoms of overtraining

▶ Identifying common swimming, cycling, and running injuries

▶ Training in extreme weather

. . . .

*N*o one likes to think about injuries, but now is the time to do so — before you start your training. With a little advance preparation and a lot of rest, you can prevent many common injuries experienced during triathlon training.

In this chapter, we offer tips for reducing your risk of injury and illness associated with overtraining. If your workouts are getting harder rather than easier, and you're finishing feeling exhausted rather than exhilarated, you may be training too hard. It's okay to take some time off to refuel your body and your mind. We show you how to recognize the signs of overtraining and tell you what you can do about it.

If you find yourself experiencing pain in the water, on your bike, or during your runs, you find help in the section on the common causes of pain and how to treat or prevent it.

In this chapter, you also find guidelines for training in extreme temperatures — either hot or cold — and tips for identifying when it's time to get back inside or to seek medical attention.

Preventing Pain and Injury

Pain is part of triathlon training — to a degree. The secret lies in knowing the difference between *normal* training discomfort and pain that indicates you're overtraining or running yourself toward an injury.

Understanding why you get cramps

At some point during your triathlon training, you may experience muscle cramps — possible in any of the three triathlon sports. You can prevent and treat cramps, and it's important to know how so that a sudden, unexpected pain doesn't knock you out of your event, even temporarily. The causes of cramps are unknown, but athletes and coaches all point to hydration as a likely cause. Drink fluids before, during, and after every training session and be sure to include electrolyte-rich sports drinks, as well as water. If you're experiencing frequent cramps, also be sure to add potassium-rich foods — such as bananas, cantaloupes, raisins, potatoes, squash or spinach — to your nutritional plan. And remember to stretch and warm up and cool down. If you do experience a cramp, gentle stretches and self-massage can help to relieve the pain and spasm.

In this section, we tell you how to prevent injuries, how to tell if you've been overtraining (and prevent yourself from doing that in the future), and how much rest you need to keep your pain and injuries to a minimum.

Preventing injuries

You can do all the right things and end up with an injury due to a fall or a twisted ankle. These acute injuries happen due to fatigue, carelessness, or sometimes just dumb luck — you know when they happen, and you know why they happened. As frustrating as these injuries are, you may have to take time off to heal.

Other injuries, however, you can actually *prevent*. Generally, *chronic injuries* (the type that are slow in coming and slow in healing) give you advance notice of their intent. It may start with a twinge or an ache. If you ignore it, the pain can become nagging or persistent, and it can worsen until it prevents you from continuing to train.

You can prevent injuries in the following ways:

- ✔ Follow an appropriate training plan, gradually increasing distance or speed.
- ✔ Stretch and weight-train to build strength and promote muscle balance.
- ✔ Be sure your equipment is in good working order (especially your cycling equipment) and fits you correctly.
- ✔ Follow proper technique and pay attention to your form during exercise.
- ✔ Learn to recognize the signs of overtraining and allow sufficient time for rest and recovery (see the following section).

With experience, you'll be able to recognize what hurts because you're facing a hill and what hurts because you're facing an injury. Your muscles will be sore at times from training. But if you experience sharp pains or repeated joint pains, your body is protesting. Listen up!

Identifying the signs of overtraining

You've been following your training plan, and you're feeling great. You haven't missed a workout, any maybe now you're thinking, "I'll get even better conditioned if I train on my day off." Please don't.

If you don't give your body time to recover, you'll be entering the overtraining zone. Overtraining can lead to injury or illness, which can sideline you and prevent you from training or participating in your event.

Undertrain for your event, and you'll have trouble finishing it — and possibly injure yourself in the process. Overtrain for your event, and you'll experience the same results. In fact, given the choice, you'd be better off being slightly undertrained as you approach race day than overtrained.

Listen to your body — it will talk to you! If you go out for an intense workout, and you're just not feeling it that day, back off and do an easy workout. ***Remember:*** Your rest and recovery days are just as important as any of your workouts.

During your triathlon training, if you experience any of the following symptoms, you could be overtraining:

- **Extended periods of fatigue:** If your legs are feeling heavy and you find yourself feeling drained of energy, take this as a sign that you should rest.

- **Difficulty sleeping:** Sufficient exercise can lead to a restful night's sleep. Overtraining, though, can lead to insomnia. Sleep is vital to adequate recovery and healing of your muscles.

- **Agitation, depression, or an inability to relax:** The correct amount of exercise leaves you feeling energized and with a peaceful, focused mind. Too much exercise can have the opposite effect, leading to exhaustion and hormonal imbalances. If you find yourself moody or irritable, or if you're having trouble concentrating, schedule some rest time.

- **Weakened immune system:** Too much exercise can stress your body's abilities to ward off colds, sore throats, or upper-respiratory infections.

- **Sore muscles and joints:** An unusually hilly ride or fast run leaves you with aches a day or two or after your training. If these muscle aches never seem to go away or your joints hurt, this can indicate that you're not allowing your body enough time to recover.

- **Increasingly difficult training sessions:** If a normally easy training session feels harder than usual, a break might be in order. Look for reduced speeds or fatigue that hits before you reach your base mileage or time.

- **Increase in resting heart rate:** Fitness _reduces_ your resting heart rate. If your heart rate takes longer than usual to return to its resting rate or if you feel your heart is racing, give yourself time in your schedule for additional rest.

- **Loss of appetite:** Training for a triathlon requires enough calories. You may notice that you eat far more than you used to, while still losing or maintaining your weight. If your appetite wanes, though, that can be a sign that you've overtaxed your body.

- **Missed or irregular periods:** Overexercising, especially without the proper consumption of calories, can lead to changes in a woman's menstrual cycle, including irregular periods or _amenorrhea_ (cessation of periods).

If you experience any of the signs of overtraining, give yourself additional time between workouts to rest and recover and reduce the intensity of your individual workouts. Take a few days off; take a week off — it won't hurt your training as much as being overtrained will.

Wondering what to do during your time off? Treat yourself well. Sink yourself into a bath; indulge in a massage. Or try yoga or other relaxation techniques to clear your mind and focus on your goals.

If your symptoms persist even after some additional rest, seek the advice of your physician.

Preventing overtraining

Your best plan is to prevent overtraining in the first place. To do so, follow these guidelines to stay healthy and energized:

- **Go at your own pace.** Training with a group can help you to increase your speed, but you may also be tempted to train harder than your body is ready to. Don't push yourself to keep up with the fastest or strongest athlete in the group.

- **Don't try to catch up.** You can't cram for a triathlon like you might for a test. If you've missed some training time or you're not starting with the fitness level you need to follow an aggressive training schedule, you can injure yourself if you try to catch up. Instead, focus on slowly building your fitness over time.

✔ **Listen to your body.** Your body is your first coach. If you're using a personal trainer or coach, he may try to push you harder than you're ready for. It's okay to ask for more time.

✔ **Reduce or change your workouts.** Ease the intensity of your training or take some time off to cross-train with another activity or sport you enjoy.

✔ **Get enough rest.** Sleep is as important to your training as swimming, cycling, or running is. During your sleeping hours, your body recuperates and regenerates. Don't deny yourself this time to build on your strengths and store energy for your next workout.

✔ **Remember your goals.** We know it's easy to get caught up in the competitive spirit of a triathlon. But when we ask people about their original triathlon goals, few people state those goals in terms of winning or placing. Remember why you are training for a triathlon. Keep your goals — one of which should be to feel healthy and comfortable — in sight.

Treating Common Swim Injuries

Injuries caused by swimming are not nearly as common as those caused by running or cycling. In fact, swimming is the sport athletes turn to when they're injured in other sports. Still, swimming injuries can happen. In the following sections, we tell you what to look for.

Swimmer's ear

You may remember this common swimmer's ailment from your childhood — the pain can be hard to forget. You spend a carefree day in the pool, splashing and jumping, only to be awakened in the middle of the night with severe pain in your ear.

Swimmer's ear is an infection caused by moisture trapped in the ear canal. It can hit swimmers of any age, not just kids. The ailment can be painful, as well as chronic, and it often requires antibiotics (in the form of eardrops) to heal.

You can prevent swimmer's ear. Sure, you can jump on one foot and bang on the side of your head to get the water out of your ears, but there are easier ways. If you're prone to swimmer's ear, look for over-the-counter drops (such as Swim-EAR) that can help dry the ear canal. Earplugs also can help to keep the ears dry while swimming.

Swimmer's shoulder

Swimmer's shoulder is shoulder pain caused by the constant repetitive over-head movement of the arm and shoulder in the freestyle stroke. Swimmer's shoulder is an overuse injury brought about by increasing the duration of your training too quickly. Poor stroke form also can lead to swimmer's shoulder. If you're experiencing swimmer's shoulder, you may have soreness and swelling in the rotator cuff.

Take some time to rest your shoulder. When you return to the water, be sure to work on the swimming drills you find in Chapter 5 to develop proper form. And remember to stretch your upper body (shoulders, arms, chest, and back) before and after each swim (see Chapter 11).

As with any chronic injury, talk to your doctor if your pain does not subside.

Avoiding Common Cycling Injuries

Accidents aside, the majority of cycling injuries are caused by poor bike fit or by improper riding technique. If your bike is not fit to your body, you may experience neck, knee, and back pain, as well as hand or foot numbness. Usually these pains cause discomfort during and after your ride, making your ride less enjoyable. Occasionally, though, the pain can signal the beginning of an injury that can prevent you from riding at all.

In this section, we cover the most common pains of pedaling and tell you how to correct them.

If rest or changes to your bike fit don't help to heal your pain, talk to your doctor.

Knee pain

If you're feeling pain in your knees when you ride, start by checking your seat height or position. If your seat is too high, you'll feel pain in the back of the knee. If your seat is too low or too far forward, you'll have pain in the front of the knee.

If your seat is positioned correctly, the cause of your knee pain can be in your foot position. If you're using clipless pedals, bring your bike and shoes to your local bike shop so that a fit professional can check the angle. Improper foot position can cause tightness or stress on the *iliotibial band* (the ITB, a band of tissue that runs from the hip down the outside of the leg and past the knee), which causes pain on the outside of the knee or hip. Stretching the ITB also helps with the tightness. To stretch it, cross your right foot over your left and reach toward the inside of your left foot as close to the floor as you can, keeping a slight bend in your knees; repeat with your left foot crossed over your right and reach toward the inside of your right foot. You should feel the stretch in your hip.

Pedaling in too high of a gear (using a large ring in the front with a small cog in the rear), which requires extra muscle power in your legs, also can cause undue stress on the knee and result in pain. If your *cadence* (the number of times one of your legs completes a pedal stroke in one minute) falls below 80 to 100 rotations per minute, remember to change your gears so that you spin quickly and lightly, without needing to push down hard in each pedal stroke.

Knee pain can also occur as a result of poor pedaling form. If you pull your knee toward the bike or let it fall away from the bike during your pedal stroke, the pressure on your knee can cause pain. Remember to keep your knee in a circle that runs parallel to your bike's frame.

Spinning in very cold weather may bring about knee pain, too. If the weather is cold enough that your muscles never fully warm up and remain tight throughout your ride, you may experience knee pain due to the pulling against tight quadricep muscles. To ward off the chill, wear cycling gear suitable for the weather conditions.

You may experience other injuries, such as iliotibial band syndrome (ITBS), an injury we cover in the running section. Familiarize yourself with the injury risks for each sport so that you can identify pain that can be carrying into another sport. Whenever you experience joint or muscle pains when you ride, check your body form and your bike fit.

Neck and shoulder pain

Neck pain is a common complaint among cyclists and can leave you feeling drained, even when the rest of your body is ready for more.

When you're riding, be sure to lower and relax your shoulders to relieve the pressure. Sometimes, neck pain can be simply a matter of getting used to the position on the bike. Other times, you may just be in the wrong position. Your seat or handlebars may need to be adjusted. If you're leaning forward uncomfortably and putting too much weight on your hands, you may end up locking your elbows and, as a result, raising and tensing your shoulders to bear the weight.

It's best to have your bike adjusted for proper fit at your local bike shop. Some adjustments may put you in a more upright position. This position is less aerodynamic, of course, but you're better off sitting upright and riding comfortably than leaning forward and aching to stop.

Numbness

Even with padded cycling gloves, you may still experience numbness or tingling in your hands, especially your fingers, as you rest some of the weight of your upper body on your hands.

Change your hand position frequently to relieve the pressure. You can also shake your hands out occasionally to get the blood flowing again. And remember to relax your elbows and shoulders to let your arms take some of the pressure, so that your upper-body weight is not all supported by your hands. Let your lower back help to carry the load by keeping your hands light on the handlebars.

The position of your seat relative to your handlebars affects the amount of weight you're supporting on your hands. If your handlebars are too far forward or your seat is too far back or sloping downward, you'll have trouble relaxing your arms and elbows. Your local bike shop can make small adjustments in your handlebar or seat position that can make your ride more comfortable.

Saddle sores

Saddle sores are minor skin irritations that can be quite uncomfortable and can lead to painful infections. They sound as awful as they are, but you can get through your cycling training without them.

To avoid saddle sores, follow these tips:

- ✔ **Check your bike fit.** Get a saddle that's comfortable for you and have it positioned correctly. Some triathletes prefer a skinny saddle with little padding, but not everyone is comfortable on this type of seat. Others find the large, gel-cushioned seats more comfortable than the smaller saddles.

  Manufacturers make so many seats in a variety of sizes and gel cushioning that a little trial and error is all it takes to find the saddle that works best for you. Women-specific seats can provide extra comfort for women.

  Also, be sure your seat is positioned correctly. A seat that's too high or that dips forward can make you slide back and forth as you pedal, increasing friction points. Seek the assistance of a person experienced in bike fitting at your local bike shop to adjust the height, level, and position of your seat.

- ✔ **Stand frequently.** You don't have to wait for a hill to stand up out of the saddle to stretch your legs and relieve the pressure on your body. Standing also helps to improve circulation.

- ✔ **Adjust your riding position in the saddle, especially as you spin up and down hills.** Slide back in your saddle occasionally to change the pressure points.

- ✓ **Buy the best cycling shorts you can afford, with seamless and comfortable chamois.** Skip the skivvies, too. You'll be more comfortable without the extra seams of underwear. Cycling shorts are supposed to be worn without them. Really.

- ✓ **Use body lubricants to prevent chafing and irritation.** Find the product that is comfortable and works best for you. Apply the product generously to areas where you're experiencing chafing or anywhere your body is contacting your saddle. The product will feel strange at first, but that will go away quickly.

- ✓ **Stay clean.** This should go without saying, but make sure your shorts are clean and dry each time you ride. If you have only one pair of shorts, and you need them again for the next day, wash them and turn them inside out to allow the chamois to dry faster.

Running Injury Free

As a weight-bearing, high-impact exercise, running causes more injuries for triathletes than swimming and cycling do. Most running injuries occur when overzealous athletes go out too fast and hard. Running injuries can also be a result of poorly fitting or worn-out running sneakers or the surface on which you do most of your running.

In running, more than in cycling or swimming, remember to progress slowly.

Check your running shoes and replace them when they show obvious signs of wear. If you press your thumb into the sides of the cushioned soles of your running shoes and the rubber does not give at all, this can be an indication that your shoes are worn and are providing little give with the impact.

In the following sections, we cover common running injuries.

You can prevent most of these injuries by training smart — stretching and using properly fitting and well-cushioned running shoes. Replace your shoes every six months or roughly every 300 to 500 miles.

As with any injury, if your pain persists, consult a physician.

Iliotibial band syndrome

Iliotibial band syndrome (ITBS) is inflammation anywhere in the iliotibial band, from your hip to just below the outside of the knee, which can cause pain. ITBS is commonly caused by increasing intensity or duration too quickly, by running on banked surfaces (such as the shoulders of roads), or by excessive downhill running.

To treat ITBS, you need to get plenty of rest and do lots of stretching. Be sure to run on flat surfaces and ice the painful area after each workout. Also, check your running shoes for wear or improper fit.

Pulled hamstring

A *pulled hamstring* is an excessive stretch or tear in the hamstring muscle, which is located just below your butt and down to the back of your knee. It's commonly caused by starting a running session too fast without a proper warm-up or increasing intensity too quickly.

To treat a pulled hamstring, get plenty of rest, and use ice, compression, and elevation (you can remember this by the acronym *RICE*). Keep your runs slow and easy until your muscle is fully recovered and no longer feels tight or painful. And when you recover, remember to stretch your hamstring before and after your runs. (See Chapter 11 for a hamstring stretch.)

Runner's knee

Runner's knee is a wearing away of the cartilage under the kneecap, which results in pain and inflammation. Symptoms include pain under or on the sides of the kneecap, as well as swelling of the knee. It's commonly caused by overtraining, worn shoes, *overpronation* (see Chapter 3), weak quadriceps, and extensive downhill running.

To treat runner's knee, you need to rest from running or any other high-impact activity, ice the knee, and strengthen the quadriceps through weight training. Cross-train with pool running, easy cycling or swimming, and slowly return to running.

Shin splints

Shin splints are pain or tenderness along the inside of the shin usually half-way between the ankle and knee. You may feel greater pain as you start your run, and it will start to subside as the muscles become warmer. New runners experience shin splits more often than experienced runners because their legs are not used to being stressed the way they are in running. You may also experience shin splits if your shoes are worn or if you run on hard surfaces such as concrete sidewalks.

If your pain is severe, stop running. If your pain is mild, cut back on duration and intensity until the pain subsides. A half-hour before running, apply heat to the area in the form of heat packs or products such as Icy Hot or Ben Gay to stimulate and warm up the muscles. Apply ice to the shins after each workout and run on softer surfaces, such as trails and tracks. Check your shoes for wear and replace them if necessary. Gradually return to running.

Achilles tendonitis

Achilles tendonitis is inflammation of the large tendon located behind the ankle, connecting the calf muscle to the heel. Symptoms include pain close to the heel, between the calf muscle and the ankle, or along the tendon. Achilles tendonitis is commonly caused by tight calf muscles, which cause strain on the Achilles tendon.

To treat Achilles tendonitis, avoid running or doing any weight-bearing exercises until you can perform them pain free. Gradually return to running. Warm up and stretch the calf muscles before running. Strengthen the calf muscles by doing heel raises.

Plantar fasciitis

Plantar fasciitis is inflammation of the tissue on the bottom of the foot that runs from the heel to the base of the toes. Symptoms include pain at the base of the heel, which is most severe when you first step out of bed in the morning and at the beginning of a run. It's commonly caused by overtraining, worn or poorly fitting running shoes, a tight Achilles tendon, and tight calf muscles.

To treat plantar fasciitis, stop running if the pain is severe. Ice the area. Check and replace your sneakers, if necessary. Return to running gradually, after the pain has subsided. As with Achilles tendonitis, stretching and strengthening the calf muscles helps avoid this injury.

Training in Extreme Heat or Cold

As part of your training, depending on where you live, you'll face all kinds of weather. You may be surprised to find that you enjoy running in the rain or cycling on hot days far more than you thought you ever would. Still, you should be aware of how changes in climate affect your training and your health. We cover all this in the following sections.

Heading into the heat

Hot and humid weather can be taxing on your body. Head out adequately prepared and aware of the risks, knowing when to turn around and head home in the shade.

You'll expend far more energy on a hot day, because your heart will pump harder, working to cool the body as well as fuel the muscles. Your heart rate will rise faster.

To prepare yourself for hot and humid weather, slowly acclimate to it, if possible, heading outside for short, easy workouts. And try these tips for staying cool and safe:

- ✔ **Do your warm-up inside or in the shade before your workout.**

- ✔ **Place a little ice at the back of your neck or under a hat to help lower your body temperature.**

- ✔ **Take in plenty of fluids.** Drink *before* you're thirsty. Alternate between sports drinks and water in extremely hot weather to restore your electrolytes and sodium.

- ✔ **Don't drink caffeinated beverages before your warm-weather workouts or during your workouts.**

- ✔ **Always use sunscreen.** Protect your skin before you head out for a training workout. Use a water-resistant product designed for sports.

Training in temperatures higher than 80°F (27°C), with humidity greater than 50 percent to 60 percent can quickly lead to a variety of heat-related illnesses, some of which can be life threatening if not identified and treated. These illnesses are caused by increased body temperature, loss of fluids, and loss of electrolytes.

Here's what to look for when you're training in hot weather and what to do if you experience any of these symptoms:

- ✔ **Dehydration:** The early signs of dehydration include thirst, loss of appetite, dry skin, dark-colored urine, fatigue, weakness, chills, and headaches. Dehydration can be the first sign of a dangerous condition, so take it seriously.

  You can prevent dehydration by drinking plenty of water and replacing your electrolytes with a sports drink after periods of prolonged exercise or training in a hot environment.

- ✔ **Heat cramp:** If you lose salt and other electrolytes during prolonged exercise in hot weather, you may experience painful muscle cramps, most commonly in the calves. These cramps can strike during exercise or in the hours after.

  If you experience a heat cramp, stop exercising and rest in a cool place. Drink a sports drink to replace electrolytes.

- ✔ **Heat exhaustion:** Symptoms of heat exhaustion include headache, pale and clammy skin, dizziness, nausea, and muscle cramps. If you suddenly feel cold during a hot-weather workout, you may be experiencing the early signs of heat exhaustion.

Stop the training session immediately. Get to a cool place, rest, and drink electrolyte-replacing fluids.

✔ **Heat stroke:** Heat stroke is the most serious of the heat-related illnesses and can cause death. A person experiencing heat stroke has an elevated body temperature (possibly more than 104°F/40°C); confusion; seizures; rapid, shallow breathing; rapid pulse; unconsciousness; and dry, hot skin.

Know how to respond if you're training with someone who is experiencing heat stroke. Have the person lie down in a cool place, elevate the feet 12 inches, and call 911. Do *not* give the person anything by mouth if he's vomiting or unconscious.

It's always a good idea to train with a buddy, but having company is especially important in extreme weather. If you're training outside when the weather falls below freezing or temperatures exceed 90°F (32.2°C), have a training partner join you for safety.

Catching some cold

Training in extreme cold actually is less dangerous than training in extreme heat, but you still need to be prepared. In fact, you may find the hardest part about training in cold weather is finding the motivation to get out there, especially first thing in the morning.

Here are some guidelines for staying safe when you train in the cold (assuming you can get yourself out the door):

✔ **Dress appropriately.** Wear layers, especially layers close to your body that wick sweat away from your body. Your first layer should be a synthetic material that pulls the moisture away from your body and dries quickly. Consider a fleece layer for warmth. And then top that with a wind-resistant layer. Don't forget gloves and a hat.

✔ **Warm up and go slowly in the beginning of your workout.** Cold muscles tend to injure more easily.

You feel the strain from the cold weather the most on your bicycle. Your muscles take longer to warm up and stretch in the cold weather, making you susceptible to joint pain.

✔ **If you have asthma or other breathing-related illnesses, get the green light from your doctor before you head out into the cold.** Breathing the cold air can lead to chest pain or trigger an asthma attack.

✔ **Use sunscreen, even in the winter.**

✔ **Continue to hydrate, even when it's cold.** You may not feel yourself losing moisture as you would in the hot weather, but exercising in the cold can still be dehydrating, sapping you of energy and making it harder to stay warm.

Knowing when to go back inside

Experience helps you decide what you want to train through, and what you should roll over and sleep through (perhaps choosing a later-day indoor training instead). But certain weather and body conditions make that decision easy for you. Stay inside or get yourself indoors as soon as possible if you:

- Exhibit any signs of heat-related illness.

- Will be riding your bike in extremely high winds.

- See lightning or hear thunder.

- See high waves or flags indicating rip tides in open water (if you're planning to swim).

- Are aware that heat advisories are in effect or temperatures or wind chills are in the single digits.

- Notice a patch of hard, very red, or pale skin. Get inside and slowly warm this area. If any part of your body feels numb, especially fingertips and toes, get to a place where you can warm them.

- Begin to shiver excessively (whether it's hot or cold out) or experience a loss of coordination or slurred speech. If you have these symptoms, seek medical attention immediately.

Part IV
Planning for Race Day

The 5th Wave   By Rich Tennant

"You'd better get some rest before tomorrow's race. Yesterday, you fell asleep in 12 minutes and 18 seconds. Let's see if we can better that."

In this part . . .

Here you create a race-day strategy for peak performance. Chapter 13 tells why it's important to taper
your training (decrease the intensity) before your event.
We also give you an important checklist for packing your
race-day equipment. In Chapter 14, we offer a timeline to
help you prepare for your race start, as well as tips on
how to prep your transition area. We also give you some
race-day etiquette do's and don'ts.

If you're like most triathletes, you'll already be planning
for your next event before you cross the finish line.
Chapter 15 helps you evaluate your performance, revel in
your achievements, and plan for your next event.

Chapter 13

Counting Down to Race Day

· ·

In This Chapter

▶ Backing off on your training intensity

▶ Maintaining your positive focus

▶ Building your confidence

▶ Packing your gear

▶ Getting enough sleep before your event

· ·

You've been counting down to race day since you selected your event, focusing on the number of months — and then weeks — left to transform your body. Time's up!

As you face the final few weeks before your event, anxiety may start to outpace excitement. That's normal. And all the triathletes participating in your event are probably feeling some degree of the same, regardless of how experienced they are in the sport.

Your triathlon is like the final exam you've been studying for — or should've been — for anywhere from 12 to 30 weeks. It's where you put all your training to the test and, right now, you're probably feeling as if your only options are pass or fail.

In this chapter, you find out what to do as you approach race day to help ensure your success. Although it may seem counterintuitive, in the weeks leading up to your event, you'll be resting far more than you may be used to. We tell you why that's important and how to make the best of it. You also find a checklist of items you need to pack for your event and tips for staying calm, positive, and focused.

Tapering Your Training: Slowing Down as Your Event Approaches

As you approach race day, your natural inclination will be more, more, more, as you think you need to fill every free moment with training. But cramming as much training as possible into a few weeks won't improve your fitness — it'll wear you out. Instead, you want to taper your training.

Tapering (pulling back on the amount and intensity of your workouts) will be harder than it sounds. As you follow your training plan (see Chapter 10), you'll exercise less in the days before your event than you did even at the start of your training. And your workouts will be easy compared to the weeks before. Sure, take a day off. Sleep late. Skip the long ride.

But if you've been following your plan, this lighter load will feel like cheating. You may fear you'll lose all your hard-earned fitness in the few days leading up to your event. Not so. In fact, you won't be ready for your event if you *don't* cut back. And if your taper goes according to plan, the day before your event, you'll feel full of energy and eager to unleash it.

The length of your taper will be in proportion to the length of your race. If you're training for a Sprint event, you'll be on the course anywhere from an hour to two hours, so resting up for a few days to a week will give you plenty of energy stores for that time frame. If you're planning on an Ironman, though, you can be exerting yourself for as many as 17 or 18 hours — you'll want to stockpile your energy stores, so give yourself more time to ease up on your workouts.

Tapering is not about returning to or embracing new coach-potato ways. You still need to move your body. The week before your event, though, is not the time to push yourself or test your limits. Save that energy for your event.

Your taper will be as personal as your training. Some triathletes find they need longer to recuperate from an intense workout. If this is you, focus on the outside range of the tapering schedules.

If you're not ready for your event the week before your Sprint distance or four weeks before your Ironman, nothing you do in the weeks leading up to your race will make the event much easier. Going out and training hard until race day, though, can do plenty to wear you out and make you *less* prepared for your event.

During your tapering, especially in the week before your event, you may feel sluggish and heavy. This doesn't mean you've lost all your fitness — it's just your body storing fuel and rebuilding.

Here are our guidelines for tapering time periods for each race distance:

- ✔ **Sprint or Super Sprint:** For a Sprint or Super Sprint event, you'll take it easy for not much more than a week. If you're following the training schedules in Chapter 10, you'll notice that your training duration peaks at around 270 minutes during Week 11. From there, you'll cut back sharply (with no long workouts) to less than half that time during Week 12, the days before your event.

- ✔ **Olympic:** For the longer Olympic-distance event, you'll slow your effort starting about two weeks from race day. In Week 18 of your 20-week training program, you should be logging eight hours or more on the roads or in the water. In Week 19, you'll cut back to about seven hours, with nothing longer than a two-hour bike ride. In the final week before your event, you'll cut this time in half to just a little more than $3\frac{1}{2}$ hours or so of total training time.

- ✔ **Half-Iron:** Gradually begin to ease the intensity and duration of your workouts for a Half-Iron event about three to four weeks before your event date. During Week 20 of your 24-week program, you'll be putting in about 13 hours of training time. By Week 21, you'll be looking at fewer than ten hours, and at Week 24, you won't know what to do with yourself and all your free time — you'll spend only about four hours swimming, cycling or running.

- ✔ **Ironman:** Yes, Ironman triathletes do rest, but rest is relative when you've grown accustomed to training for 20 hours a week. As an Ironman-to-be, start to think about slowing down five weeks from your event, focusing on your final long runs and bike rides, and then cutting the time and distance starting around three weeks before race day.

Your easiest week of Ironman training is about equivalent to your toughest week in Sprint training. When you reach Week 26 of the 30-week Ironman program, you'll be racking up the miles, spending as many as 20-plus hours training. By weeks 27 and 28, you'll be reducing that time to about 17 hours each week. Two weeks before your event, you'll "slack off" and train for about eight hours. The week before your event, you'll be twiddling your thumbs after only four hours of training. (To put that in agonizing perspective, that's the same time as your *peak* training week for a Sprint.)

Maintaining your nutrition

Cutting back on training during your taper doesn't mean you cut back on calories or nutrition. Continue to eat sensibly, including carbohydrates, proteins, and fats in your diet.

When preparing for your triathlon, you need to stay hydrated, but don't drink so much water that you over-hydrate and potentially deplete your potassium or sodium stores. Drink water, as well as sports drinks with electrolytes and sodium.

Don't step on a scale. You may put on a few pounds during your tapering period because you won't be burning as many calories as you were just a few weeks before. But you'll need these calories for your race. Don't skimp on your nutrition.

Tapering is not the time to cram in more work or run around doing errands. It's time to relax, focus positively on your race, and get plenty of rest.

When you're not filling your days with laps in the pool and loops on the road, you'll have some extra time to practice your transitions. Set up your transition area and make sure everything is in the order that works best for you. The more you go through the motions of transitions, the more they become a routine, leaving you one less thing to stress over.

Staying positive and focused can be your greatest challenge during your taper period. Without the regular workouts to reassure you that your muscles will perform as they've promised to do over the past few weeks, it's easy to second-guess your readiness for your triathlon. Don't be tempted to squeeze in one final test run at a fast pace just to know you can do it. Trust your training. You've stocked up on fitness for the past few weeks. Think of this week as your time to let it earn dividends.

The ultimate goal of your taper is to ensure that you're ready for your event — in mind and body.

Getting into Your Head: Staying Positive and Focused

As race day approaches, you may start wondering, "What was I thinking?" During your tapering session, when you're not as focused on maintaining proper training form and fitting in the training minutes, your mind may begin to wander. In this quiet time, fear and self-doubt can work their way into your head, and as you plan out your race day — when to arrive, where to go, what to do — all the scary what-ifs can create a day of high waves, high winds, and even higher hills.

If you let your fears take over, your fitness won't serve you as well as you'd like. Everyone, from the veteran triathlete to the first-timer, has fear and self-doubt when it comes to race day. If you're a new triathlete, you'll battle the fear of the unknown, as well as your fear of failure.

Some of your worries will be conquered only by crossing the finish line. Others you can overcome with planning and focus.

Overcoming common fears

Now that your event is only days away, you may be thinking, "What have I gotten myself into?" It's normal to be nervous. If you find yourself anxious enough that you're losing sleep worrying over an aspect of your event or are distracted by fears, this section helps you break down those fears and put them in perspective.

Many first-timers are afraid that they'll find themselves in the middle of a body of water with no way to get back to shore. Even after training for the swim, especially in open water, you still may be dreading this first leg of your triathlon. Plus, you may find yourself standing at the water's edge for up to an hour waiting for your wave to start — which gives your mind all kinds of time to work itself up into a frenzy.

Regardless of your event distance, the swim is the shortest leg of your triathlon and will be over before you know it. The difference between the swim and the bike and run legs of the triathlon, though, is that you can't just stop and stand still to catch your breath. You can stop pedaling on your bike and coast for a while. You can stop running and walk. These are comfortable movements most people are familiar with. But being in the middle of a body of water is not an everyday happening for most people. It's easy to understand how the swim concerns many first-timers.

You can take a break, and many swimmers do. Whenever you need to catch you breath, calm your nerves, or make sure you're heading in the right direction, lift your head out of the water and do a breaststroke or even a dog paddle. You can also float or do the backstroke or hold onto a guard boat or buoy.

Make transitions simple

Very few first-timers are as concerned with their performance in the three sports as they are fearful of fumbling through the transitions, forgetting something important, or finding themselves in an empty transition area while the rest of the triathletes have gone on without them.

If the potential intensity of getting all your gear together during the transitions makes you sweat, the best solution for this is to go outside, even in your driveway, and set up a mock transition area. Practice going from one sport to the next as simply and quickly as possible, and consider having a friend or family member time you, just for fun.

When you get to the point that you can reach for your cycling shoes and strap on your helmet without even thinking, you'll have less to worry about and more energy to enjoy your event.

Focus on how far you've come

When you're only days away from your event, it's easy to fear that you could've trained better and that you may not be well enough prepared.

Use the downtime during your taper period to think about all the great runs you've had, the ride when you felt as if you could climb hills forever, the time when swimming seemed effortless — and imagine feeling that strong as you complete each leg of your event.

Meet up with friends you've made through your triathlon club and talk to others who may be feeling the same way. Someone may remind you of your first run, when you thought you'd never complete a mile, and point out how you can now comfortably run 5 miles.

To keep the negative thoughts out of your head, focus on all you've accomplished by getting to the *starting line* on your race day. You will have self-doubt — everyone does. What matters is how you *respond* to the self-doubt.

Be prepared and on time

If you're having dreams about pulling into the parking lot of your triathlon as the swimmers plunge into the water or arriving in the transition area without your bike, you're not alone. It's common to worry that you won't have all your equipment or enough time to set up. Or that you'll wander the event grounds not being able to find the portable bathrooms.

The more prepared you are for race day, the less anxiety you'll have. Mentally plan the day well before it arrives. Imagine yourself calmly:

- ✔ Arriving at your triathlon site with time to spare
- ✔ Setting up your transition area
- ✔ Knowing exactly where to find your bike
- ✔ Looking strong and confident as you wait for your wave to start
- ✔ Sighting easily throughout the swim
- ✔ Pacing yourself on the bike and in your run

Don't even think about what can go wrong — there's no point in letting your mind go there.

If you have the opportunity, go to the race site ahead of time and check out the course to get familiar with it. Or consider volunteering at a local triathlon to observe how everything works. Knowing as much as you can about the energy and activity of races will help you feel more like you belong when your race day arrives.

Practicing pumping yourself up

No matter how prepared you are physically and mentally, participating in a triathlon will give you the jitters. Your stomach will have butterflies; your hands will be shaky or sweaty. It's all normal. But letting it get the better of you can cause you to run out of steam before you even get started.

You can measure your fitness gains over the course of your training. But race day is where you measure your character. Embrace this moment. Accept your feelings and take that step toward your fear. The tools you've acquired during your training will carry you through the miles.

If you still have doubts, try one of the following techniques to get you through the rough moments:

- ✔ **Remember to breathe.** When you're stressed, you may be holding your breath without even realizing it. Use standard relaxation techniques — such as deep, controlled breathing or meditation — to help calm your nerves in the days before your event and as you stand around waiting for your wave.

- ✔ **Believe it.** This is not the time to think about the training session you missed or the session in which you could have pushed yourself harder. Your body is far stronger than you think it is. Know that the strength is there.

- ✔ **Relive your successes.** Remember your toughest training. Think about what got you up that hill or through that last lap when you wanted to stop.

- ✔ **Repeat a mantra to yourself.** If you don't have a mantra, take ours: You can do this. When the going gets tough, get the focus back on the positive. Cheer yourself on. Count. Calmly tell yourself "You can do this" again and again in time with your pace — anything to keep your mind off your fears and on your performance.

- ✔ **Be kind.** Imagine you're actually the person standing next to you. Would you tell that person to worry or that he may not be ready? Would you tell her that she should've trained harder? Encourage yourself, just as you would anyone else.

- ✔ **Laugh.** It's remarkably stress relieving. Enjoy this experience. Don't take it — or yourself — too seriously. Remember to have fun.

✔ **Think of a past challenge you can call up at will.** When self-doubt threatens to steal your confidence, focus your thoughts on how you felt when you mastered this task.

✔ **Shake it out.** Take a moment to think about where your shoulders are. If they're hunched up close to your ears, you're wasting energy and creating tension in your muscles. Lower your shoulders and breathe. Swing your arms and shake out your legs. Imagine all the tension rolling down through your fingers and toes and out onto the ground.

✔ **If all else fails and you feel yourself slipping, remember not to let anyone see it.** Think like a duck — calm and composed on the surface; paddling with everything you've got underneath. Don't let others know how exhausted or nervous you are. That gives your feeling more power than you may like it to have. If you pretend you're unruffled, you'll start to believe it, too.

✔ **Stop and assess.** Sometimes, you'll just want to plow through without over-thinking your next step. But know that it's okay to stop to compose yourself. If you're feeling overwhelmed and can't get your focus back, stop moving. Take a drink if you need to. Breathe. Take the focus away from your movement for a moment to allow yourself to get your mental focus back.

Packing for Race Day

Pack for race day when you're relaxed and not rushed. Use a checklist to help you pull together your gear. If you haven't worn it, eaten it, or used it, don't bring it.

Visit the race Web site or contact the organizer to find out what they'll be serving at your event — including gels, sports drinks, and, depending on the length of your race, any solid foods. If what they're serving is what you've been training with, then that's less that you have to pack. If it's not, then pack all your favorite and training-tested energy aids and make sure you have enough — bring more than you think you'll need.

Checking your gear for wear

Check your gear before you even begin to pack for your event. Closely inspect any equipment that's essential to your race — bike, helmet, wetsuit, or running shoes.

Tuning up your bike

Take your bike for a tune-up at your local bike shop a few weeks before your event. If you can't get to the bike shop, be sure to:

- ✔ **Check your tires for wear.** Rub any debris — such as glass, metal, or rocks — off the tires.

- ✔ **Check your brake pads for wear.** Roll your bike forward and squeeze the front and rear brake levers separately to be sure that they stop your bike.

- ✔ **Inspect, clean, and lube your chain.**

- ✔ **Check your seat height.**

Three or four days before your event, head out for a short, easy ride to make sure you're comfortable and that your bike is operating correctly.

Inspecting your swim gear

Goggles are easy to toss in your bag and forget about, but if you haven't checked them for wear, they can seriously impact your swim. Your goggles can lose suction as they get old. Wear them one last time in a swim during your taper weeks, paying attention to how they fit:

- ✔ Adjust the straps for comfort.
- ✔ Check the nose pad for areas that may be rubbing.
- ✔ Notice whether water is seeping past the seals.

If your goggles need to be replaced, purchase the same type as you used in training and try them out in the water before packing them in your race bag.

Reviewing your clothing

Pull out every item of clothing you'll wear — socks, shoes, tri suit, wetsuit, hats, sunglasses, gloves. Make sure they're all clean and ready to go. Be sure you've worn each item a few times during training so that you know that it fits comfortably without any *hot spots* (areas that rub or chafe).

If you notice just days before your event that your running shoes have excess wear, don't panic — and don't replace them. Now is not the time to buy anything new. If you wore the shoes recently on a training run and didn't notice the wear as you ran, then don't worry. You're better off running in your current shoes than in a new pair.

Knowing what to pack

Your equipment checklist is probably one of the most important lists you'll make prior to packing for race day. For help in creating a packing checklist, go to `http://triathlon.racechecklist.com`. Select items from its list of essentials and add your own. Print your checklist and keep it with your bag as you pack. The best checklist will be one that breaks down your gear into each leg of the race and identifies the must-haves and the nice-to-haves.

Get a large gym bag into which you can pack all your gear. Make sure the bag is easy to carry or roll because all your gear can get heavy, and you'll have to get your bike to the transition area. If you're traveling, plan to bring a bag separate from the clothing and personal-care items you'll need for your stay.

Pack the items in Table 13-1 into your race day bag and check off the Packed column as you do. Add your own items, as needed.

Table 13-1	Your Equipment Checklist		
Swim	**Must-Have**	**Your Call**	**Packed**
Swimsuit	X		
Goggles (two pairs)	X		
Wetsuit		X	
Earplugs		X	
Body lubricant		X	
Tri suit		X	
Anti-fog for goggles		X	
Bike	**Must-Have**	**Your Call**	
Bicycle	X		
Helmet	X		
Gloves		X	
Tubes and tools	X		
Tire pump or CO_2	X		
Protective glasses	X		
Cycling shoes		X	
Socks		X	
Water bottle	X		
Cycling clothing		X	
Race belt		X	

Run	Must-Have	Your Call	
Running shoes	X		
Swim	**Must-Have**	**Your Call**	**Packed**
Socks		X	
Hat		X	

General Race Day Items	Must-Have	Your Call
Towel for transition area	X	
Sunscreen	X	
Directions to event	X	
Photo ID	X	
Race packet/number	X	
Favorite nutrition/drinks	X	
Pre- and post-race clothing	X	

Check, double-check, and triple-check your list to make sure you have everything you need and want.

This is not a cruise, so over-pack if you need to. A triathlon is one of those rare times when it's better to pack and haul around too much than to go light and forget something.

You don't have to pack all in one day. Set aside time without distractions and keep your checklist handy to make sure you don't forget anything.

One Sheep, Two Sheep: Logging Enough Shut-Eye

Your week of tapering may not be as restful as you imagine. As you reduce your training time, you may see an effect in your ability to sleep. Maybe you're not as tired at the end of the day as you were during your peak training. Maybe you're not relieving as much stress as you have been in the past week. Or maybe your mind is racing — taking you through your event over and over again.

Trying to sleep before your event is a little like trying to sleep before the first day of school. Your clothes are set out. You're excited. You're nervous. You've been waiting for — or dreading — this day for weeks. You've bought supplies. You've packed your bag. You may be looking forward to seeing old friends or to making new ones. You'll be going to bed early and probably checking your alarm every few minutes, or even throughout the night.

If sleep doesn't come easily to you, or it's interrupted during the night, try these tricks for getting some shut-eye:

✔ Avoid training for at least three to four hours before going to bed.

✔ Skip the caffeine, alcohol, or any other stimulants after 4 p.m.

✔ Don't go to bed full or hungry.

✔ Limit TV time and don't watch it in your bedroom.

✔ Use your bed solely for sleeping.

✔ Try old-school remedies, such as a warm bath, warm milk, or caffeine-free herbal tea.

✔ Keep your room as dark as possible.

✔ Relax your body one part at a time. Start with your toes — squeeze them tightly for 10 seconds, and then release. As you release, exhale and feel yourself melting into your bed. Then squeeze your entire foot. Move up to your calf, and continue to all your body parts.

If you're traveling for your event, your location may present an additional sleep challenge. You're in an unfamiliar bed, maybe even in a hotel with a raucous wedding party. If you're in a different time zone, you may be going to bed at what feels like dinnertime. Try these tips for getting some sleep away from home:

✔ **Arrive two to three days before your event.** This will give your body more time to adjust.

✔ **If you've traveled far, jump onto the schedule where you are.** Reset your watch and don't calculate what time it is back home. Live as if you're in the zone.

✔ **Go to bed when the clock, not your body, says so.** If you've traveled east, your body may be telling you it's 7 p.m., but the clock says 10 p.m. A few hours before your bedtime, draw the curtains and lower the lights to prepare yourself for sleep.

Chapter 14

Race Day: Ready, Set, Go!

In This Chapter

▶ Knowing when to arrive at your event and how to spend your time

▶ Picking up your race packet

▶ Prepping your transition area

▶ Minding your manners at every stage of the event

*Y*ou've trained and prepared for this day, and it's finally here. If you're a little nervous, don't worry — that's normal. Even experienced Ironman triathletes get race anxiety. Trust in your training and think positively. You worked hard to be at the start line, and you're going to finish with a smile on your face. John Wayne once said, "Courage is being scared to death but saddling up anyway!" Doing anything for the first time can be scary. But the hard part is over — the training. Now comes the fun!

In this chapter, you get a feel for what to expect when you arrive at your event, from checking in to staging your transition area. We also give you tips for staying focused and positive while waiting for your start time. There are race day rules of etiquette you should know and follow, and you'll find them at the end of this chapter.

By understanding what you need to do before the event, you'll lessen your anxiety and give yourself more time to savor each moment of your big day.

Picking Up Your Packet

Event organizers put together a *race packet* for each participant. A race packet is an envelope containing race day instructions, your race number, and other items you'll need at your event (see the next section for more on what's in the packet). Depending on the size of the race, you'll most likely need to pick up your race packet a day or two before your event.

When you go to pick up your packet, be sure to bring photo identification (a driver's license will do), as well as any necessary association membership cards that you may have used for your race registration or discounts.

Many popular triathlons conduct expos the day before or even two days before race day. Make sure to go to this expo — not only to scope out the area and collect tons of free stuff — but also because this is where you'll need to pick up your race packet.

Often race directors organize a pre-race meeting during the race expo, and sometimes this meeting is mandatory for participants. Even if it's not, plan to attend. You'll get specific instructions on preparing for the event, where to rack your bike, and where to go for your start time. You'll also learn important information about the course and route changes or hazards. All this will help you feel more prepared and confident about where to be and when on race day.

Many events do not allow you to pick up your race packet on the day of the event. Find out in advance of your race day by calling your event organizer or checking the procedures on the event Web site. If your event is far from home, you have already made arrangements to arrive at least a day before your event, so you should have time to pick up your packet.

What's in your race packet and why you need it

Your race packet contains all kinds of important information you need in order to be prepared on race day. Here's what you'll find in it:

- **Race number and safety pins:** Also sometimes called a *race bib,* your race number identifies you in the event so that race organizers know who you are and that you're a registered participant. Race numbers are printed on durable, weather- and rip-resistant paper and usually also identify the event and event date. You'll use the safety pins or a race belt to attach your race number to your tri suit or shirt.

  Race numbers are fun to collect, so hold on to yours after the event!

- **Wristlet:** Some event organizers provide a paper bracelet that you must wear to any race-related activities, including events and workshops at the expo and the race meeting. The wristlet may be required for entrance to the transition areas.

- **Numbers for bike and helmet:** Many race organizers supply bike race numbers. The bike number will have adhesive strips at the top and bottom — you wrap the number around your top tube, and remove the paper from the sticker and press the two pieces together. Or your number may come with plastic ties so that you can secure it to your bike. You may also receive a number to attach to the front of your helmet.

✔ **Timing chip:** Timing chips give you a more accurate measurement of your individual race time than the race clock you see at the finish line. The timing chip records the time you start the event and when you finish, as well as tracks when you enter and exit transition areas, so you'll know how long each leg took and how much time you spent transitioning. When you complete your event, you return the timing chip to volunteers.

✔ **Swim cap:** If the event organizer requires a swim cap, most likely they'll provide one. The caps will be color-coded for your *wave* (the time you start your swim).

✔ **T-shirt:** Many events offer T-shirts to participants, which are often given to you when you pick up your packet. We don't recommend wearing this shirt during your event. Stuff it into your bag and wear it proudly in the days following your event.

✔ **Flyers for more fun:** In your packet, you may find flyers and registration forms for triathlons or road races. Tuck these back into your bag for now. You can plan your next event after you finish this one.

✔ **Race instructions:** Often, you'll find a printed instruction list for your event, including the course map or any changes to a map you've received from the event organizer. Review this carefully and hold on to the instructions if they contain information you may need later in the day or on race day.

✔ **Transition info:** This includes information on the location and structure of the transition area and where to set up, if necessary.

Event organizers often spend a great deal of time obtaining free stuff to give to triathletes. On race day, you'll receive a bag in which they've placed all the goodies or in which you can collect them as you make your way around the check-in area or the expo. Some people call these items *swag*. Free stuff is great, but don't use any of it on race day unless it's product you've already tried and tested. Save any nutrition bars or blister pads for a future training day. You may also be lucky enough to find coupons or maybe even a discount for a massage at a local spa in your bag.

Steps to a stress-free packet pickup

The steps to your packet pickup may vary slightly from event to event. Here are the basic steps in the order that they're most likely to occur in a triathlon. You can get more information on your specific event by checking online on your race's site.

1. **Locate your race number.**

   For large events, organizers often have sheets of paper listing participants' names, alphabetically by last name. They'll tack these onto boards set up outside the tents where you'll pick up the first pieces of your race packet or on the walls outside the room where you'll get your race packet. Find your name, and then look next to it for your race number. Remember your number or write it down. On-site computer searches also are becoming a popular way for users to look up their race numbers in popular triathlons with thousands of registered racers. But smaller events may process packets by last name. If you don't see listings of race numbers, your event may have lines split into alphabetic ranges (A–E, F–J, and so on).

2. **Proceed to the appropriate line.**

   You need your race number to find the appropriate line in which you can pick up your race packet. Volunteers will have set up tables for ranges of numbers — for example, 100 to 199, 200 to 299, and so on. Find the range of numbers in which your race number falls and get in that line for your race packet.

3. **Pick up your timing chip.**

   You may need to go to a separate table or tent in the check-in area to pick up your timing chip. If so, you'll need to present your race number or wristband as evidence that you're a registered participant.

4. **Pick up your other goodies.**

   Some event organizers give you everything at one table. Others have you move from area to area to collect all your stuff and possibly wait in long lines for the best free products.

5. **Cap it off.**

   If your swim cap was not included in your race packet, you'll need to proceed to the table where you can collect your cap and present your race number or wristband here as well.

6. **Get ink.**

   All participants in the event will need to be "marked" with their race numbers. Volunteers will write on your skin with a permanent marker. You'll leave the marking area with your race number and your age and gender marked on your body — for example, 3213 F41, for participant 3213, who is a 41-year-old female. If your event features more than one distance, you may also receive a letter (*S* for sprint, *O* for Olympic, and so on). Elite athletes may be marked with an *E*. The marked number is a way of identifying you in the swim or if for some reason your number falls off during the race. The coding can also help you identify who you're passing or who's passing you.

7. **Talk it up.**

Review your race instructions or the postings around the check-in area to find out when the pre-race meetings will take place and find a time that fits into your schedule, especially if the meeting is mandatory.

For safety reasons, you won't be permitted to race if you haven't attended a meeting that was identified as mandatory.

Arriving on Race Day

Awaken at least three hours prior to your event, plus the time you need to travel to the event location. If your wave starts at 8 a.m., and you live an hour from the event site, you'll want to be up by 4 a.m.! Here's how you'll spend that time, assuming an 8 a.m. start time and a one-hour drive:

Time before Race Time	Estimated Time	Activity
4 hours	4 to 5 a.m.	Awaken, eat a light breakfast, drink a glass of water, and prepare for departure. Don't forget to make one last visit to your bathroom before you leave.
3 hours	5 to 6 a.m.	Travel time (assuming an hour's drive — adjust according to your distance from the event).
2 hours	6 to 7 a.m.	Arrive at event location, park, and get your gear to the transition area and set up. **Note:** If you haven't checked in and picked up your race packet, allow another half-hour for this process.
1 hour	7 to 7:30 a.m.	Stretch, warm up, focus your thinking, and visit the portable restrooms one last time.
30 minutes	7:30 to 7:50 a.m.	Put on your wetsuit, if you'll be wearing one, and your swim cap.
5 to 10 minutes	7:50 or 7:55 a.m.	Arrive and get set at your designated start area for the swim.

The morning of your event, plan to put on at home what you'll wear for the event — a swimsuit if you've decided that works best for you, or your tri suit. Do not put on your wetsuit — do this just before the swim. Over your swimsuit, put on clothing appropriate for the weather.

Before you leave, double-check your gear, pump your bike tires, and make sure you have everything you'll need before heading out the door. If you've already picked up your race packet, be sure you have that with you as well.

Plan to arrive an hour to two hours before your event start time, depending on how much you accomplished the day before. Do you have anything else to pick up? Do you still need to be marked? If so, give yourself the full two hours. The bigger the race, the more time you should leave. Consider that you may have to battle traffic and find parking, and then get from the parking lot to the event start with all your gear.

It may seem as if we're suggesting leaving a lot of time pre-start, but you won't want to feel rushed when you're getting ready. You're better off sitting around with some extra time to stretch and tweak your transition setup than having to throw things together and race off.

Preparing for Your Start Time

You've arrived at your event, parked your car, and pulled all your equipment out of the trunk or off the roof. Now what? It's time to have your bike checked, get your gear ready in the transition area, stretch, and focus on the race ahead.

Having your bike checked and approved

Take your bike for a safety check, if necessary. Your event may require that your bike and helmet be approved before you participate. If so, before you enter the transition area, volunteers will perform a quick safety check on your bike and your helmet. They'll test the brakes to be sure they work and other parts to make sure they're secure. They'll evaluate your helmet to ensure, at least visibly, that it's in good shape and meets safety-code certifications.

Staging your transition stall

The *transition area* is where you'll stage your bike, shoes, helmet, hydration, and nutrition for the cycling and running legs of your race. Each individual section of the transition area is called a stall; basically, a stall (like the one shown in Figure 14-1) is the small amount of space to which you lay claim. If you've battled your way into a popular class at a gym trying to squeeze weights, a step platform, and your body into an area not big enough for *you* let alone you moving, then you're prepared for claiming space in a transition area.

Get your gear to the transition area as early as you can. Give yourself 30 to 60 minutes to find a transition stall and set up your equipment.

Put on blinders as you walk through the transition area, especially if it's your first triathlon. As you pass all the other triathletes, you'll no doubt assume that they're more experienced, less nervous, and better equipped than you are. And you'll forget what you do have and start to worry about what you don't. You'll distract yourself, thinking, "Why don't I have that?", "Should I have that?", "Where did he get that?" Don't look. You have what you need; you have what you trained with; it's served you well. Relax.

Figure 14-1:
Although it may not appear so if you arrive early, the transition area gets crowded — and quickly.

© 2008 Stacey Smith

Setting up your transition area should be something that you've practiced a number of times in your training. We offer our recommendations, but after your training, you may have determined a system that works best for you. If you have a system, go with it. If not, try ours and adapt it to suit your needs.

Both transition areas, especially for sprint-distance events, are usually in the same location. For longer distances, though, sometimes your bike and run transitions can be in different locations. Ask your event organizer in advance. You'll want to be prepared if you need extra time or equipment to stage two transition areas.

Here are our recommended steps for staging your transition area:

1. **Find your transition stall.**

   Transition stalls are often assigned by race number. Look for a range of numbers at the end of each transition row, and find the row in which your race number falls. Depending on the event, you have only a designated row or an assigned spot.

If you're assigned a row only, bikes will be racked first-come, first-served. Spots closest to the transition exits are more desirable, but don't feel as though you have to shuffle and scurry. You'll be fine wherever you rack your bike. Find a spot that feels comfortable, not competitive.

If your event allows you to rack your bike in any available spot, the earlier you arrive, the better chance you'll have of getting a spot near an exit.

2. **When you get to your spot, rack your bike.**

Racks generally are constructed of pipes or wood, much like sawhorses. The best way to rack your bike is to push your bike, rear wheel first, under the bar, and then pull your bike toward you and lift it up to rest the nose of the saddle on the bar, lifting the rear wheel off the ground (as shown in Figure 14-2).

Figure 14-2: To position your bike in the transition area, push your bike under the bar of the rack, rear wheel first, and then pull your bike toward you, lifting the saddle up and placing the nose of the saddle onto the rack.

© 2008 Stacey Smith

3. **Load your bike.**

Equip your bike with the hydration and nutrition you'll need for the ride. Put full bottles in the bottle cages of your bike. Tear open a corner of each gel pack or nutrition bar so that you can open it easily with one hand while riding. Tape the gel packs or nutrition bars to your handlebars or top tube, positioning the tapes on the tops of the wrappers so that you can pull the packs or bars to you, leaving the top sections of wrappers on your top tube. Also, make sure you've added an additional tire tube, CO_2 cartridge, and tire-changing tools to your saddle bag.

4. **Check your tires for rough spots or road debris that can puncture one of your tubes.**

5. **Pick a side.**

   Now that you have your bike racked and ready, take a look at where everyone else in your row is setting up their equipment — to the right or left of their bikes — and do the same.

   Keep your wetsuit, goggles, swim cap, and timing chip in your bag for now — you'll take the bag out of the transition area with you to get ready for your swim. Remember, though, when you return to the transition area after your swim, you'll be leaving behind your swim gear. Think about where to best position this so that it's not in the way of reracking your bike or putting on your running shoes.

6. **Lay down a towel.**

   Start by spreading a small towel onto which you can set your shoes. Most transition areas are set up on grass, gravel, or dirt. A towel protects you and your equipment from pebbles where you don't need them (in your shoes) and helps you stake out a small space on the ground as yours. On this towel, you'll set up your gear in the order you're going to use it, except your swim gear, which you'll be taking with you out of the transition area.

7. **Set out your cycling shoes.**

   You require the most equipment for the cycling portion, and it's what you'll need first after your swim, so arrange it for easy access and in the order you'll put it on. When you come back to the transition area after your swim, you'll be taking off your swim gear and setting that aside and putting on your cycling shoes or running shoes, so place them on the edge of the towel closest to you.

   Open your shoes as wide as possible so that you can slip in your feet quickly. If you're wearing running shoes for your bike leg, place your sneakers at the edge of the towel and open them wide with the tongues pulled up and out so that your feet can slide right in. If you plan to wear socks, place these on top of your shoes.

   Some experienced and competitive triathletes clip their cycling shoes onto their bike pedals to save time. Then they walk barefoot out of the transition area, slide one foot at a time against the opposite leg to brush off dirt or gravel, slip one foot into a shoe on the pedal, give themselves a push off with the other foot, swing the leg over the back of the bike while moving, start pedaling and then slip the other foot into the shoe. If you decide to try this method, be sure to practice it a lot and often during your training.

8. **Get your helmet ready.**

   Set your helmet on the handlebars of your bike, with the chin strap open and pulled to the outsides of your helmet. Be sure you've adjusted the straps to fit before the event. Be sure your helmet is secure on top of the handlebars, or loop a strap over a brake lever to help ensure it'll still be there when you return and not on the ground after being knocked off by another bike as it was removed quickly from the rack.

9. **Position your sunglasses.**

   If you wear sunglasses while cycling — and you should — they'll be next. Place your sunglasses with the arms straddling the saddle, in a way similar to how they go on your head, so that they don't fall off if someone bumps your bike. Or you can place them in your helmet so that you can take them out first and put them on before you strap on your helmet.

10. **Set out your gloves.**

    Wearing cycling gloves during a triathlon is a personal preference. Donna doesn't wear them for Sprint- or Olympic-distance events but wouldn't go without them for a Half-Iron or full Ironman.

    Weigh the time it will take you to get them on and off against the comfort they provide to you when riding. If your hands are uncomfortable when riding without gloves, and you don't mind spending the seconds it will take to put them on, wear them. If you can ride without gloves and do so often, you can choose to skip them.

    If you decide on gloves, open the glove for your right hand and slide that onto the end of the handlebar on the right side of your bike. Put the glove for your left hand on the left handlebar. Be sure the gloves are as far up on the handlebars as they can go so that they don't fall off if your bike is bumped.

11. **Get your running shoes ready.**

    If you're wearing cycling shoes for the bike leg, place your running shoes on the opposite end of the towel in the direction in which you can step into them, laces open and tongues pulled out.

12. **Pin on your race number.**

    Use the safety pins in your race packet to pin your race number to the back of the shirt you'll wear while running, or ask for assistance to pin the number onto the back of your tri suit.

    Do not pin your race number to your wetsuit. The safety pins will damage the wetsuit material. And you'll have to fumble with pins when you're wet and rushed to get your number off your suit and onto your cycling jersey or shirt.

TIP

On the bike leg of your triathlon, you'll want your race number on your back. When you run, though, your race number needs to be in the front. Some triathletes use a *race belt,* a narrow elastic strap that clips together quickly and has two snaps that hold your race number. Attach your number to the belt and drape the belt over the top tube of your bike. When you strap it on for the cycling leg, you can maneuver the number around to your back. When you set out to run, you simply pull the number toward your front. Practice riding and running with a race belt to ensure it's comfortable before your event.

13. **Place your shirt on your saddle or across your top tube.**

If you'll be adding a shirt before you get on the bike, place it on your saddle, front side down. Or drape it over your top tube if you have sunglasses on your saddle.

14. **Get your heart-rate monitor ready.**

If you plan to wear your heart-rate monitor during the event, open the strap and drape that onto your saddle on top of your shirt.

15. **Check and recheck.**

Your transition area is set (see Figure 14-3). Go over your transition area visually. Imagine coming back to the stall after your swim. Lay your eyes or your hands on every piece of equipment you'll need in the order in which you'll need to use it. Do the same for when you return from cycling and need to get ready to run.

Figure 14-3: Lay out your transition area using the method that works best and makes the most sense for you. This is a guideline that works well for most triathletes.

Photo by Ed Pagliarini

Stretching and focusing

As you prepare your transition area, you may notice other triathletes heading off to run, bike, or swim — or all three. Sometimes, another triathlete's warm-up can seem like your workout.

The best solution: Just don't look. Pay attention to what works for *you*. You'll want to warm up your muscles, and doing so will help relax your mind, too — and keep you focused.

Warm up

Give yourself 30 minutes to move your muscles. Then take your bike for a short spin — and we mean spin. Use a low gear and a high cadence. You want to warm up your legs, not wear them out. If you can't get your bike from the transition area, run off the pre-race jitters with a short jog.

When you're moving around on the bike or on your feet, the trick is to not focus on the anxiety or that feeling that has come over you yet again that makes you think you need to find a restroom and fast. ***Remember:*** Everyone, even the experienced triathletes, is feeling the same. And you're probably keeping company with many more first-timers than you can guess. Look confident like they do — and you'll feel confident.

Get into the water

Some races allow you to warm up in the water only prior to the race start, so if you're in one of the later waves, you may have to get in the water, and then stand around for a half-hour until your wave starts. Other events designate a small area for participants to jump in and swim for a few easy minutes at any time before their wave starts.

When you're in the water, you can't see or hear anything that's going on around you, other than the water below you and the water ahead of you. It's a great way to clear your head before the start and to stretch your muscles, too.

Try to get in the water at some point before the start of the race. It helps to get a feel for any currents or waves and to be prepared for the water temperature. Donna has participated in triathlons in early June. The water temperature was a breathtakingly cold 55°F (13°C), so she knows firsthand that if you get in before your swim and let the cold water seep into your wetsuit, you'll have time to get over that initial shock without worrying about swimming, too.

After you've arranged your transition area, walk down to the spot where you'll enter the water. After doing any warm-ups in the water, walk or slowly jog the route you'll take back to the transition area, paying attention to the terrain. Know if you'll be climbing steps or running on sand or rocks or across a grassy field, and look for areas or obstacles you'll want to avoid when you return from your swim.

Stretch it out

After you have the blood flowing in your legs, do some gentle stretches. Remember to breathe and relax. Use this time to focus on how good you feel — and how flexible you've become and how strong and toned your muscles look.

Getting ready to start

About 30 minutes before your start time, head to the portable bathrooms one last time. (Nerves will probably have you feeling like you'll need to go again as you enter the water, but one last stop can't hurt.) Refer to your race instructions for the correct time to report to the pool or to the water.

Then find a spot with some space for yourself and start putting on your wetsuit. Follow these steps for getting into your wetsuit and getting your swim gear ready:

1. **Place your goggles on top of your swim cap with your timing chip so that you don't forget any of these items.**

2. **Apply lubricant and put on your wetsuit, if you're wearing one, just as you have during your training sessions.**

3. **Secure your timing chip around your ankle.**

   The timing chip will have a Velcro strap that wraps around your ankle. Secure it tightly but not so it's cutting into your ankle. You'll leave your timing chip on for the entire race.

Finding your wave

Most triathlons with open-water swims group swimmers into *waves* — groups of swimmers who will enter the water at the same time. Waves help to avoid the crush of every participant battling for first position in the water (see Figure 14-4). You'll be placed in a wave based on your age, unless you elected to register in a multi-age group so that you could participate with your friends.

Don't worry if you're not in the first set of waves. You'll be wearing a timing chip, so your actual start time and finish will be recorded.

In an open-water swim, you'll start either in a shallow section of the water or on the beach. Plan to hang back toward the end of the pack or to the side. You'll be less likely to be accidentally shoved and kicked in these positions. Expect arms and legs to be moving in all directions and water to be splashing.

Getting into your lane

If your triathlon has a pool swim rather than an open-water swim, you'll be placed in groups based on your predicted swim time when you completed your registration. Generally, groups of two will enter the lanes together at their assigned times.

In a pool swim, you'll start in the water holding onto the wall.

© 2008 Stacey Smith

Figure 14-4: Triathletes will enter the water in waves, or groups of swimmers who will start their triathlon together.

Where to put items you don't need during the triathlon

You may have your race packet or bag, clothing you wore to keep out the morning chill, your car keys, and other items you don't actually need for the event. Here are some options for storing your stuff:

✔ **Check your bag.** Some event organizers offer a secured baggage-check area for participants. After you've picked up your race packet and set up your transition area, if you have a bag you don't need, you can place it in the baggage-check area. You simply give the volunteers your bag, and they'll identify it in some way, usually with your race number. After the event, you can return to this area to pick up your belongings. Be sure to leave enough time to wait in line when checking your bag.

✔ **Store it in your car.** If you drove to the event and parked close enough to walk back to your car, bring the belongings you don't need back to your car and store them there, preferably locking them in the trunk. Be sure to keep your key with you somewhere safe; place it in the saddle bag of your bike or a zippered pocket or give it to someone who's there to support you.

✔ **Ask for help.** If friends or family have come to cheer you on, ask them to hold your bag or the gear you won't need for your event.

Taking You through the Tri

You've trained in each of the legs of the event and even put two together with a well-planned transition in the middle. So, think of your event as just another training session. Use all the tools you developed in your training, keep your cool, and have fun.

In this section, we take you through each leg of your triathlon on event day, offering some last-minute tips that will have you feeling like an experienced triathlete.

At the start

A start gun or siren will signal the beginning of your swim leg. When you hear the gun, enter the water and settle into a steady pace, paying attention to your own rhythm, not the pace of everyone around you. There will be faster swimmers and slower swimmers, and the person you thought you'd surely beat can be the first person to pass you, and vice versa.

The first few minutes of the swim are the most frantic. *Remember:* Everyone is there for the same reason, and they're all just trying to move ahead. Kicking and hitting is not intentional. It's part of swimming in a tight pack. Stay relaxed. Take a break and change your stroke for a second if you need to until you have some space to get back in your stroke and on your pace.

Look up often (every 8 to 15 strokes) to be sure you're heading in the right direction. Use a buoy or guard boat to guide you.

In some triathlons, you'll be able rest at buoys, on lane lines, or at guard boats. If you need to, take advantage of these spots to catch your breath. Some events even offer foam flotation noodles. There's no shame in taking a noodle. *Remember:* You're in the water, swimming in whatever way you can to the finish — that's far more than the majority of the population can say.

When you reach the end of the swim leg, if you're in open water, stand when you feel the ground under your stroke and walk out of the water.

At the first transition

When you reach land, your first transition, known as T1, begins. You start the process of peeling off your wetsuit if you're wearing one, as you jog slowly to your transition stall. Take it slow. Give your legs a minute to adjust.

Place (not propel) your wetsuit, goggles, and swim cap in your transition stall. Don't drop and throw your gear. Yes, you may see where it lands at that moment, but who knows where it can end up after you've completed your transition and the hundreds of others behind you have done the same.

On the bike

As you leave the transition area, be cautious and aware of those around you and how your legs feel. It can be tempting to power out of the transition area, especially to the cheering and applause of spectators. But take your time; give your muscles the time to get accustomed to the change in motion.

As soon as you feel comfortable on the bike, grab some of your hydration or your nutrition. Even if you feel you don't need it, remember: Drink before you're thirsty; eat before you're hungry.

At the second transition

As you approach the second transition area (this transition is known as T2), get off your bike and walk or slowly jog to your stall. Rack your bike first, and then remove your helmet. Take off your shoes if you've worn cycling shoes and slip into your running shoes. If you didn't need to wear your race number for the bike leg, be sure to grab it now. Take some water or other hydration if you have some left on your bike in your transition area. If not, don't worry. You'll encounter a hydration stop on your bike leg. Take advantage of it.

On the run

Although the swim is the most difficult physically, you'll feel most fatigued at T2, making the run, at least the first yards, more difficult than your typical run. You'll be battling the accumulated fatigue of the entire event and asking your legs to move in yet another direction. If you've trained using bike-run workouts, or *bricks* (training sessions involving cycling and then running), you'll know your legs will feel like they're filled with bricks. Keep moving, they'll loosen up.

Minding Your Manners: Race Etiquette

Emotions run high during a triathlon — you'll feel everything from fear and frustration to complete elation. There's a lot to take in, and everyone at your event is feeling the same. You can help to make everyone's day more enjoyable and memorable by considering those around you. It not only can make for a more pleasant event, but it can keep you or a fellow participant safe.

Each triathlon has its own culture and set of rules. Know the race rules you received in your race packet and follow them *all.* If any of the following tips are not on the event's list, add them to your own personal list:

- ✔ **Spread some cheer.** You know what it took for you to get to where you are. Your fellow triathletes experienced the same — or more. Say hello, smile, and be friendly. If a conversation starts, enjoy it for the moment. If not, don't take it personally. Your head may be somewhere else the next time someone says something to you, as well.

- ✔ **Be aware of how much room you're taking up in the transition area.** Be careful and respect everyone's equipment. If someone seems rushing to get by you to a transition stall, let him. Don't be distracted by someone else's anxiety.

- ✔ **Don't be a litterbug.** Yes, during the run, it's acceptable to toss your drink cup off the side of the road where volunteers pick it up, but that doesn't make it okay to trash the course. During your bike leg, don't toss your nutrition packs and wraps onto the ground. And don't leave litter behind in the transition area. Leave the event with whatever you brought with you.

- ✔ **Keep your clothes on.** Be courteous of others around you — participants and spectators. Don't strip down in the transition areas or strip off your shirt in the run.

- ✔ **Position yourself for the swim where you belong — for yourself and those in front of and behind you.** If swimming is not your strongest leg of the triathlon, stay to the back of your wave. Doing this will keep swimmers from bumping into you or swimming over you at the start. Just the same, if you're a strong swimmer, consider moving up in the pack or to the side so that you don't swim over slower swimmers in front of you.

- ✔ **Whenever you're on your bike or moving your bike to get on it, have your helmet on and buckled.** Not just on — *on and buckled.*

✔ **Keep to the right except to pass.** The same rules of the road apply to the bike and run legs of triathlons. Then when you do pass, look over your left shoulder quickly to make sure you're clear. Then let the person you're passing know you're on the left —common expressions are, "Passing on your left," or a simple "On your left." Be cautious but pass quickly. And be prepared. A cyclist or runner who sees you on his left can temporarily get distracted and step off to the left into or in front of you. Be ready just in case.

Do not pass other triathletes in your event by crossing the center line on a road, unless you're confident the entire road has been closed for the race. Remember that roads usually are open and traffic blocked only temporarily as the cyclists or runners go by. You may encounter traffic, so be especially aware of oncoming vehicles if you intend to pass. If there's no room to pass without crossing the center line, wait.

✔ **Whether you're passing or being passed, a word of encouragement is always welcome.** Try "Way to go!", "Looking good!", or "Keep it up!"

✔ **If you experience mechanical problems with your bike, signal to other riders nearby or speak loudly (say, "Pulling off") to let those around you know your intention to leave the race course.** Move all the way off the course to be conscious of the safety of other riders.

✔ **If you plan to stop during the run to tie your shoe or catch your breath, remember there may be a runner behind you.** If you stop suddenly to bend over to tie your shoe, another runner can end up falling over you. Be considerate. Look behind you, and when the lane is clear, move off to the side to slow down or stop.

✔ **If you're stopping at an aid station, move to the side quickly, off the course, grab your drink, and go.** As you toss your cup, remember, there may be a runner behind you who may not want to be showered with your backwash. Be sure to toss your cup to the side carefully and not to drop it where it can be in the path of another runner.

✔ **Don't draft on your bike.** Drafting is fun and can be a welcome break during group training rides, but drafting during your triathlon can get you disqualified. Drafting is not allowed on the bike. If you can get behind someone to draft in the swim or on the run, have at it.

Chapter 15

After You Finish Your Triathlon

Congratulations! You're about to achieve what only a small percentage of the population even dares to consider. We can't fully explain the exhilaration you'll feel when you see the finish line of your first event and hear people cheering you on. No matter in what place you finish, you'll have completed a triathlon, and you should be proud of yourself.

In this chapter, we tell you how to cross the finish line. Yes, there's a correct form for this, too — a way to do it correctly and with respect for those still on the course and for the volunteers helping you through this final stage.

After you've had some time to bask in your achievement, you need to begin the process of recovering, so that you can enjoy more celebration later in the day and the next day, too. In this chapter, we let you know what to eat and drink after you finish and why stretching at the end of your event is so important.

Finally, we fill you in on how to prepare for your next event. Yes, we know you haven't finished the first one yet. But trust us — cross that finish line, and one of the first thoughts to cross your mind just might be, "Next time, I'll. . . ." Here we help you sort through the "next time" (or the unlikely "never again") and create a plan for maintaining your fitness level or building on the foundation you've created.

Smile and say "triathlete"

Many event organizers arrange to have photographers at the event to capture images of the participants in the three legs and at the finish. You won't always know where the photographers are hiding along the course, but you can be sure they'll be at the finish. Your collection of pictures will be available for you to purchase on the photographer's Web site a few weeks after the event, searchable by your last name or your race number. The photos taken throughout the event may capture you looking strong or looking silly (even if you felt strong). If you run with a friend or helped someone through a rough moment (or they've done the same for you), it's great to have a photo of the two of you crossing the finish line, so feel free to stick together. When you look at that picture, you'll relive those feelings of joy and accomplishment. *Remember:* These are not glamour shots, nor should they be. You worked hard out there, and you're going to look like it. Be proud of that.

Crossing the Finish Line

As you approach the finish area, you'll see supporters on either side of the course, cheering for you and all the participants. If your friends and family have come out to support you, you'll be eager to see them. Some participants will head off to the sides to their loved ones for high fives or hugs. Before you indulge in too much celebrating, though, don't forget to actually cross the finish line.

After the event, hundreds, if not thousands, of people will be searching for their friends and families. Before the event starts, determine a place to meet to eliminate walking any more steps than you have to after you complete your event.

You won't be counted as a finisher until the race organizers have a record of you stepping onto the *timing-chip pad* (the electronic device that records your time from the chip you'll be wearing) or until you return the detachable portion of your race number.

Depending on the size of your event, the finish line can be a simple area with a clock timer and a few banners or an elaborate area with a stage, music, and a person announcing your name or number as you cross the finish. In an Ironman event, every participant will cross the finish line and break through a winner's ribbon. Don't worry if your event skimps on the pomp and circumstance; you'll be feeling so great, it really won't matter to you.

Here are some tips for finishing with style and good sportsmanship:

✔ **Move through the finish quickly.** Regardless of the distance you just completed, you'll experience a wide variety of emotions upon finishing. You set a goal, and you achieved it. You certainly have reason to celebrate, but remember that there are participants right behind you — or far behind you.

Don't stick around to bask in the glory of the finish line. Clear the area quickly to allow participants behind you to enter and enjoy their moments at the finish line as well. Certainly, you can cross the finish line with your arms raised in the air — just keep moving through as you do it.

After you cross the finish line, a number of volunteers will be waiting for you. If you need help, for any reason, you'll find someone there to assist you. And if you need medical treatment or feel nauseated, dizzy, or cold but sweaty, be sure to let them know so that they can guide you or take you to a medical tent or the event's medical personnel.

✔ **Enter the chutes in the order you finished.** When you cross the finish line, you may be directed into *chutes* (lines designed to keep participants in the order in which they arrived at the finish). As you enter the chute, stay in your finishing order — do not pass anyone here.

You may be asked to rip off the bottom perforated portion of your race number (if there is one) and hand that to a volunteer.

After the chutes, you'll also need to stop at the timing-chip removers to return your timing chip. Remember how flexible you were at the beginning of the event when you strapped your timing chip around your ankle? Don't be surprised if your ankle feels like it's moved farther down your body than it was at the race start. If you're too tired to bend over and remove the chip yourself, you won't be alone. That's why volunteers will be there to help you.

If you're caught up in the moment and forget to remove your timing chip, and it's still on your ankle when you get home, you'll have to mail it back or pay for it. Try your best to remember to take it off and return it as soon as you finish your event.

After you remove your chip, continue through the finish chute, and you'll be presented with your finisher's medal, if your event offers it.

✔ **Thank the volunteers.** As you continue through the chute, don't forget to thank the volunteers who are there helping you and cheering you on. The volunteers put in a lot more time on that course than any of the racers, and they stay long after all the finishers have left.

✔ **Keep moving.** Don't walk away from the finish and sit down or dramatically drop to the ground, even though you may want to. Your muscles will stiffen, and that will add to any soreness later. Walk around until you feel your heart slow to its normal rate.

✔ **Cheer on your fellow triathletes.** You'll know how good it felt to finish to cheers and applause. It's likely the participants finishing behind you need that motivation and recognition just as much as you did, or even more. While you're relaxing, they'll still be out there digging deep. Stick around and help to make their moments as special as yours was.

Making the Most of the First Hour after Your Finish

You've crossed the finish line, but you're not done with this event just yet. Post-race activities are a big part of the fun of triathlons. Knowing where to go and what you need to do will help ensure you have the time and energy to stick around and revel in your achievement.

Hydrate and eat

Replacing the fluids and nutrients you used during the event will speed your recovery. Even though you will have been drinking and eating throughout your triathlon, you'll still finish in a degree of dehydration.

Often, as you proceed through the race chute and into the area just after the finish, you'll find tables set up with plenty of food and drinks. Help yourself.

Sports drinks are the best post-race drink, because they contain sodium, an electrolyte that you need to replace. They also taste good, so you'll be likely to drink more.

Although you may feel like chugging that first icy-cold bottle of a sports drink, don't. You'll end up with stomach cramps, or the liquid will end up on the ground in front of you. Sip a little at a time, but make sure you drink enough to feel satisfied. Avoid alcohol and caffeine immediately following the race — these beverages will increase your need to urinate and add to your dehydration. Skip the soft drinks as well, even caffeine-free ones — these drinks are loaded with sugar, which do nothing to help replace your electrolytes. Instead, they may set you on a sugar rush that will leave you feeling more exhausted later in the day.

You'll also want to replace your *glycogen stores* (fuel used by your muscles to assist in muscle recovery) within 15 to 20 minutes of completing the race. Most races will have choices of foods that will be easy to digest and help to boost your fuel stores. Grab granola bars, bananas, bagels, fruit juice, or muffins.

M-a-s-s-a-g-e spells relief

Many event organizers set up massage-therapy chairs or tables. If yours does, take advantage of them! Immediately after your event, you may feel fine — but you may be surprised by the soreness you feel as you get your massage. Working out muscle knots and deposits of lactic acid now will help you feel better later. Head to these tables early, because the lines get long as people finish the event (or realize they used and abused their muscles more than they had planned so they could finish early).

In you can't get a massage, take a shower or a warm bath as soon as you can after your event to relax your muscles.

Stretch

Most people finish a race and get so caught up in the moment that they grab their gear, get in the car, and drive home. Unless the race is in your home-town, you're going to sit in your car for maybe an hour or more, and the muscles you just worked so hard are not going to be happy when you get back out. In fact, they'll be screaming at you.

Take a few minutes to stretch all your major muscles. Find a spot along the race course where you can move around without knocking into people and gently stretch. You'll feel much better when you get out of your car and much better the next day. Plus, if you position yourself along the race course, you can cheer for people heading toward the finish as they pass by.

Collect your gear

After you've relaxed a little, hydrated, eaten, congratulated other racers, given and received hugs and pats on the back, and stretched, it's time to collect your gear.

If you plan to stay for the awards ceremony after all the finishers have completed their events, collect your gear and load it into your car. If you're leaving before the race is finished, you'll be the only one allowed in the transition area to get your belongings. When the race is over, you can ask a friend or family member to assist you with your gear in the transition area.

Some event organizers won't allow anyone back into the transition area until all participants have finished their T2 transitions (bike to run). This rule ensures that no one gets in the way of the participants still on the course.

Leaving before the end of the race is not considered good race etiquette. And it's certainly not going to do much for fellow triathletes' morale to see you packing up your gear while they're transitioning from the bike to the run.

To re-enter the transition area after you complete your event, you'll need to show your race number or bracelet. Volunteers will check your number against your bike number to be sure it belongs to you.

When you return to the transition area, you'll find your belongings not nearly as neat as you left them, or thought you left them. All the clothing that was folded and dry in your gear bag when you arrived will be wet, dirty, and thrown on the ground now. You'll need to stuff that all back into your bag as best you can. Plastic bags can help keep wet clothing from soaking your cycling shoes or other gear you'd prefer to keep dry.

Make sure you clean up everything around your transition stall, including garbage, even if it wasn't yours. Pitch in to help the volunteers who helped you.

If there's a volunteer who helped you during the event — maybe he pointed you in the right direction when you set out on your bike or reminded you to take off your helmet before you started your run — look for this person at the end of your event to thank him for his help. As you're leaving, thank any volunteers you pass on your way to your car, along with the race director, if you can identify her. Putting a race together takes a lot of work.

Know where you placed

Now that you're away from the finish line, you can act like you just won the Tour de France. After all, one person's Tour de France is another's Sprint triathlon. Walk around with a big smile and take in all the attention. How often does that happen?

Shortly after all the finishers cross the finish line, the event organizer will post a computer-generated printed listing of times and order of finishers. These results will be posted on boards outside or on a wall inside. You can review the race results to find out where you placed overall and in your age group. Event organizers give awards for first-, second-, and third-place overall finishers, male and female, and for *age groupers* (amateur athletes, like you, who are grouped according to their ages into age brackets, such as 20 to 24, 25 to 29, 30 to 34, and so on). Events provide separate awards for male and female age groupers. So, if you place 216 in your event overall, but you're the first 42-year-old female to cross the finish line, you'll receive an age-group award.

The best goal for your first triathlon is to finish the event, not to have a specific place in mind.

Award presentations, where you receive a prize if you're eligible, generally take place immediately after the event finish. These presentations can be fun, and sometimes event organizers pull race numbers for random prizes, so it's worth sticking around even if you didn't place.

Regardless of where you placed, be proud. You're a triathlete.

Evaluating Your Performance

Regardless of how proud you feel, we know you'll soon (if not right at the finish) begin to analyze every aspect of your race, thinking you could have saved time in your transitions, spun faster on that last straightaway, trained harder, hydrated better. Stop! You did it. Don't worry right now about how you could have done better or how you'll do better next time.

Yes, it's likely you'll have a "next time." We've never heard someone at the end of an event saying, "I'll never do *that* again." More likely, you'll be recruiting friends and family and checking the schedule in your race bag for your next event. It's *that* fun.

Give yourself some time to appreciate what you did right. Then before your next event, take an honest, not overly critical, evaluation of your performance and your training, focusing on the following:

- **Your pre-race preparation:** Did you give yourself enough time to check in, set up your transition stall, warm up, stretch, and still have time to relax before the race?

- **Your starting position:** Did you set yourself up in the right position for the swim start? Did you feel comfortable with your placement in your wave?

- **Your T1 time:** How was your transition from the swim to the bike? Did you set up efficiently and find everything you needed? Should you have worn a wetsuit or skipped it?

- **Your cycling leg:** How did you feel during the bike leg? Did you train well enough? Did you struggle on hills? Did you encounter any technical problems that you could have prepared for?

- **Your T2 time:** How was your transition from the bike to the run? How fast were you? How did your legs feel on the run start? How long did it take your muscles to adjust to running? Could you have trained with more bike-to-run workouts?

- **Your running time:** Did you give it your all on the run? Did you have any kick left toward the finish?

> ✔ **Your finish:** How did you feel when you crossed the finish line? Did you feel well hydrated? Or did you feel drained?

Of course, there's always room for improvement in all aspects of what we do, triathlons included. Everyone, from the elite triathlete to the once-a-year racer, hopes to better his performance.

Don't make it your obsession to recount everything you could've done better. Keep your focus on what you enjoyed and what you can do to enjoy your event even more next time.

Planning for Your Next Event

Maybe completing a triathlon was on your list of things to do, and now you can check that off and go on to the next item on your list. Maybe you loved the experience and can't wait to do another one to see if you can do a little better or a little longer.

If it's early in your area's triathlon season, you can sign up for another event even as soon as a few weeks away. If you'd like to tackle a longer-distance event, though, give yourself a week to recover and to begin training for the additional miles.

You'll already have your fitness base, so it won't take as much effort to get ready for your next triathlon as it did for your first. As long as you don't take an extended rest from training (two weeks or more), you can schedule triathlons throughout the season and maintain or build on your excellent fitness level.

With the sport's growth, you'll find many events to try, but often registration closes early, so complete and submit your application as soon as you pick your next event.

What to consider before you register again

If your event took place toward the end of the triathlon season, you'll have to focus on the following season and decide which races you may want to conquer. When considering an event for the next season, ask yourself:

> ✔ Was I able to fit in all the training for the distance I did?

> ✔ If I want to attempt a longer distance, does my schedule allow for the additional training time?

> ✔ Do I need to increase the intensity of my training — was it too easy or not enough of a challenge?

✔ How would my family feel about my spending more time training, especially during the spring and summer months?

✔ Am I happy doing one "special" triathlon a year with my friends and having fun, or would I prefer to pack as many events into a season as possible, even if it means traveling solo?

Whatever you choose to do, make the decision based on what you want from the sport, not what you think is expected of you. You don't have to increase your distance or your number of triathlons in a season. Don't take on so much that you're going to feel stressed and overwhelmed. You'll stick with the sport if it stays fun.

Overcoming burnout

It's possible that after your event you won't want to train for another event . . . or for anything. This is called *burnout.* The best way to handle burnout is to give yourself the mental and physical break your body may be craving.

After a week, try one of these tips for getting past burnout:

✔ **Take the pressure off.** Pick the sport you enjoyed most and head out for a short, easy run, ride, or swim. Find a comfortable pace and enjoy your surroundings.

✔ **Try a new sport or set a new goal.** Select one sport and add a distance — a 1-mile swim, a century bike ride (100 miles), or a marathon (26.2 miles). Or try adding three similar sports with some variation, such as an adventure race of mountain biking, trail running, and kayaking.

✔ **Enlist the help of friends.** Meet with a group of former triathlon-training friends or even just head out for a walk in a new area or on new trails to remind your body — and your mind — how good it feels to be moving.

✔ **Cross-train during your off season.** Pick a new sport for the off season, something that keeps you moving but is fresh.

Your triathlon training has given you a fantastic foundation of fitness. You won't need to continue to train four or more hours a week if you don't plan to participate in another event, but you know you can find the time to exercise three to four times a week, even if only for 20 to 30 minutes at a time, so keep with it.

Adjusting your diet

During your training season, you may have returned from a swim or a *brick* (bike ride and run) to a bowl of rice and beans suitable for a family of four. You burned many calories during training and needed to replenish them. If you reduce your training, adjust your caloric intake, too.

Yes, your metabolism will have increased with your increased activity level and muscle mass, but without continued training, this level won't stay the same. If you reduce your activity, you won't be burning as much fuel, so you won't need as many calories.

Finding other ways to stay involved

If you don't plan to become a race junkie, but you enjoy the atmosphere of the triathlon and all the excitement, you can sign up to volunteer at local races. Check the event's Web site for information on volunteering.

After you've completed your first triathlon, you'll have a good sense of how important volunteers are to an event. Volunteer to support an event. You'll know what the triathletes need before *they* do — you've been there. And if you're on the fence about racing again, sometimes just being there can reignite that spark.

Remember all those experienced triathletes who mentored or encouraged you in your training? You're an experienced triathlete now. Return to your triathlon club (or join one now if you haven't already) or your first-timers club and share your knowledge with those just starting out.

Part V
The Part of Tens

The 5th Wave   By Rich Tennant

DESPITE HIS INITIAL CONFUSION WITH THE NAME, SCOTT FINISHED 13th IN THE IRONMAN COMPETITION.

In this part . . .

Every For Dummies book ends with a Part of Tens, and in this one, you find ten life-changing benefits of participating in a triathlon. Still nervous? Look to Chapter 17, where we debunk ten triathlon myths, and you'll see that you're not the only one. Here, you find the truth about the most common misconceptions about triathlons and the people participating in them. In Chapter 18, we offer a list of extras you'll want to bring with you on race day to make your event more fun and easier to navigate. And, if you haven't yet chosen your event, we tell you about ten Web sites that list local and international triathlons, as well as women-only triathlons and those that raise funds for charities.

Chapter 16

Ten Reasons You Should Do a Triathlon

. . . .

In This Chapter

▶ Having fun while improving your health

▶ Finding a fitness program you can stick to

▶ Motivating others and yourself

. . . .

*I*n this chapter, we share our ten favorite reasons for doing a triathlon. Triathletes train with individual goals, but the results are universal: improved health and well-being, reduced stress, and a new outlook on life and on exercise.

Bragging Rights: Having the Chance to Be a Finisher

We certainly don't expect that you'll set out obnoxiously relating your final steps to the finish amid cheering and applause to everyone you know. We think you'll be bragging to yourself, about yourself.

The thrill of the finish is that no matter where you finish, you know that every day during training you had to push past challenges and excuses. And the thrill of your finish will be in direct proportion to how you hard you fought this struggle.

Completing a triathlon is not something everyone does. Although it may seem as if everywhere you look, people are training for triathlons, remember that's only because you've surrounded yourself with these people. Only a small number of people can call themselves triathletes.

When you cross your first triathlon finish line (or your 50th), you'll find yourself filled with emotion, adrenaline, and pride. People will be cheering for you, applauding, telling you they're proud of you. Believe it. You deserve it! Share the bragging rights of your finish. Let them tell you how great you did, let them tell their friends, and, at your next event, you may find a familiar face or two standing next to you.

Moving Out of Your Comfort Zone

It's easy to say, "I can't do it" and roll over and go back to sleep. To get out and train, you'll be tapping into a strength, determination, and discipline that you may not have known you had.

Everybody has athletic strengths, whether they use them or not. Some bodies are designed better for swimming than others. Some athletes race up hills as if they're going down them. Multi-sport training allows you to take advantage of these strengths and use them as a springboard to the other sports.

And combining all three sports into one event forces you to demand more of your body and your mind than one sport ever can. As a personal trainer and wellness director, Donna has watched people in gyms repeat the same workouts year after year without realizing that their bodies have become accustomed to the actions and that they're no longer seeing significant results from their efforts. There's no challenge. And where there's no challenge, there's no reward. You don't have to worry about not being challenged as a triathlete — and rewards are all around!

Every day, you have to overcome the mental obstacles that keep you comfortably in your bed, on your couch, in a place where you can't fall or fail. That's one of the thrills of completing a training session, and that's the mindset that will take you to the finish line. You may start a training session or enter your first triathlon thinking, "I don't want to do this." If you keep pushing through, you won't end a training session in that same mindset. More than likely, you'll say, "I'm so glad I did that."

A triathlon asks the question: Do you have what it takes mentally? Not physically — you'll train for that. But can you convince yourself you can do this? Overcome your fear of swimming? Believe you can ride and then run? Be confident you can get out there with all those other triathletes and manage your way through the transitions? When you do — and you can! — you'll find it easier to convince yourself you can tackle just about any goal.

Finding Focus and Relieving Stress

Training for a triathlon forces you to concentrate on your body in a way you may not be used to. As you train, you'll be thinking about how your body *works,* not how your body *looks,* and you'll vividly experience the power of your thoughts — good and bad. Think negative thoughts, and you slow down. Focus on your form, and you move forward.

By concentrating on the moment — how your body feels, how to pace your breathing, or how to increase your cadence — your thoughts about whatever may be bringing you stress fall into perspective . . . or fall away.

Triathletes will tell you that their Zen moments — when everything stops hurting and they fall into a smooth, effortless rhythm — come at different times and for different reasons. No matter the method, training can bring a feeling of quiet self-awareness and a connection between your body and your surroundings.

When you become so completely engrossed in an activity, you give your mind a break from the onslaught of negative thoughts that sometimes take control of a day. You finish your training sessions feeling energized and positive. Chemical changes in your body promote and support these feelings: Exercise releases endorphins, your body's natural stress and pain relievers. And just ask any triathlete — endorphins are addictive.

You'll begin to crave that peaceful, feel-good state, and as you face a day of deadlines and demands, you'll change your thinking from "I don't have time today" to "How will I *make* time today?"

Improving Your Health and Well-Being while Having Fun

While you're busy having fun and reaping the rewards of a clear head and energized body, your muscles will be building strength, your breathing will relax, and your heart will pump more efficiently.

As you track your performance during training, you'll see results that quickly impact your day-to-day life, not just your waist size. You'll feel the difference in your mood, your energy level, and your productivity. Training will become part of your life, and you'll miss it even on your rest days.

The benefits of training are immediate — if you're looking in the right place. Ask yourself two questions before and after every workout:

✔ How did I feel when I started?

✔ How do I feel now?

You'll start to eat better — not because you *should*, but because you *need* to. You'll feel the difference when you don't fuel your body effectively for training. You'll find stairs easier to climb, groceries easier to lift, daily chores easier to manage. Your increased muscle mass will boost your metabolism. And all of it will make you feel healthier and happier. And that's contagious.

Add to all this the well-known health benefits of exercise, and it's easy to see why triathlons are so popular:

✔ They lower your blood pressure.

✔ They strengthen your heart, lungs, and bones.

✔ They reduce your risk of heart disease and stroke.

✔ They reduce your risk of diabetes, cancer, and other chronic and life-threatening conditions.

✔ They improve your sleep and mental awareness.

Achieving Total-Body Fitness

When you train in three sports, you achieve a level of total-body fitness you can never achieve with only one.

Swimming alone is perhaps the best single sport for whole-body conditioning. We've all admired the swimmer's physique — long, lean, and toned muscles. Swimming is a highly aerobic exercise that builds endurance, great posture, and flexibility. By nature, swimming is an easy sport on the body in terms of injuries — there's no relentless pounding on the pavement.

But pounding on pavement has its positives, too. Weight-bearing exercises, such as running, help create strong bones. In addition, runners develop endurance, a strong core (important for posture and back health), and strong muscles.

Throw a 50-mile training bike ride into the weekly mix, and you have a recipe for weight loss. Nothing burns calories quite like a long-distance, good-tempo bike ride. There's a reason cyclists have pockets in their jerseys — they like to pack food. And there's a reason they pack food — they're always eating. So, cycling does wonders for flabby abs, core strength, and overall balance and coordination. Cycling also is kind to your joints — exercising them without jarring or compression.

Combine those benefits, and you've not only exercised your joints and every major muscle group in your body, but you've improved your cardiovascular health.

Reducing Exercise Burnout

Triathlon training varies your weekly routines to keep exercise interesting and fun. Who wouldn't dread going to the gym every day to repeat the same pointless circuits? Or running the same 3-mile loop? Or swimming countless laps to nowhere?

It's no wonder so many people don't stick to their exercise routines in gyms. The air is forced. The machines are lined up in strict rows. The people face mirrored walls or televisions that feed them news and information about what they should know or have or do. If you're lucky, you may get a window view.

Triathlon training gets you outside. You run, jump, ride, and splash. You play with "bricks," talk about fartleks, and slurp sweet, gooey stuff. You race down hills and sing up hills (it's a rhythm thing). You talk technology and buy cool clothing you can easily justify by trying it out in training.

Or you can count reps and sets. Sure, you may find yourself in the gym for strength training or stretching or to escape a snowy day, but we guarantee you'll be looking around, thinking, "People, get outside and play!"

Reducing Risk of Injuries by Cross-Training

Cross-training gives your body adequate time to recover following a training session, while you work on another sport or another body part. If you start to feel pain or need to take some time away from the pounding of running, you can add mileage to your cycling. If your joints are sore or you're experiencing back pain, head to the pool for an easy, relaxing swim.

Enjoying the Camaraderie of the Triathlon Club

A triathlon is not a team sport — finishing your first triathlon is a personal achievement — but *training* for a triathlon is very much a team sport.

Triathletes know that meeting a friend for an early-morning swim, ride, or run will give them that extra incentive to drop their warm feet onto the cold floor. Triathletes are eager to pull together for motivation. The support of other triathletes during training swims, group rides, or runs makes it easier to stay on track and to achieve higher levels of fitness than you may have achieved on your own.

If you attend group-training events, you may even find yourself in the company of elite athletes and age-group finishers from whom you'll learn and improve your own skills. The group's collective energy pulls you along, and the group's success becomes your success.

By deciding to train for a triathlon, you've immersed yourself in a new world — one that's about fitness, nutrition, hydration, heart rates, and one that your main support group (your friends and family) may not always understand. Honestly, they won't share your fascination with your new bike's compact gearing unless they're getting on their bikes in the morning, too. You'll have your triathlon friends for that.

And your club or training friends probably will also get together after training to rehydrate and eat. Groups sometimes host parties to celebrate the start of the season, the longest day of the year, or even a *transition party* (when a group of triathletes get together and practice their transitions and time each other). Your club can also organize bike-repair, fix-a-flat, or swim clinics.

Every triathlete in a training club will not be an experienced or elite athlete. A new crop of clubs are targeted specifically to first-timers, novices, or women. There's a bond that forms when you're with people who feel the same as you do. Everyone shares a fear of not finishing, and they're all seeking help and encouragement. Veteran triathletes often mentor these clubs to share their knowledge and experience and to help everyone find their way to the finish.

So, if you've signed up for your event alone, be sure to seek out the support of a local triathlon training club. You can find many resources online, or check with your event organizer, local YMCA or similar organization, or the gym where you train. Depending on where you live, an Internet search for tri-athlon clubs in your town or a city near you may yield results.

If there aren't any clubs in your area, check in with your local swimming club, bike shop, or running store. They'll know who's training for an event and have suggestions for getting together with a group You may even have a triathlon shop nearby that supplies everything you'll need for training — and maybe even some contacts or clubs to train with.

Motivating and Inspiring Others

You're stepping into the world of elite athletes and showing the people around you that it can be done. People will admire and respect your determination.

The first triathlon club Donna organized started with only 25 scared athletes, 15 of whom were participating in their first triathlons. After their events, Donna asked them to share their stories of their journeys to the finish line. A local newspaper even picked up the stories and published them. The following year, 160 athletes joined Donna's club. At the season's first club meeting, a woman stood up and said, "I can't swim, bike, or run, and you mean to tell me I'll be able to finish a triathlon?" In response, Donna asked everyone in the room who had completed their first triathlons — and who felt the same before they did — to stand up. All 25 triathletes from the previous year stood.

If you've asked around for friends to join you, many may have laughed or thought you were crazy. But sign up for a triathlon alone, and we're sure you won't train or finish alone. When friends witness your increased energy, your positive mood, and your excitement, it won't be long before they're asking, "How can I have that, too?"

And this is how triathlons have become a collection of every body type and shape, all levels of fitness and athletic ability. Someone watching at the finish line may see himself in you and realize that he can do this, too. And that's what makes triathlons such a popular and growing sport.

There's only one feeling better than knowing you did it: It's having someone come up to you at the finish to say, "Thanks for helping me believe *I* could, too."

Changing Your View of Yourself and the World

Training for a triathlon teaches you not to accept excuses, and you'll recognize and appreciate when others do the same. Have you ever seen someone running in big, clunky shoes or jeans? And have you thought, "What is she doing?" What she's doing is not accepting excuses. She's getting out to exercise regardless of the weather or the clothing she has. As a triathlete, you'll recognize and appreciate that — because you'll be making those same daily choices yourself.

You'll pay more attention to what people are doing, instead of what they're not doing. And you'll start to notice people on the roads and encourage them up a hill as you drive past.

You'll want to surround yourself with people who talk about what they *can* do — not what they can't. Setting your body into motion sets your life in motion. As you set priorities and goals, recognize your weaknesses, and build on your strengths, your self-confidence grows along with your fitness level.

And this you carry with you into every aspect of your life.

Chapter 17
Ten Triathlon Myths Debunked

In This Chapter
▶ Sizing up the competition
▶ Calming your nerves in the swim
▶ Accepting your place in the pack

Despite their growing popularity, triathlons carry a degree of mystique. Some people think they're only open to the fittest athletes or the athletes with the best gear. Others believe that triathlons are long, grueling events that can take entire days and require travel to Hawaii. In this chapter, we dispel these and other myths about triathlons.

Triathlons Only Take Place in Hawaii

Say the word *triathlon* and most people think of the Ironman — specifically, the Ironman in Kona, Hawaii. The one in Kona is the World Championships, so it's the race that most triathlete hopefuls are most familiar with. Although you'll find great Ironman events in Hawaii, Arizona, New York, Australia, New Zealand, Malaysia, France, Germany, Switzerland, and China, among other places, you won't have to travel far to find a Sprint-distance event close to home.

In fact, depending on where you live, especially if you're in a warm climate near open water, you can fill your season with triathlons and never leave your state.

Triathlons Take All Day to Complete

Unless you're participating in an Ironman, you won't need from sunrise to sunset to finish your triathlon. It's true: An Ironman can take 15 hours or more to complete, especially for a first-timer. But you can participate in an Olympic-distance event, covering more miles than you would in a marathon, in less time. And the average time for a Sprint distance, the most popular triathlon distance for a first-timer, is 1 hour and 45 minutes to cover approximately 16 miles.

Triathlons Are for Elite Athletes Only

You don't have to be an experienced triathlete — or experienced in any one of the three sports — to succeed in a triathlon. What you're likely to find, depending on the event you've selected, is a group of helpful, happy, welcoming, and supportive people just like you. Some will be first-timers, some more experienced, but you'll all be working toward the same goal — finishing.

That's not to say you won't encounter the occasional high-octane athlete focused entirely on time and a personal best. Our best advice to you: Just get out of the way and go back to enjoying your event.

The field will be made up of athletes at every fitness level. You'll spot elite racers at your event, but they'll most likely be the minority. Most of the triathletes will look like average people. In fact, some of the athletes will have you thinking to yourself, "If *that* guy can do this, so can I."

Elite athletes started the same way you did, maybe just before you did. They know what it takes to find the discipline to train. And most will respect that you're out there giving it your all. Don't be afraid to approach an elite athlete and ask questions or talk about what to expect on the course.

All Triathletes Look Fit and Thin

Weight loss is an obvious perk of training in three sports. When you train for a triathlon, you'll lose weight and tone your muscles. But not everyone who competes in a triathlon sports the sleek swimmer's physique. You'll find triathletes at your event in every size and body type.

Don't assume that the person who looks the least fit will be the last to cross the finish line. Just the same, the toned and fit athlete next to you at the beginning of your event may just finish far behind. You won't be able to predict performance based on how a person looks.

Triathletes Spend All Their Free Time Training

Some triathletes *do* spend all their free time training — that's true. In fact, some triathletes manage to turn their training and competing into careers. This is not *your* career, though. You have a life — a job, family, friends, other hobbies and interests. Triathlon training should *enhance* your life — your fitness and well-being — not overwhelm or overtake it.

When you set your triathlon goals, remember to do so with a realistic understanding of the time you have available to train in each sport. With a basic foundation of fitness, you can train for a Sprint-distance triathlon in four hours a week. As you increase your distance and your personal goals, you can add training time, focusing on the sport in which you feel you have the most room to improve. (But if you decide to train for an Ironman, you can expect it to take a considerable portion, if not all, of your free time.)

Training for a triathlon is not about intensity. It's about making smart decisions and using your time to your best benefit. Consistency is more important than blasting out a few weeks of three-hour workouts day after day, followed by time spent nursing an injury — physical or psychological. Don't burn yourself out. Maintain a balance, and budget the time you have. Don't worry about how much someone else may be training — just focus on yourself and enjoy *your* training.

I'll Panic in the Water

Swimming is perhaps the most anxiety-producing sport of the triathlon. It's the leg that most triathletes fear, even those who were swimmers first. That's why triathlons are designed with the swim first — it's a tough leg, and it's good to get it over with early in the event.

There's no denying that triathlon swimming is hard, but it's not impossible.

The list of worries for the water is long:

- ✔ Will I get kicked?
- ✔ Will I get lost?
- ✔ Will my goggles leak and my eyes sting with the salt or chlorine?

> ✔ If I don't swim fast enough, will other participants swim right over me?
>
> ✔ Will I take a breath and get a mouthful of ocean?

We can't promise that you won't get kicked or hit, or that you won't swallow water or get water in your goggles. But we can tell you that there's no need to panic in the water. And we're sure you won't get lost. The course will be buoyed and maybe even roped off. You'll learn how to sight during training, and guards will be on duty to keep you on course.

If you've trained and practiced with the gear you'll use during the event, you'll be well prepared and comfortable with your goggles, and you'll know how to tread water to clear them out and get them back on if you have to.

Still, the first few yards of your swim can be nerve-wracking as everyone heads out together. Just remember to breathe and relax. In a few strokes, the pack will loosen, and you'll find some space.

Triathletes Have to Swim Long Distances without Stopping

During training, you'll learn how to take breaks between laps, even while you keep moving. You can change your stroke — using a backstroke, breast-stroke, or even dog paddle. You can float for a bit. And in your event, you can do the same.

If you plan to rest throughout your swim leg, be sure to position yourself at the back of your wave or to the side so that you don't block other swimmers.

In some triathlons, especially those that welcome first-timers, you can even use a foam flotation aid, such as a swim noodle. And guards will be in boats or on surfboards in the water to give you a place to hang on and catch your breath.

I Don't Need to Practice Transitions

You can save time in your event more easily during transitions than in any other area of a triathlon — which means you should practice transitions often before your event. Before you arrive on event day, know how you want to arrange your transition area. You don't want to be fumbling with your wet-suit zipper or your laces for the first time while you're nervous.

The average first-time triathlete can spend five minutes or more in a transition area. Streamlining your transition is the easiest way to shave minutes from your overall time. It would be much harder to increase your speed in any of the three legs than it would to practice getting your cycling shoes on and off faster.

Triathletes Need Expensive Bikes

You do *not* need to spend thousands of dollars, or even a thousand, on a bike for your first triathlon. You can participate in a triathlon using the bike you have in your garage or the bike you ride around your neighborhood, and many first-time triathletes do so.

Whatever bike you choose, be sure to have it tuned up and checked out by a mechanic at your local bike shop.

At your event, you'll probably see riders on bikes equipped with the best components. Their frames alone may cost more than double the cost of the average bike used in a triathlon. But don't assume that the rider of this bike is any more fit or capable than you are.

Spending a lot of money won't make you a better triathlete. Training will.

I'll Be the Oldest, the Slowest, or the Last to Finish

You won't. Well, we don't know this for certain — *someone* has to be the oldest, the slowest, or the last to finish. But many events, especially those geared to first-timers, have got you covered. Often, well-known event organizers or volunteers with the events will participate in the event and keep company with those who need it most — the back-of-the-packers.

Perhaps the best known of these participants who sets out to be last is Sally Edwards, a long-time triathlete who has competed in more than 100 Danskin women-only Sprint events. Edwards started competing in triathlons shortly after the event was first created in 1974. Since then, she has crossed the finish line of 16 Ironman events and has won 100-mile endurance runs. Now, Edwards, a speaker and author of 20 books on fitness and triathlon training, makes it her mission to be last in these women-only, first-timer-centric events to help eliminate first-timers' fears.

Since Edwards's first triathlon in the 1970s, the number of triathlons taking place each year has increased. So, too, has the age of the oldest participant. Don't be surprised to see triathletes in their 70s or 80s. So, unless you're an octogenarian, you won't be the oldest participant. And if you are, congratulations! Be proud and shout it from your transition stall, your bike seat, and your swim wave!

You'll notice, as you review the race results, that as the participant ages go up, the number of participants goes down. Triathlon is a tough sport. If you're the oldest participant at your event, not only will you feel like an elite athlete no matter how fast you finish, but you may even feel like a rock star. People will spot you, respect you, and cheer for you loudly.

And if you're the slowest? Again, congratulations! Know that other triathletes recognize the effort it takes you to get to the finish. Never be embarrassed by your time. An elite triathlete can finish a Sprint triathlon in under an hour, and you may be expecting to take up to three hours. So, while the elite athlete is done and lounging around, you're still out there working — and most athletes recognize that. You'll have *been* working — swimming, cycling, and running — for more time than the elite athletes did.

And you'll likely finish to loud applause because you deserve it. Many of the athletes who finished before you will stick around to cheer you on, and the announcers will help get the crowd excited. The back of the pack can be a fun and inspirational place to be — and Sally Edwards is not the only one to realize this. It's not unusual to see triathletes helping each other. On occasion, you may see an experienced triathlete running, jogging, or even walking alongside an athlete who needs some support.

Chapter 18

Ten (Or So) Items to Bring on Race Day

In This Chapter

▶ Adding comfort to your triathlon

▶ Saving seconds in the transition areas

▶ Personalizing your event

*L*ong before you start packing your gear for your triathlon, you'll have selected and tested your race day essential equipment: swim gear, bike, cycling shoes, helmet, clothing, and a great pair of running shoes. In this chapter, you find ten (or so) items to add to your race day list that can help bring comfort, safety, support, and even a little speed to your event. You don't absolutely need to bring what's outlined here, but *we* wouldn't compete in a triathlon without this stuff.

Your Cheering Section

Triathlons come stocked with cheering sections. In the transition area preparing for your triathlon, you'll find yourself looking at the bikes, the equipment, and the people, thinking, "What am I doing here?" But those athletes who may leave you feeling intimidated at the beginning of your event will likely be the same athletes you'll find cheering you on in the end. They've been where you are, and they know that applause fuels a finish-line kick.

Still, there's nothing like seeing a familiar face in the crowd, someone who's there just for you, cheering your name and not just your race number, especially if you're thinking you may never see the finish line.

Invite your friends and family to the event, especially those who supported you during your training. Just knowing there's one person you know waiting outside a transition area, along the route, or at the finish line provides some added motivation: You want to get there and get there looking strong.

The same person or group of people who supported you during your training will want to be there to celebrate your achievement. Don't be embarrassed to ask. Having been on both sides of event fences, we know that onlookers often are more impressed and enthusiastic to cheer on the last people to cross the finish line than they are the first.

And, if you can imagine an extra bonus to having someone clapping just for you, remember: You'll have a bike and all your gear to gather up and get back to your car. As great as you'll feel emotionally, you'll have far less energy and adrenaline than when you arrived at the event. You'll be relieved to have an extra hand to get you back to your car and an extra ear to listen to you rave about your experience on the way home.

A Race Belt

A *race belt* is a narrow elastic strap that clips together quickly and has two snaps that hold your race number. It's a great addition to your race wear and makes attaching your number in the transition area quick and easy.

You aren't required to wear your number in the swim because you'll have your number marked on your body. Still, many triathlon organizers require racers to wear their numbers on their backs while they ride and in front while they run. (This way, participants can be spotted and identified easily during both legs.)

If you don't wear your number in the swim, you won't want to fumble with safety pins to attach your number before you get on your bike. And you won't want to worry about how to get it from your back to your front as you set out to run.

Instead, attach the race number to the race belt when you set up your transition area. Drape the belt over the top tube of your bike so that when you arrive in the transition area, you can grab it, wrap it around your waist with the number on your back, and quickly clip it closed. As you set out to run, simply pull the number around your waist to your front.

A Tub and Towel for Transitions

Depending on the location of your event, when you complete your swim, you may find a beach between you and your bike. Your wet feet will gather sand as you run to the transition area. And if you put socks and cycling shoes on sandy feet, you won't want to travel far from that spot.

If you'll exit your swim onto a beach, add a tub, bottles of water, and a towel to your event-day packing list. Place the tub and towel near your bike and shoes in the transition area. Before you head out, fill the tub with water from the bottles you brought with you. When you return to the transition area after your run, dip your feet into the basin, and then dry them quickly with a towel. Slip your feet into your socks or directly into your cycling shoes if you've decided to go sockless, and head out feeling refreshed (or as close to refreshed as you can feel after your swim).

Sometimes, race organizers will provide rinse tubs for participants to dip their feet into. But having your own supplies will be faster — not to mention cleaner. If you come out of the water in a group and you have your own tub, you won't have to wait for others going through the tubs ahead of you.

A Way to Identify Your Bike in the Crowd

If you've ever stared anxiously at the carousels full of black suitcases in an airport and thought, "I'll know mine when I see it," just as your bag chugs past, then you have a taste of the wonder that awaits when you splash out of the water and drip your way from your swim to the transition area to find your bike.

You think you'll remember. You'll pick out landmarks. You'll count how many bikes are on the racks next to yours. But after your swim — and after the other 300 to 3,000 triathletes in your event have joined the transition area and set up their bikes and their gear just like yours — the hardest part of your triathlon can turn out to be finding your bike.

To help you find your bike in the crowd, bring helium-filled balloons to the triathlon and tie them onto the spot where you rack your bike. Choose colors or characters you'll spot easily. Be careful not to accidentally tie the balloons onto your bike. Riding with balloons on your bike would obviously slow you down — although it *would* make it easier for your cheering squad to find you!

If you don't like the idea of bringing balloons to your event, apply a piece of neon or brightly colored tape to your handlebars to make your bike stand out from the others. Even a brightly colored bandana tied to the rack in front of your bike can help.

Also, bring a striped towel or one with bold colors. If you have children, this is a great place to "bring them along" to the event with you — grab one of their favorite character beach towels and use that to mark your transition area.

Finally, bring some brightly colored sidewalk chalk and, if your transition area is on blacktop or pavement, draw yourself a picture, scribble your initials, or even write a motivating message to yourself with an arrow to your bike.

A Road ID Bracelet

If you have specific medical needs — such as severe allergic reactions to environment, food, or medicine, or diabetes or a heart condition — medical personnel need to be aware of your situation if you require medical attention. Wear a *road ID bracelet,* a wrist strap with an area on which you can write. On the bracelet, indicate your name, an emergency-contact phone number, and any other critical information. Medical personnel are trained to look at people's wrists for medical ID bracelets.

Even if you don't have a medical condition or an allergy, it's always a good idea to wear an identification bracelet to facilitate contact with people who will be at the event with you, in case you need medical attention.

A Waterproof Sport Wristwatch

When your wave starts, you probably won't be the first person in the water when the timing clock starts ticking. If your event has chip-timing, you'll have a timing chip in your race number or that you've strapped around your ankle. This will keep track of the exact times you cross the start line, enter and exit the transition areas, and complete your race.

Some athletes like to know their times as they participate to help them monitor their pace. You can easily do this with a sport wristwatch. You can buy a watch that allows you to monitor your time — all you have to do is remember to start it by pressing the designated buttons to start the timer and to start and end *splits* (the individual segments or legs of your event).

Expect to pay from $30 to $100 for a good watch and look for the following features:

- ✔ **Waterproof:** Look for a watch that's *waterproof,* meaning it can be submerged into the water. (*Water-resistant* watches can only withstand rain or other splashing.)

- ✔ **Digital, easy-to-read numbers:** Digital watches allow you to keep track of split times easily. Look for numbers that are big and bright.

- ✔ **Ease of use:** Select a watch with buttons that are easy to press and accessible at the sides of the watch or on the watch face.

Be sure to read all the instructions on your watch and know how to use it long before your event. You won't want to be fumbling with buttons and timers that can distract you from what you should be doing.

If you're into high-tech gear to boost your performance, watches are available with advanced features including an altimeter; heart-rate monitor; compass; features you would find on a cycling computer such as a cadence counter, speedometer, and odometer; and a wireless computer connection to log and evaluate your training. The capability can cost you, though, with prices in the hundreds of dollars.

Sun Stuff: Sunscreen, Sunglasses, and a Hat

Although most triathlons start in the early morning, by the time you're into the bike and run legs, the sun can be blazing. You'll want to stay cool — and *looking* cool doesn't hurt either.

Protect your skin from the sun by wearing a sweat- and water-resistant, high-SPF sunscreen. Be sure to apply it liberally, especially to your shoulders, back, the back of your neck, and the tips of your ears.

During your training, you probably already selected sunglasses or protective eyewear for cycling. Find out before your event if you can run with these, too. You don't want to be distracted by slipping shades.

Keep a lightweight hat in your transition area. Choose a mesh cap for breathability if your event takes place in warm weather. A hat worn during the run leg can help protect your head and eyes from the sun, and it's a great coverup for hair that's been wet and stuffed into a sticky swim cap and then tucked under a bike helmet. You'll look cool and collected crossing the finish line.

Body Glide

Body Glide, or a similar lubricant, makes it easy to get your wetsuit on before the event and to get it off again when you're in a hurry. Place some on your wrists and ankles so that the suit slides off these difficult parts. You can also apply a little to areas that tend to chafe when you're riding or running. It's a mess-free way to stay comfortable.

Some triathletes make themselves more slippery by spraying on Pam or a similar cooking spray. Yes, it's low in fat, but it tends to make everything slippery and doesn't feel good on your skin. Also, never use petroleum jelly near a wetsuit; it can dry out a suit, causing cracks. Instead, stick with a lubricating product designed for athletes.

Your Favorite Fuel

You need to fuel your body during your event just as you would during your training, so bring your favorite fast nutrition. Many triathletes choose gel or blocks of energy-filled gummies and take them on their bikes. Toss some into the pocket of your shirt or tape partially opened packets to your bike's top tube or handlebars so that you can grab one while riding. One triathlete we know even sticks the gummy block directly to his top tube.

Load your bike water bottles with your favorite sports drink. You'll find water stations throughout the race course, but to stay fueled, you need the electrolytes only a sports drink can provide. Be sure to use a sports drink you've tested during your training.

Lucky Charms

A lucky charm can provide a connection for you with someone you find inspirational. Your charm, also referred to as *mojo,* can be a photograph, a written message, a favorite T-shirt, a pair of socks, or even shoelaces — anything that makes you feel as though you have an edge because you have it with you. Lucky charms provide more security and comfort than they do luck in finishing — you have your training for that.

Triathletes use whatever small amount of space they have to attach their lucky charms. Here are some perfect places for your personal items:

- ✔ **Helmet:** Your helmet can be a mini billboard for your motivation. You can attach stickers or write on it with a marker.

- ✔ **Saddle bag:** Tuck mementoes inside your tool bag under your seat or pin them to the outside of the bag.

- ✔ **Bike:** Securely tape a small item to your handlebar stem, seat post, or top tube.

- ✔ **Hat or shirt:** Attach your charm or motivational memento to your hat or shirt with a pin so that you have it with you when you run.

Shoes and Clothing for after the Event

You've taken great care to select race wear that's comfortable and that'll take you from your swim through to the finish. But no matter how good your clothing feels going into the event, when it's over, you'll want it off.

Don't assume you'll comfortably slip back into whatever you wore on your way to the event. That early-morning chill when you picked up your race packet can give way to a post-event, midday steam.

Bring comfortable clothes and an extra towel to dry yourself off. Remember, though, that places to change will be limited in most cases, if they exist at all. Expect to just pull on track pants or a fresh T-shirt.

Toss a container of powder or some deodorant into your race day bag to use after the event for a quick freshen-up. Also, consider bringing a container of wet wipes to use after the race, to wipe away sweat and road debris from your face, neck, arms, and legs. It's no shower, but it can make your ride home more tolerable. Or if your swim was in fresh water, don't be afraid to take a quick dip in the lake or river to wash off the salty sweat and cool your muscles.

Pack a pair of after-sports shoes, such as flip-flops or other comfortable footwear. Slide off your sneakers, peel off the sweaty socks, and slip your tired dogs into your favorite slides or sandals. Let your feet breathe. If you find yourself with hot spots or blisters after the event, especially if you skipped socks, you'll be relieved to walk without backs or sides of shoes rubbing your heels or toes.

Chapter 19

Ten (Or So) Resources for Finding Triathlons

*Y*our local triathlon club is a great resource for you when you're ready to register for your first triathlon — or ready to schedule a season full of events. Experienced triathletes know which triathlons are best for first-timers and where to go for the best courses or the best-organized events, so ask around before you register.

If you haven't met any triathletes yet, or you're ready to branch out to other locations and become the triathlete from whom others seek advice about the not-to-miss events, read this chapter for a list of event calendars, searchable by location or date. We also include sites that offer news on the sport. You'll find a sample of women-only events and a selection of regional events to get you started in your search for the next great triathlon.

The American Triathlon Calendar

On the American Triathlon Calendar (www.trifind.com), you can search for an event by state, using the links on the left-hand side of the home page. The site also offers tips for beginners and information on identifying and treating injuries.

Be sure to click the Triathlon: The Early History of the Sport link on the home page; it offers a fun look at the early history of the triathlon, written by one of the sport's founders and the organizer of the first event in 1974. (You can also get there directly by going to http://home.san.rr.com/johnstone.)

USA Triathlon Calendar

USA Triathlon (USAT) sanctions more than 2,000 triathlons across the country. The organization selects and trains teams for international competition, including participation in world championships and the Olympic Games, but membership is open to triathletes of all ages and abilities. Members often receive discounted registration fees for USAT-sanctioned events, among other benefits. On `www.usatriathloncalendar.com`, you'll find small-town races with 300 participants, as well as large, well-known events that draw thousands of participants from around the country. Events are searchable by date, distance, USAT sanctioning, prize values, and child-friendliness.

TRImapper.com

Go global. Use TRImapper.com (`www.trimapper.com`) to locate a triathlon anywhere in the world. You can find events on six of the seven continents. (Who would actually do a triathlon in Antarctica?) Search by continent, by date, or by event distance. The home page features two maps:

- **World Triathlon Map:** This map is speckled with markers for event locations, color-coded by distance. The World Triathlon Map is a fun tool because it lets you look at the overall map or zoom into a specific area and select the icons for your desired distance. A pop-up window gives you a quick look at the event name, date, location, and distance, as well as a link to the event's Web site. It's an easy and fast way to see what's near your desired location.

- **Triathlon Clubs around the World:** This map displays markers identifying the locations of — you guessed it! — triathlon clubs around the world. A box at the upper-right corner of the screen shows a breakdown by type of club, including collegiate, youth, and women-only. The site doesn't offer a comprehensive list, though, so if you don't find a group in your area on this map, don't give up hope.

Inside Triathlon

Inside Triathlon (`www.insidetri.com`) is the online version of the triathlon magazine, *Inside Triathlon: The Multisport Life,* which is published 11 times a year. Although this site does feature a calendar, searchable by date or state, you'll find the content even more useful. The news section features the usual who-won-what-event listings, as well as a look at the growth of the sport itself and fun, informative feature stories. The site is neatly divided into departments such as Race Reports, Gear Reviews, Events, Photos, Training, and Buyer's Guide (giving you comparisons of new products for each sport).

Triathlete

Triathlete is a monthly magazine, and www.triathletemag.com is its online version. On the Web site, you can find an event calendar (partnered with Active.com), as well as event photo galleries. These photos are not the inspirational, set-to-music, promotional images you often find on event organizers' sites. Instead, they're the out-on-the-course shots of people pushing past their limits. Blogs and podcasts give the site personality.

Race360

Race360 (www.race360.com) offers a calendar of more than 2,000 endurance events — not just triathlons — across the United States. Select the Triathlon tab at the top of the home page for a chart of upcoming races, including dates and distances. Along with the chart, the site offers short reviews of upcoming events, as well as links to event details, photos, and videos, and a list of local triathlon clubs to keep you motivated.

Active.com

Active.com is a well-known site packed with information and events across the country. The triathlon portion of the site (www.active.com/triathlon) features training tips, expert advice, and gear guides. Enter your zip code for a scrollable list of events near you. Links take you to a registration page with a brief description of the event and a link to the event's Web site. And if your event is a fundraiser for a charitable organization, Active.com provides a donation page through which you can request and track donations.

Team In Training

Sometimes motivation for training for a triathlon comes from a greater cause. Doing something far outside your comfort zone is a popular way to raise funds for a charitable organization, such as the Leukemia and Lymphoma Society. When you register for the popular Team In Training event (www.

`teamintraining.org`), you'll be hooked up with a team led by an experienced triathlete. Visit the site for more information on how the events work and where they take place.

GetSetUSA

GetSetUSA (`www.getsetusa.com`) features an easily searchable map of the United States. On the home page, click on your state, and then select your sport for a listing of events in your area.

Slowtwitch

The term *slow twitch* refers to the types of muscle fibers that are most efficient for endurance events. Muscles comprise slow-twitch and fast-twitch fibers, but it's the slow-twitch ones that help you go for a long time before tiring. The Slowtwitch site (`www.slowtwitch.com`) is a resource for everything triathlon. On the home page, you find a list of ten U.S. regions and the number of triathlons, some in the hundreds, listed for that area. Triathletes rate an event based on the number of competitors on the course, safety, and even food and bathroom accommodations. Aside from the calendars, you can spend a day on the site poring over the informative articles, custom-fit bike calculator, and discussion forums.

Women-Only Events

If you're seeking the supportive and encouraging environment of a triathlon just for women, you won't have to look far. Check out these sites for more information:

✔ **Danskin Women's Triathlon Series (`www.danskin.com/triathlon.html`):** Registering for one of the eight Danskin women-only Sprint-distance triathlons is a little like getting tickets to a rock concert. Some of the events, such as the New York Metro event, sell out in hours. The site displays a map of the eight events across the country — Orlando, Florida; Austin, Texas; Disneyland (Anaheim, California); Aurora-Denver, Colorado; Chicagoland; New England; Seattle, Washington; and New York Metro — and calls the Danskin triathlon "the longest-running multisport series in the world." We call it girl power. The Danskin triathlons are fundraisers for breast cancer research. The positive energy of the weekend-long event draws participants back year after year.

- **SheROX Triathlon Series (`www.sheroxtri.com`):** SheROX is a three-event series with Sprint-distance triathlons in Tempe, Arizona; Philadelphia, Pennsylvania; and Charlotte, North Carolina. These women-only events are organized specifically to inspire and encourage women to give the sport a try. The event features a mentor program in which experienced triathletes lead first-timers through the training and the event.

- **U.S. Women's Triathlon Series (`www.uswts.com`):** The U.S. Women's Triathlon Series offers four events — one each in Naperville, Illinois (near Chicago); Federal Way, Washington (between Seattle and Tacoma); San Antonio, Texas; and San Diego, California. The events raise funds for ovarian cancer research and are designed to be supportive for first-timers and women of all ages and abilities.

- **Women-Only Triathlon Calendar (`http://hertri.trifind.net`):** This site lists women-only events by year, with links for general information, as well as links to the events' Web sites and registration pages.

Regional Events

There are loads of region-specific triathlons. Here are some ways to find the ones in your region:

- **East:**

  - CGI Racing (`www.cgiracing.com`): Features registration and event information, including course details, activities for children, open-water group swims for the New Jersey State Triathlon, North East Maryland Triathlon, Philadelphia Women's Triathlon, and Black Bear Triathlon. A fun feature of the site is the Tri Tube, a multimedia journey through the course with inspirational photos of finishers — it's a great motivator.

  - Finish Strong (`www.fsseries.com`): Finish Strong puts on multi-distance events throughout North Carolina.

  - Lin-Mark Computer Sports (`www.lin-mark.com`): This site lists events of all distances, including triathlons. It's searchable by date and features a great photo album of event participants. Click Links for a long list of training clubs and groups.

- **Midwest:**

  - HPF Racing (`www.hfpracing.com`): This event-organizing company manages races throughout Ohio, Michigan, Wisconsin, and West Virginia. Through easy-to-navigate links, you'll find one-click access to information on course distance, awards, registration information, and directions, as well as a few sentences about what makes each event a must. The site lists triathlons, duathlons, and special events, such as the perennially sold-out De Soto American Triple T, a three-day "team triathlon tour," as well as the Wheelie Fun six-race triathlon/duathlon point series, with events for children and for women only.

- Ultramax Events (www.ultramaxtri.com): This is an event organizing and production company founded by a ten-time Ironman competitor. On this site, you'll find events throughout Missouri.

✔ **West:**

- RaceCenter.com (www.racecenter.com): Check out this site for multi-sport events in Washington and Oregon.

- Tri-California Events (www.tricalifornia.com): California was built for triathlons — the weather, the water, the stunning vistas to distract from your aching muscles. In fact, it's the birthplace of the sport. Check out this site for information on five popular triathlons, including the Escape from Alcatraz. Easy-to-navigate links take you from event to event, with video and inspiring photos, and offer information on every aspect of the events, from how to register to how to ship your bike.

- TriUtah (www.triutah.com): These event organizers pull together races from Sprint distance through Ironman.

Index

• *D* •

BUSINESS, CAREERS & PERSONAL FINANCE

Accounting For Dummies, 4th Edition*
978-0-470-24600-9

Bookkeeping Workbook For Dummies†
978-0-470-16983-4

Commodities For Dummies
978-0-470-04928-0

Doing Business in China For Dummies
978-0-470-04929-7

E-Mail Marketing For Dummies
978-0-470-19087-6

Job Interviews For Dummies, 3rd Edition*†
978-0-470-17748-8

Personal Finance Workbook For Dummies*†
978-0-470-09933-9

Real Estate License Exams For Dummies
978-0-7645-7623-2

Six Sigma For Dummies
978-0-7645-6798-8

Small Business Kit For Dummies, 2nd Edition*†
978-0-7645-5984-6

Telephone Sales For Dummies
978-0-470-16836-3

BUSINESS PRODUCTIVITY & MICROSOFT OFFICE

Access 2007 For Dummies
978-0-470-03649-5

Excel 2007 For Dummies
978-0-470-03737-9

Office 2007 For Dummies
978-0-470-00923-9

Outlook 2007 For Dummies
978-0-470-03830-7

PowerPoint 2007 For Dummies
978-0-470-04059-1

Project 2007 For Dummies
978-0-470-03651-8

QuickBooks 2008 For Dummies
978-0-470-18470-7

Quicken 2008 For Dummies
978-0-470-17473-9

Salesforce.com For Dummies, 2nd Edition
978-0-470-04893-1

Word 2007 For Dummies
978-0-470-03658-7

EDUCATION, HISTORY, REFERENCE & TEST PREPARATION

African American History For Dummies
978-0-7645-5469-8

Algebra For Dummies
978-0-7645-5325-7

Algebra Workbook For Dummies
978-0-7645-8467-1

Art History For Dummies
978-0-470-09910-0

ASVAB For Dummies, 2nd Edition
978-0-470-10671-6

British Military History For Dummies
978-0-470-03213-8

Calculus For Dummies
978-0-7645-2498-1

Canadian History For Dummies, 2nd Edition
978-0-470-83656-9

Geometry Workbook For Dummies
978-0-471-79940-5

The SAT I For Dummies, 6th Edition
978-0-7645-7193-0

Series 7 Exam For Dummies
978-0-470-09932-2

World History For Dummies
978-0-7645-5242-7

FOOD, GARDEN, HOBBIES & HOME

Bridge For Dummies, 2nd Edition
978-0-471-92426-5

Coin Collecting For Dummies, 2nd Edition
978-0-470-22275-1

Cooking Basics For Dummies, 3rd Edition
978-0-7645-7206-7

Drawing For Dummies
978-0-7645-5476-6

Etiquette For Dummies, 2nd Edition
978-0-470-10672-3

Gardening Basics For Dummies*†
978-0-470-03749-2

Knitting Patterns For Dummies
978-0-470-04556-5

Living Gluten-Free For Dummies†
978-0-471-77383-2

Painting Do-It-Yourself For Dummies
978-0-470-17533-0

HEALTH, SELF HELP, PARENTING & PETS

Anger Management For Dummies
978-0-470-03715-7

Anxiety & Depression Workbook For Dummies
978-0-7645-9793-0

Dieting For Dummies, 2nd Edition
978-0-7645-4149-0

Dog Training For Dummies, 2nd Edition
978-0-7645-8418-3

Horseback Riding For Dummies
978-0-470-09719-9

Infertility For Dummies†
978-0-470-11518-3

Meditation For Dummies with CD-ROM, 2nd Edition
978-0-471-77774-8

Post-Traumatic Stress Disorder For Dummies
978-0-470-04922-8

Puppies For Dummies, 2nd Edition
978-0-470-03717-1

Thyroid For Dummies, 2nd Edition†
978-0-471-78755-6

Type 1 Diabetes For Dummies*†
978-0-470-17811-9

---

* Separate Canadian edition also available
† Separate U.K. edition also available

Available wherever books are sold. For more information or to order direct: U.S. customers visit www.dummies.com or call 1-877-762-2974.
U.K. customers visit www.wileyeurope.com or call (0)1243 843291. Canadian customers visit www.wiley.ca or call 1-800-567-4797.

INTERNET & DIGITAL MEDIA

AdWords For Dummies
978-0-470-15252-2

Blogging For Dummies, 2nd Edition
978-0-470-23017-6

**Digital Photography All-in-One
Desk Reference For Dummies, 3rd Edition**
978-0-470-03743-0

Digital Photography For Dummies, 5th Edition
978-0-7645-9802-9

**Digital SLR Cameras & Photography
For Dummies, 2nd Edition**
978-0-470-14927-0

**eBay Business All-in-One Desk Reference
For Dummies**
978-0-7645-8438-1

eBay For Dummies, 5th Edition*
978-0-470-04529-9

eBay Listings That Sell For Dummies
978-0-471-78912-3

Facebook For Dummies
978-0-470-26273-3

The Internet For Dummies, 11th Edition
978-0-470-12174-0

Investing Online For Dummies, 5th Edition
978-0-7645-8456-5

iPod & iTunes For Dummies, 5th Edition
978-0-470-17474-6

MySpace For Dummies
978-0-470-09529-4

Podcasting For Dummies
978-0-471-74898-4

**Search Engine Optimization
For Dummies, 2nd Edition**
978-0-471-97998-2

Second Life For Dummies
978-0-470-18025-9

**Starting an eBay Business For Dummies,
3rd Edition†**
978-0-470-14924-9

GRAPHICS, DESIGN & WEB DEVELOPMENT

**Adobe Creative Suite 3 Design Premium
All-in-One Desk Reference For Dummies**
978-0-470-11724-8

**Adobe Web Suite CS3 All-in-One Desk
Reference For Dummies**
978-0-470-12099-6

AutoCAD 2008 For Dummies
978-0-470-11650-0

**Building a Web Site For Dummies,
3rd Edition**
978-0-470-14928-7

**Creating Web Pages All-in-One Desk
Reference For Dummies, 3rd Edition**
978-0-470-09629-1

**Creating Web Pages For Dummies,
8th Edition**
978-0-470-08030-6

Dreamweaver CS3 For Dummies
978-0-470-11490-2

Flash CS3 For Dummies
978-0-470-12100-9

Google SketchUp For Dummies
978-0-470-13744-4

InDesign CS3 For Dummies
978-0-470-11865-8

**Photoshop CS3 All-in-One
Desk Reference For Dummies**
978-0-470-11195-6

Photoshop CS3 For Dummies
978-0-470-11193-2

Photoshop Elements 5 For Dummies
978-0-470-09810-3

SolidWorks For Dummies
978-0-7645-9555-4

Visio 2007 For Dummies
978-0-470-08983-5

Web Design For Dummies, 2nd Edition
978-0-471-78117-2

Web Sites Do-It-Yourself For Dummies
978-0-470-16903-2

Web Stores Do-It-Yourself For Dummies
978-0-470-17443-2

LANGUAGES, RELIGION & SPIRITUALITY

Arabic For Dummies
978-0-471-77270-5

Chinese For Dummies, Audio Set
978-0-470-12766-7

French For Dummies
978-0-7645-5193-2

German For Dummies
978-0-7645-5195-6

Hebrew For Dummies
978-0-7645-5489-6

Ingles Para Dummies
978-0-7645-5427-8

Italian For Dummies, Audio Set
978-0-470-09586-7

Italian Verbs For Dummies
978-0-471-77389-4

Japanese For Dummies
978-0-7645-5429-2

Latin For Dummies
978-0-7645-5431-5

Portuguese For Dummies
978-0-471-78738-9

Russian For Dummies
978-0-471-78001-4

Spanish Phrases For Dummies
978-0-7645-7204-3

Spanish For Dummies
978-0-7645-5194-9

Spanish For Dummies, Audio Set
978-0-470-09585-0

The Bible For Dummies
978-0-7645-5296-0

Catholicism For Dummies
978-0-7645-5391-2

The Historical Jesus For Dummies
978-0-470-16785-4

Islam For Dummies
978-0-7645-5503-9

**Spirituality For Dummies,
2nd Edition**
978-0-470-19142-2

NETWORKING AND PROGRAMMING

ASP.NET 3.5 For Dummies
978-0-470-19592-5

C# 2008 For Dummies
978-0-470-19109-5

Hacking For Dummies, 2nd Edition
978-0-470-05235-8

Home Networking For Dummies, 4th Edition
978-0-470-11806-1

Java For Dummies, 4th Edition
978-0-470-08716-9

**Microsoft® SQL Server™ 2008 All-in-One
Desk Reference For Dummies**
978-0-470-17954-3

**Networking All-in-One Desk Reference
For Dummies, 2nd Edition**
978-0-7645-9939-2

**Networking For Dummies,
8th Edition**
978-0-470-05620-2

SharePoint 2007 For Dummies
978-0-470-09941-4

**Wireless Home Networking
For Dummies, 2nd Edition**
978-0-471-74940-0

OPERATING SYSTEMS & COMPUTER BASICS

iMac For Dummies, 5th Edition
978-0-7645-8458-9

Laptops For Dummies, 2nd Edition
978-0-470-05432-1

Linux For Dummies, 8th Edition
978-0-470-11649-4

MacBook For Dummies
978-0-470-04859-7

Mac OS X Leopard All-in-One Desk Reference For Dummies
978-0-470-05434-5

Mac OS X Leopard For Dummies
978-0-470-05433-8

Macs For Dummies, 9th Edition
978-0-470-04849-8

PCs For Dummies, 11th Edition
978-0-470-13728-4

Windows® Home Server For Dummies
978-0-470-18592-6

Windows Server 2008 For Dummies
978-0-470-18043-3

Windows Vista All-in-One Desk Reference For Dummies
978-0-471-74941-7

Windows Vista For Dummies
978-0-471-75421-3

Windows Vista Security For Dummies
978-0-470-11805-4

SPORTS, FITNESS & MUSIC

Coaching Hockey For Dummies
978-0-470-83685-9

Coaching Soccer For Dummies
978-0-471-77381-8

Fitness For Dummies, 3rd Edition
978-0-7645-7851-9

Football For Dummies, 3rd Edition
978-0-470-12536-6

GarageBand For Dummies
978-0-7645-7323-1

Golf For Dummies, 3rd Edition
978-0-471-76871-5

Guitar For Dummies, 2nd Edition
978-0-7645-9904-0

Home Recording For Musicians For Dummies, 2nd Edition
978-0-7645-8884-6

iPod & iTunes For Dummies, 5th Edition
978-0-470-17474-6

Music Theory For Dummies
978-0-7645-7838-0

Stretching For Dummies
978-0-470-06741-3

Get smart @ dummies.com®

- **Find a full list of Dummies titles**
- **Look into loads of FREE on-site articles**
- **Sign up for FREE eTips e-mailed to you weekly**
- **See what other products carry the Dummies name**
- **Shop directly from the Dummies bookstore**
- **Enter to win new prizes every month!**

* Separate Canadian edition also available
† Separate U.K. edition also available

Available wherever books are sold. For more information or to order direct: U.S. customers visit www.dummies.com or call 1-877-762-2974.
U.K. customers visit www.wileyeurope.com or call (0) 1243 843291. Canadian customers visit www.wiley.ca or call 1-800-567-4797.

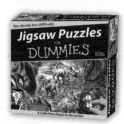